Inshallah

Odyssey to the Middle East

Kevin Jones

With best Wishes

K Jones

Home made Books
Telemation Publishing
www.tele-mation.co.uk

Home made Books
Published by Telemation
30 Pine Gardens, Upton on Chester, Chester CH2 1DB
www.tele-mation.co.uk

First Published 2003

The moral right of the author has been asserted

Printed by Home Made Books

ISBN 0-9545128-0-4

This book is for Hanna who has been my guiding light and loving partner since we first met in Nepal and who, through her many letters brought so much comfort to me in my travels throughout the Middle East.

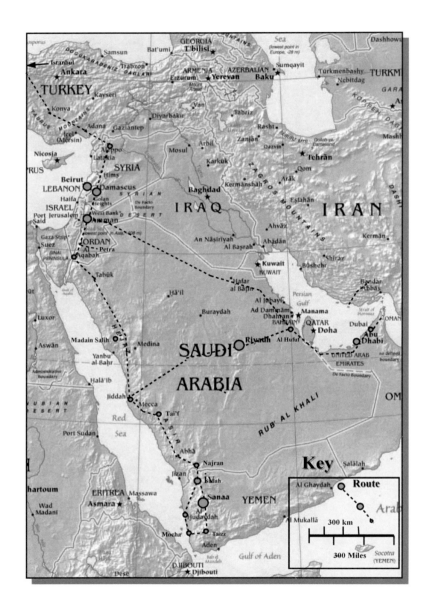

Contents

List of Illustrations

(copyright ©author's collection)

Acknowledgements

The preparation of the text and illustrations for this book were facilitated in many ways by various friends and contacts.

I would like to express my thanks to Peter Hamblin for his

freely given help and advice on the layout, presentation and printing of this book which must surly have saved me from the costly pitfalls that can beset an author and who sustained my faith in its eventual production.

Also my thanks to Peter Lang, my very good friend, journalist and former travelling companion, whose unstinting perseverance in the editing of this text helped immeasurably to bring a sharper focus to the writing of this adventure.

Finally I would like to thank Hanna, for believing in this book and for her help in reading the many versions over the months it took to write.

Introduction

Inshallah - a philosophical perspective

This is the first day in the start of my new life. With my university department closed, due to the funding crisis in higher education, I now have the freedom to recall and finally tell my own true adventure story which began 24 years ago. It was to be such an important part in the forming of my future life that I hope my brief jottings and memories from that time, which only now I am fully committing to paper, will be shared with others who either dream of, or long to savour the moment when adventure beckons…Inshallah.

To write about these adventures and re-live them, they are once again becoming fundamentally so much a part of my soul. As the journey through the lands of the Middle East unfolds, I can once again live those moments and am reminded that life can have many paths but that either by accident or design it becomes an adventure. Also one needs a life guide, a truth to believe in and I found this through the people who helped us so much in the countries I visited throughout the Middle East.

After I returned from Nepal, a few months before, I had a clear aim to change direction away from the sciences in which I had trained and make my love of photography my "life" and profession. When I eventually took on the project to photograph Arabia in those early days as a photographer, nothing seemed impossible. Even to travel 30,000 km in an ageing Volkswagon combie van, to take it across unmarked desert tracks or through unimaginable chaos such as the city of Beirut, seemed possible.

The hard endurance was to be rewarded by instances of sheer joy. Such as the time John Macmahon, my companion photographer and I, lay atop the V.W., in the enveloping dark but tranquil night of the Saudi desert, star gazing amongst the crystal clear pinpricks of light above us, from the cozy warmth of our beds on the roof rack, leaving us to drift off into a deep sleep in the balm of the cool night air.

Most memorable of all though, was the hospitality of the people of the Middle East, whatever their ethnic origin or religious beliefs. Instances such as the politically powerful Imam of Damascus, engaging us in philosophical discussion, or the Phalangelist family in Beirut, who provided a safe base from which to explore their war ravaged but once beautiful city, continue to stir emotions after all these years. We were also humbled by the friendship of the shepherd family tending their flocks in the scrub of Yemen with whom we shared the delights of our mint infused tea; and the Saudi border guards, who provided us with free board, petrol, oil and clothes for our onward journey.

We found the curiosity of our hosts and numerous questions about our beliefs, families and above all opinions of Middle East life were sincere and always rewarded by kind hospitality, mutual trust and respect together with a genuine concern for our well being .

During the long path we took by road, across both verdant and barren areas, with a beauty all their own, we eventually discovered more about our inner selves, throwing away fears of the unknown and coping with the realities of exploration. Life, which often seemed to conspire to thwart the best of intentions, provided opportunities that often saved the day. In this respect we developed a positive mental attitude which on many occasions throughout the venture, helped us to win against the odds.

Our dictum on the road was "always go forward, never back" but this was sorely tested at times. Life simply dictated its terms and often provided the means to overcome the daily obstacles put in our path and this was to be rewarded by the successful completion of the eventful journey, six months later. I am not a fatalist but from our experiences I believe even more firmly that you can take even the worst moments, turn them around and put them to the best advantage that suits at the time. As time marched on I adapted to this philosophy so that I became more accepting to the way things are, in very different lands to the one where I was brought up.

The belief that life itself will so often provide a solution to the dire problems we were presented with, was not based on any particular religious philosophy but on the way I experienced the journey in often harsh and challenging geographical and climatic areas that exist in those countries which we were fortunate enough to visit.

As photographers we explored our own leads and planned our own routes, to document aspects of Middle East life through the countries we visited. On our own we became more self assured and self reliant but often became tied to events that were seemingly out of our control, requiring clear choices to be made. As a general rule we discovered that no matter what the impenetrable difficulties were, we found solutions to these situations ourselves. Moreover, they very often found us, turning out to be right for that particular moment and we seemed to be guided, as perhaps Allah willed it, unharmed in any way, to meet the gruelling schedule that was to be our life for those six wonderful months .... that to me is embodied in the term ..... "Inshallah."

Inshallah

Chapter 1

Wanderlust and the big break

My first journey to whet my appetite and provide me with the crucial photographic portfolio to obtain further work, came about whilst working temporarily on a traffic census based around Harrogate. This job introduced me to other colleagues "passing through" who like myself were confirmed travellers. One of them, Brian Harrison, showed me his wonderful colour photographs of Nepal, which inspired my long felt desire to travel and see the mountain ranges of the Himalayas first hand that I had read so much about in the books of Chris Bonnington and others.

Whilst living in Leeds, Miriam, a friend and neighbour, introduced me to Peter Lang, a rather eccentric journalist who like myself wanted a companion with whom to travel to India and Nepal. After three months spent in cars, buses, trains and lorries, we eventually arrived in the Kingdom of Nepal. During the eventful few months in which I travelled the breadth of Nepal with Peter, I became totally absorbed in recording aspects of the culture and life there. I also spent time working for the natural history museum in Swayambu on the outskirts of Kathmandu, helping to establish a national collection of insects. I took part in expeditions to the beautiful Himalayan mountains which I also documented with many photographs along the way.

With a tin full of Kodachrome film in my rucksack I was now keen to process them and establish a portfolio with which to gain further work on my return to England. I also wanted to travel a lot more to build up my collection of documentary photographs. At the time another important development to my life came when I met a Dutch woman. Her name was Hanna Bastiaansen.

We had met by chance on one of my expeditions to buy groceries in the city. Standing next to her at another stall I related the true cost of some coins she wanted to buy from the market, after which we decided to go for a coffee and a chat to get acquainted. Though we did not know it our next meeting was not to be for another 10 months.

Hanna was to play a crucial part not just for me and my future happiness but also as a point of contact with home, through her regular letters that I miraculously received throughout the Middle East. For the most part I shared them with John, my companion on the journey, on the many occasions he received nothing, as they provided a much needed psychological warmth from the Netherlands.

Returning from Nepal, full of renewed enthusiasm to make a life change into photography, I knew I needed a project of some kind, something to concentrate my energies and one that would consolidate some of my hitherto unfulfilled wishes.

The only glimmer of hope to satisfy my wish for travel and finding a "proper job" was through an application to the Antarctic Survey organisation for a six month tour as an entomologist, based with the research unit there. This would include travelling out over the snow wastes in search of indigenous species and also collecting specimens of those migrating to warmer climates.

I had recently received a wonderful series of photographs from Steve Hutchinson, a co-student during my degree re-sits, (for the third time) who had also been "selected" and who was obviously having a ball. The photographs proved it by showing him crossing the stark white hills of the Antarctic with a snowmobile full of equipment and what's more being paid for it!

At this same time I was having a brief romance with Gill, a separated but still married woman who I met that Christmas whilst visiting Mike and Linda, some very close friends from my Harrogate days the year before. The relationship seemed to be going nowhere. The day I arrived to find yet another lover, just leaving the flat was the last straw. I felt humiliated and rejected and made my mind up to do something about it and soon.

And then it happened! A seemingly total change of tack offered itself. Mother and I were sitting in a coffee shop just off the main

Wanderlust and the big break

high street in Sutton, close to home and whilst deep in thought over a cup of Kenyan best, I casually turned through the pages of the January issue of Amateur Photographer. I was keen to have some slides I had taken in Nepal converted to prints, as these were the days before computer scanners and cheap colour printers. It was while looking through the small ads section to find a suitable contact that my eyes became riveted on a small advert with just a few lines of text.

Photographer needed to develop a picture library depicting Middle East life. Must have full driving licence and an aptitude to take quality photographs. Please apply to Miz Rhamen c/o Islamic Information Services Limited, 101 Praed Street, London W2Y 1NT

I could not believe my luck and flushed with excitement, I saw a possible solution not only to a roller coaster love life but also for my wanderlust, which was beckoning impatiently once more. In this case it was eventually to result in a 30,000 kilometre tour through countries I had only heard of on the radio or television, which provided a most memorable and exciting journey. My other side however had doubts.

The recent memories of making sightseeing journeys in the appalling heat and humidity of Delhi, made me wince as they had me scampering out of my six rupee a night room, at some god forsaken hour in the cool morning, to visit say, the new city or the Red Fort and later return to my hotel room and flop thoroughly exhausted on the bed by 10 am. Only the swish of the ceiling mounted fan and accompanying whirlwind it generated kept me company. Dripping with sweat I could only stare at the geckos silently pattering across the walls and ceiling, in their unswerving quest to catch a food morsel.

I kept asking myself, how on earth would I cope in the Middle East? Mother of course thought the whole thing was a complete fantasy and that I wouldn't enjoy the heat at all. There were the pressing and personal matters with Gill, which I kept to myself and the prospect of further travel away from my seemingly hum-drum life outweighed the geographical and climatic conditions I was going to have to put up with. Full of optimism, this was an opportunity not to be missed and on our return home I soon had a typescript application in the post and had contacted the office to arrange a meeting for a few days hence. It was now looking as though I may have the possibility of either freezing to death in the Antarctic on the one hand or roasting alive in the heat of the Arabian peninsula on the other. A temperature range from 50 degrees below zero to 50 degrees above. What a contrast!

The interview with my prospective employers, Islamic Information Services, was held over lunch in a well appointed Chinese restaurant in the centre of London. There was John Macmahon (to be my companion and fellow photographer), Miz Rhaman the director of Islamic Information, whose brother was later involved in the spectacular collapse of the Bank of Credit and Commerce International, (BCCI) and Jim, the other half of the publishing business and partner to Miz in this project. We sat eating a most delicious meal but all through this informal but crucial meeting, I felt entirely at ease. This is the way things are supposed to be, I thought because since graduation I had my belly full of stuffy interviews and moronic selection panels, who really could not care less about me as a person and whose rhetoric clearly displayed a minimal enthusiasm for their job.

In the restaurant it could not have been more different. We had a pleasurably relaxed talk about ourselves, with John describing his photographic work and darkroom experience and me talking enthusiastically about my travels to Nepal. Showing the group some sample photographs, Miz and Jim, to my delight, seemed genuinely interested in them, asking questions of the camera and lens settings used, film preferences and so on. These treasured slides had been hiked (literally) round a succession of photo libraries and studios in London with a lot of interest but very little in financial reward to show for it.

Now at last they were being put to good use (or so I hoped). I was especially keen to explain a rather graphic "lightning strike". A silhouette shot taken at night with forked lightning illuminating the valley surrounding the "chai" or tea shop in which I had been staying whilst backpacking in Nepal. I held back on any elaboration under the circumstances in which it was taken as it had been under the influence of a few puffs of Hashish.

Hashish or Ganja is a well known medicine for the hill tribes there, providing herbal relief for many ailments. For me at the time, this happened to be a bout of muscle cramps and a touch of sun stroke. So one night during a severe downpour and well under the influence, I held my Pentax camera up against a window sill, whilst holding my breath to keep the camera steady. I took an exposure of about 10 seconds, during which I captured a flash from the electrical storm that forked so beautifully for me across the resulting, pin sharp photographic slide.

During the meal we talked at length about the project, to learn that it was to be an expenses paid photographic expedition to some of the classical and also more remote parts of the Middle East. It was planned to take three months and its purpose was to establish a quality documentary photo library on aspects of Middle East life. The modest finance available, supported by the BCCI, was just enough to equip two photographers and a vehicle. They were to travel entirely overland and to take opportunistic photographs of people, buildings, places of historical and cultural importance, as well as recording typical landscapes from the geographical areas they encountered. For this, twelve hundred rolls of Kodak Ecktachrome 120 film were available to record as many quality medium format photographs in the time allowed, I just couldn't wait!

We were, in hindsight, like the proverbial lamb to the slaughter, as I now recall how naïve our perception of the task was that lay ahead. After the exhilaration of this first meeting but ever cautious, I was stunned to have an offer of employment and was invited to attend a further meeting in the offices of Islamic Information to tie the knot, so to speak and agree terms.

On arrival in Miz's office, we learned that the project had begun several months before but that the previous incumbent who had purchased the current expedition vehicle, a Volkswagon combie camper van, had for one reason or another decided to leave by "mutual agreement", wishing the project well but still contactable if needed. The itinerary had been worked out and agreed prior to our meeting. It was to involve a journey passing through Europe to cover Turkey, Syria, Lebanon, Saudi Arabia, Yemen, back through Saudi, Oman, The Arab Emirates, Bahrain, Kuwait and, if possible, through Iraq and thence Syria and Turkey over the Bosphorous and back into Europe and home.

That in just three months, yes, 100 days, to travel well in excess of 30,000 km. That would be a schedule of 300 kilometres or 187 miles a day. Oh, ignorance is such bliss!

At the time this represented a journey from Leeds to London each day. We were later to learn the impossibilities of this but at the time and with optimistic smiles we set about discussing other parts of the expedition.

As we were to learn later, the frustration our predecessor had encountered in setting up the project were over details such as the inadequacy of the expedition vehicle. We appealed to Miz and Jim's senses to buy a four wheel drive vehicle such as a long wheel based Land Rover but for "economic" reasons this was turned down flat and so we were stuck with a dilapidated VW.

After signing our fate (and our right of copyright) away, John and I arranged to meet first at his house near Hove on the south coast and later at his mother's flat, situated close to Finsbury Park in London. Here we discussed all the tasks we needed to carry out, such as obtaining the necessary documentation, jabs, visas, other essential items of equipment and of course getting the vehicle ready for the expedition.

We eventually picked the camper van up and decided to give it a run to my parents house in Tadworth, situated about 12 miles south west of central London. This was also a chance for John to reciprocate introductions to my parents, so that we and our families were by now both satisfied that whatever the outcome of this trip was to be, we were both in it together on equal terms and not companion to some suicidal adventurer!

Any doubts about each other were soon dissipated within the first few weeks as we became more and more absorbed in getting the project resurrected and worked together to get all the crucial visas arranged.

After a run of just a few miles to my parents house in Tadworth John and I soon realised that the vehicle we had inherited wasn't even fit to make the journey to the ferry on the south coast of England, let alone through the deserts and hills of the Middle East! The crunch (literally) came the following morning after a rather charming evening with all of us talking about the expedition and the itinerary we had developed.

John decided to "leap" through the drivers (left hand) side door to make a perfect landing (Butch Cassidy style) into the saddle. This John accomplished in part but was brought up short with great embarrassment by promptly stepping right through the floor pan.

Laugh, we nearly died crying in the process and to quote Victor Mildrew from the TV program "One foot in the grave", "I simply couldn't believe it!".

At this point it started to dawn on us that the organisational skills of our employers weren't all they were cracked up to be. From now on we were going to have to be far more circumspect about accepting arrangements on face value! The set up at Islamic Information definitely appeared to be just that... a set up and with it, our paranoia went into overdrive.

For our part we were happy to go along with events just for the ride, a free meal ticket and some adventure, as we would certainly not make a bean out of our contracts, but this vehicle was plainly ridiculous! I discovered on closer inspection (as the expedition mechanic) it was full of rot and I took a dim view of being able to break great chunks of our "home" away in my hands, leaving a rusty mess on the well swept road.This did not bode well for the condition of the rest of the vehicle and John decided that we could not let this issue go by without a fight.

At this crucial point in our preparations a spanner in the works of my carefully laid plans, appeared in the form of a letter from Cambridge inviting me to an interview with the Antarctic Expedition...wow! Two great choices had now arisen, so life seemed to be synchronising with my wishes after all this time.

Inshallah

I now had to make a decision. We were due to leave in three weeks just before the due date for interview. However the Cambridge organisation stirred a much greater degree of confidence in their ability to guarantee my survival, so what to do? Do I cancel the Middle East trip? It already seemed to be on very shaky ground and by this time the large distances we were to travel in a rustheap of a vehicle seemed to be turning the whole project into a shambles from the start. So now a clear choice had to be made and pretty soon.

I felt that I daren't tell John as I would let him down as even with our doubts we both accepted the challenge of the journey and were looking forward to setting off to ventures new. I decided to mull these options over in my mind to see how things would develop over the next few days. I therefore wrote to Cambridge and accepted the interview but was also determined to see how far we could go in resurrecting the Middle East project.

Determined to succeed, we yet again put forward the case for a four wheel drive Land Rover and despite the terrible state of our present vehicle all our efforts were to no avail with Miz threatening to call the whole thing off. Miz argued that a four wheeled drive vehicle would be overkill as there were roads throughout the Middle East (yes, but at the time many were joined up by long and hazardous rough dirt tracks) and it would be too costly on fuel. However Miz did see that to break down somewhere in England did not bode well for the future of "his" project and so with cash advance in hand, John and I set off to pick up a more sturdy camper van.

In the late 70's, Australia House on the Strand in central London was "the" place for erstwhile travellers to buy and sell vehicles. These generally ranged from complete no-hopers, having taken the "grand tour" of Europe several times over, to sometimes extraordinarily well equipped expedition style 4X4 vehicles, covered in tools, spare wheels, storage hatches, spare fuel and water tanks and so on. These as it turned out were unfortunately well out of our price range.

Wanderlust and the big break

We paced up and down looking in, under, and on top of a variety of suitable options but the best of all for our budget was another series II left hand drive, VW Combie. The people selling it seemed genuine enough and whilst running up the 1.6 litre air cooled engine which turned over nicely, we inspected the other recesses of what appeared to be a very tidy and most important of all, rust free vehicle. Importantly the front cab was a walk through type, allowing the co-driver to gain access to the rear compartment whilst on the road. We would be able to fix a cup of tea or food for the driver or to change cassette tapes which invariably turned out to be Vangellis, Simon and Garfunkel or Abba.

The conversion to a camper from a van had been fairly basic however, having a sink unit placed behind the right hand side passenger seat, with a galley area along the driver's side, and a bed at the rear. All however were hand made from plywood and chipboard, obviously primitive D.I.Y. but functional.

After a satisfactory test run and a lot of bargaining, the £700 float from Miz changed hands and we became the proud owners of a much younger vehicle than before. Moreover one that we had convinced ourselves would get us round! Read on........!

Full of renewed confidence we decided to leave nothing to chance and so arranged to have a complete systems check by VW agents and have new tyres fitted. The work seemed to drag on, so in the meantime we obtained our vaccinations, driving from embassy to embassy in a mad paper chase to obtain our visa stamps and also arrange the purchase of other equipment.

On a typical day, John would travel up to London by train from the south coast as his ageing Citroen was too poorly to make the journey. I would pick him up in my humble but reliable Morris Minor saloon, usually from Waterloo and we would set about our chores. On one particular day when we really were pushed for time, fate again seemed to take a hand.

I was pulled over by two very young P.C.s on the beat near Sloane Square. Whilst one gave me a grilling about the general condition of the 12 year old Morris, the other inspected the underneath. To our astonishment he reported the fact that six inches of tail pipe were absent from the rust encrusted exhaust system and then berated me for not having a catalytic converter. This was 1978 remember and these were unheard of then in Britain, especially for a 1966 D reg Moggie.

Driving to the nearest exhaust centre we were again stopped, this time by a police motor cycle patrol man.

In a very friendly manner I was told "not to panic" as he merely wanted to point out that the drivers side wing was "flapping about" a bit and needed something like a pot rivet to secure it safely.

He seemed genuinely concerned that we had been treated harshly in Sloane Square but clearly the two young PC's were not yet qualified to hand out tickets on "construction and use" of vehicles and should have called out a trained officer. He said "he would be having a few words with them when he got back to base." Cheered up somewhat by this, we set off once more to an exhaust centre and I had a new system fitted for the exorbitant but discounted price of £22, almost a week's wages at the time!

To add insult to injury, after returning from the Middle East six months later, I found that the new exhaust had rusted up through lack of use. I therefore had to go out again and buy yet another new one. Oh the injustice of it! Well some you win and some you lose, Inshallah!

Meanwhile the work was finally completed by the VW agents who assured us that the van was well equipped for Middle Eastern conditions. "Oh yes sir, definitely expedition ready" the service manager assured us. "Perfect vehicle for the Middle East. We have them going all over the world," he continued

With the paperwork finalised and assurances given, we visited the offices of Islamic Information once more to set the financial and insurance details in order, as well as to make sure that a bulk purchase of Ectachrome film, had arrived from Kodak.

It turned out that we would each receive £30 per week, out-of-pocket expenses to cover food and drink. A separate budget would pay for fuel and any other transport or visa costs. That was

Wanderlust and the big break

to be our lot as no further fees, commission or royalties would be forthcoming since we had signed the copyright over to the company without reservation......in hindsight a bad mistake, considering the risks we were to take to obtain them. We would however receive a bonus of £500 each on completion of the project.

John was the proud owner of a Swedish Hassleblad C.M. with standard 50mm wide angle and 120mm telephoto lenses that I could only drool over. This level of equipment unfortunately was way beyond my pocket at that time. I therefore persuaded Miz (fortuitously as it happened) to advance the £500 for me to purchase a suitable medium format camera for the project. Having toured the second hand shops, John and I eventually entered a small glass fronted store in the Strand. Here we looked at several cameras and with John's advice I spent the entire advance to purchase a twin lens Rolliflex f 2.8 sport. This had a faster than average lens and also boasted a built in light meter and was to prove such a reliable camera that I grew to trust it like a close friend.

On our return from the expedition the Rolliflex had taken perfect photographs, indistinguishable in quality from John's even though, as the camera mechanic in Finchley was to discover on servicing it, the mechanism contained about a thimble full of sand!

The next task on the agenda was to procure a new set of tyres. The old ones badly needed replacing and so after picking up the Volkswagen we found a fitter near the city centre who had the Michelins we were after. The tyres were eventually to prove very satisfactory but unbeknown to us they had stangely become contaminated with small black grains of anthracite coal when fitted. These became crushed between the outer tyre and the inner tube causing the subsequent punctures.

We had only just fitted them and were returning to John's mother a few miles away, when outside the buildings of Capital Radio, off Marylebon road, we had our first flat tyre (see photograph). Later, within the first two days of the expedition we had three more punctures within hours of each other, during the short drive from France to Germany.

During the whole trip which eventually took six months we ran into a lot of vehicle problems. The only puncture however, was through letting too much air out of the tyres to gain extra "flotation" on the sand in the desert crossing back from Yemen to Saudi.

The new vehicle was now ready and our departure was getting close. We had arranged all our visas, including the entry permit to Yemen. This country was to be the highlight of our 30,000 km journey only reached by driving over the sands and mountains that separate Yemen from Saudi Arabia. Yemen offered the potential of some really interesting photography but to get there we had to go via Saudi, a country closed to tourists and only possible to enter if on official business with local firms.

These difficulties had been foreseen and a rather "loose" contract was offered by Miz, to photograph a building site for a construction company which was to allow us entry. This, as it turned out, was to be our saviour in more ways than one, as the British contact there became a close friend of ours and provided much needed information, shelter, food and a base to work from, on the return journey when we had severe problems with the vehicle.

Saudi therefore represented a major obstacle and it took quite an effort in London to convince them of our bona-fide intentions before they would provide just one entry and exit visa. This presented a logistical conundrum as we would need to cross and re-enter the kingdom several times over the coming months. What we didn't say, and what was not requested from us, was that we intended to exit via the southwest border, near the town called Najran and cross over to Yemen by land. The Saudi embassy assumes all travellers from England travel by air. This route, we were later to learn, was for commercial lorries and official vehicles only, since the Saudi government could not guarantee the safety of travellers. Our story had us officially staying only briefly in the Saudi Kingdom which satisfied the authorities and so our passports were duly stamped.

Similarly, the North Yemen Embassy were convinced we would be working for a local contact in Taiz and would presumably be flying in (they did not ask) and again we struck lucky and were given a single entry and exit visa.

The fact that Miz and Jim had arranged local contacts, who would get us out of trouble, turned out to be more a figment of their imagination. When we did eventually arrive, they might just as well not have bothered for all the help they gave. Sadly this was to become a familiar trait along the whole journey, which required John and I to become resourceful in making our own local contacts and negotiating our way through the many customs posts, embassies, and a host of other red tape that threatened to thwart our photographic exploits, whilst seriously delaying the project.

Now that we were so close to departure on what at the outset looked to be a very promising if not relaxed work brief, I eventually came to the conclusion that what I had now in terms of employment was the best I could hope for and that the Antarctic Survey was a possibility and only that. We had got the expedition off the ground, having overcome seemingly insurmountable logistical problems at the start. Everything was covered to the best of our abilities, even armed only with the scant knowledge of the countries that we were to visit.

We would pay the price for this later on but the departure date had been set, the ferry crossing fixed, so at last our hard efforts were not to be in vain. Cambridge and the Antarctic Survey would have to wait. I wanted to carry on as a photographer and here was the heaven sent chance....Inshallah!

Having spent the best part of six weeks organising the journey we were finally off on Sunday March 12th and all that lay ahead was to be our adventure. We said our goodbyes to loved ones and with our intended itinerary impressed upon one and all, we looked forward to the challenge ahead but also to hearing news from home during our journey. Although apprehensive about the

Inshallah

future and what we would encounter, we were determined to complete the trip come what may.

To the amazement not only to many good friends, our families and acquaintances but also ourselves, we had just embarked on an adventure of a lifetime and were to survive the journey despite confrontations with the Syrian Army, endless searches at borders, trouble with the engine and running the gauntlet of Yemeni bandit country. If, that is, you can call a twelve year old Yemeni, heavily laden with a very worn but nevertheless lethal looking AK47, a bandit!

Looks though can be deceptive in the Middle East as he turned out to be one of the more helpful and understanding examples of his country folk. In those parts, hostility towards westerners who crossed his land was notorious. Indeed we learned that only a week before we made the crossing, a Swiss family had been shot up, making the same journey as us, through the same mountains and over the same unmade dirt track, from Saudi to the northern Yemeni capital, Sana.

Whether their deaths were due to any provocation on their part, we never found out. However we decided to obey the customs and practices in dress and behaviour of the countries we passed through. By going "native", we truly enjoyed the company of local people whilst drawing the least attention to ourselves and our potentially controversial photographic work.

With hindsight our decision at a very early stage not to carry arms of any kind also turned out to be justified, despite John's enthusiasm as a collector and the ease with which guns can be obtained for just a few pounds in open markets that abound in many parts of the Middle East. This was probably one of the better decisions we made as it took all temptation away from us to play with, brandish, or use the damned things, which would inevitably have resulted in attracting quite a different experience, tough though the going was to be at times. I am sure that any weapons found would have meant severe penalties in any of the ensuing searches of our vehicle. Such as the time at the Lebanese

Wanderlust and the big break

and Syrian borders on the road from Beirut to Damascus, where I was threatened by the border guards on the look out for hashish. For now we were at the start of our big adventure and were primed with cameras, sand ladders and a host of paraphernalia. We made our farewells to friends, colleagues and families to embark on our photographic mission come what may. With the first step of the journey being the drive south to the ferry, we constantly talked over our check lists until the ferry crossing had us blissfully committed to travelling east, through mainland Europe and then Istanbul, the gateway to the Middle East and the long drive through Arabia ....Inshallah!

Chapter 2

The Journey Begins - The first faltering steps

Sunday, 12th March was the first day of the journey and we had first travelled from my parents house down to the south coast, to catch the short "flight" by hovercraft across the channel. Sitting in the cabin watching the waves sweep by outside and with the condensing water leaving salt marks on the glass, I had a great feeling of relief now that I was committed to the project which seemed to be getting off to a splendid start. Events, however, were soon to shock me back to the real world. After the fairly routine crossing from Dover to Calais, I remember the first piece of road being very straight and with John driving, I peered out into the overcast day to see the endless line of telegraph poles blurring their way past me. Slowly, one by one they counted off the kilometres that reminded me of the enormous distance we had yet to travel. From the beginning, we pushed ourselves to cover as much distance as we could manage to arrive as soon as possible on the borders of the Middle East. We were taking turns at driving which we hoped would take us well past our estimated 300 kms per day schedule in this European leg of the journey, leaving more time for photography later on. However whilst in France and only two hours into the journey the first of three punctures occurred. Was this an omen?

Still wondering about the possibilities that the Antarctic Survey could have offered, for better or worse, I was now resigned to see the project through as far as I could but at the time it had got off to a rather ignominious start.

We overcame what in hindsight were trivial problems compared to those that would follow, attending to each puncture and in turn repairing them as soon as we were able, since we already knew by this time that others were imminent. Breaking for stop-overs by the side of the road, the journey continued through Germany with a stop at Hoebach. Here we found a bakers which made delicious bread and all manner of chocolate cakes, whilst over the road we ventured into a general store to stock up on cheese and sausage. We pulled off the road near an open field and sat blissfully enjoying fresh coffee with some warm bread covered liberally with butter and bovril. Our first break and we were already feeling the strain of the past month giving way to the routine of the nomad. "Oh, this is the life," we thought.

Whilst waiting for the kettle to boil, John and I decided to play frisbee (relatively new in those days) and with our excess energy burnt off, returned to the van when the whistle of the kettle beckoned. We were horrified to find the large glass jar of bovril had slipped off the galley and onto the floor where it had smashed itself to pieces amongst the other items stored on the floor. This created a huge pool of brown viscous lava, within which broken glass was embedded along with any piece of debris it came into contact with. With gusto we set to with loo roll and brush and managed to scrape the sticky glue like mess from all and sundry until quite exhausted we settled back in our seats to talk.

By late afternoon we passed through Nuremberg, picking up water from a very helpful gentleman at Rosenheim, then on up through the mountains to reach the Steigerwald area by 9.30 pm. Here we filled our thermos with fresh, scalding hot water at a motorway café and continued into Austria.

At 2.20am we passed surprisingly quickly through the German - Austrian Customs on a very dark and rain laden night and from there were swiftly on our way through the mountains. After a further 100 km of night driving through slush and snow we had had enough for one day and decided to back the VW into what appeared to be a very unused track within a Tyrolean ski resort. Though foggy outside we could see the dim outlines of expensive looking wooden chalets but the village itself seemed to be lifeless and shrouded by fine mist that drifted in the utter still of the chill night air. With a mixed day behind us we were able to write up the first entries in our diaries and prepare letters to loved ones.

Inshallah

With the ritual of diary keeping completed, I drifted off to sleep, still thinking of the three month itinerary and wondering if the pace of travel wasn't just a wee bit over taxing! Oh well, we were on our way and I had no need to worry about anything till the morning! I awoke to two amazing sights.

The first was of a freezing but gloriously brilliant morning with the noise of a ski lift close by and a woman scraping leaves from the lawn in her front garden. Wiping the condensation from the inner window above our bed, I could just make out the snow capped peaks, set in relief against a cobalt blue sky surrounding the village of Haltelett where we were now camping.

The second was seeing John busily making the tea and cooking fried eggs. Well at least I seemed to have him house trained, I thought but this gift from heaven was not to last and it was I in later days who was up first.

Cooking, as it turned out, was to be a pleasure we both often enjoyed, as it brought relief from the tedium of driving and became a ritual in which we both attempted to excel with our culinary expertise. Whilst in Europe, we experimented a great deal and I gained a reputation for the curries that I made from the real spices I used with fresh ingredients. Later I'm sorry to say, we avoided eating local produce especially meat, as the hot climate, sometimes reached 130 degrees Fahrenheit inside the van, precluding any thought of "freshness" remaining more than just a few minutes!

In addition we simply couldn't afford the delay for one of us to become seriously ill as we were not tourists and had a job to do and a project to finish. In these times, on the hot and dusty roads, we stuck to a seemingly monotonous but well tried diet such as chips, eggs and baked beans when we could get them. Even in 1978 these were hugely expensive depending on the location. The record was about £5.00 for a genuine tin of Heinz baked beans, purchased from a little store outside Tobuk in Saudi but after several parched days in the summer heat of the desert, baked beans never tasted as good as the ones we cooked that night.

The Journey begins - The first faltering steps

We passed on through the picturesque towns and villages of Austria and on into Yugoslavia, a beautiful but poor country, beset as it had been with internal conflicts. We found the people in the countryside were open and friendly but passing through Ljubianka there was a very oppressive atmosphere, born out by a strong military presence.

Staring apprehensively through the grey drizzle at what resembled a typical concentration camp, we could make out the dim outline of jackbooted guards, barbed wire and sentry posts. Distracted for a brief moment, we nearly crashed headlong into another vehicle coming in the opposite direction and were woken out of our musings by the loud screeching of brakes and a hand pounding hard on a car horn. That was a close call but by good fortune we had just missed being involved in a major pile up. Shaken, we pressed on into the early evening dusk to follow the road some distance further before deciding to rest in a lay by and start afresh the next day.

The roughness of the cities in Yugoslavia in the seventies contrasted so very much with the beautiful countryside which reminded me of the Yorkshire Dales back home. On waking the next morning I was amazed to see a "carpet" of wild crocuses and yellow flowers in a rain soaked wood close by the van.

All I needed now was a good hot shower and the travellers world would be my home. As it was, we had to press on with the schedule and continue with a tiring regime along often dangerous, rain soaked roads. We stopped briefly at a café called the *Brodvin Restaurant* to pick up sandwiches and fill up with petrol. The prevailing weather was in stark contrast to my previous visit whilst on my journey out to Nepal, courtesy of the infamous Magic Bus company. Then, we had slept outside on the grass, exhausted after a gruelling journey in a battered vehicle, bearing as much resemblance to my idea of a coach as water to wine. Clinging to the rear seats for sheer life we gasped as "spaced out Pete", the perpetually doped up driver, forced his way along the fast moving conga line of trucks, cars and other suicidally driven varieties of transport. We all gratefully fell asleep outside on the grass to the hum of crickets and the dancing of moths which obsessively flew around the wall lights. Only then did sleep bring back some sanity to our lives.

Now it was cold and the wet clinging rain seemed interminably present. Even the owners of the café didn't seem to be too bothered about our custom. Could this last for the whole journey I thought? We were praying for warmer weather and fate was to oblige us very generously in the Middle East. With hindsight I can conjure up a conversation with fate that might have gone something like this.

Us. "God, when is this rain going to stop. Oh for some really hot sunshine to sooth away the aches and the chill."

Fate. "Right then so you want it hotter, all rightly, no sweat, well yes actually there will probably be quite a lot of that. Yours in fact, not mine you understand. And dust, oh yes indeedy, quite a lot of that as well but then it will take your mind off the heat, but then digging the VW out of the sand will do that, mmmm ..... (pause for effect) maybe not, ok then .... mmm ah yes and not to mention flooding of the engine in a waddi, sorry ! Sorry ! I said I wouldn't mention that !"

We reached the outskirts of Belgrade, a city with three mosques but a blossoming and modern metropolis of skyscrapers, many only partially built as were the new road systems under construction. No one had told the engineers that motorways shouldn't have road workings across all three lanes. Optimistically we entered a newly finished section of motorway, complete with freshly painted road signs, high quality lighting, an altogether different looking Yugoslavia from the year before.

 Our hopes of good roads ahead were dashed however when just a few kilometres further on it ended in a rough, makeshift track. In fact the whole traffic stream was diverted around a remote and very poor housing slum and with all three lanes now converged to one tiny dirt track, we were held up by a single peasant, leisurely driving a pony and rickety wooden cart.

We took a side road and using my army compass we eventually negotiated our way back to the remainder of the motorway and

The Journey begins - The first faltering steps

continued on our way. We managed to avoid any more peasant traffic more by luck than anything else as the services had not been brought to this section of road. This meant that the lack of street lighting, combined with the blinding spray from trans continental juggernauts provided the ideal ingredients for a major pile up. An accident looking for a place to happen for sure.

We avoided any mishaps only by keeping a strict vigilance and with noses set as close to the windscreen as possible. At long last we pulled into a motel for a welcome rest and food. Here, John discovered what a really hot chilli is like as he was caught totally unawares whilst eating some garnish on a mixed grill, almost choking in the process. We both finished off our first "night out", with chocolate pancakes and plenty of beer. We had covered an astonishing 800 odd kilometres that day, exhausting under these driving conditions, which were soon to deteriorate even further as we moved ever eastward. So we decided that for safety this pace would have to slow down. However, we desperately wanted to see our first mosques and sand dunes (oh the poor misguided fellows I think now) and prepared ourselves for another long day.

Yugoslavia in the late seventies was recovering once more from its war-torn past with building projects like the one in Belgrade pushing away the dark cloak of the past. The military presence was quite another thing and it served to remind us to be cautious as I had to persuade John not to photograph some rather unsavoury looking guards who looked exceedingly trigger happy.

I think the magic of travelling through regions unknown to oneself, is in the meeting of fellow travellers, or local inhabitants, especially the children and their reaction by them to your presence.

Our first such encounter happened shortly afterwards. We had been looking for a shop to buy provisions and were directed down a very rough dirt track off the main road to *Scopje*.

The shop was an absolute Aladdin's cave, full of merchandise from raisins to shovels. It resembled a wild west emporium with the proud owner, a middle aged and attractive woman dressed in simple but functional clothes and standing behind a very gnarled wooden counter. We described the project we had just embarked on in sign language and some English, pointing frequently to cameras, and a picture of a mosque in the shop. Eventually she smiled in understanding, being helped by her children who spoke some English

That she barely knew us, made a gift of salt from her all the more significant and for our part instilled hope for the future as we were still wondering about the sense of taking on this project. I took some photographs of her beside her ecstatic children who were shouting for the sheer joy of seeing two foreign faces. In return we offered them some Polo mints out of our supplies when, as if by fate, the sun broke through, bringing the first warming rays that we had felt since entering Yugoslavia.

We thanked the woman and pointing to the sun we all agreed how wonderful it was that the rain, still dripping from the new seasons growth on the trees close by, had stopped.

Pressing on through the Yugoslavian customs we stayed on the main road to the large city of *Thessalonica* in Greece. I remembered it from the previous year when hitching with Peter to Nepal. It was still as dirty and dusty as ever, in stark contrast to the brilliant and immaculate villages we passed through further along the coast.

One of these, *Kavalla,* nestled in the coastline containing a compact but busy harbour. I had fond memories of eating a freshly caught seafood salad under the cool awning of an open café. By fresh seafood, I mean that it was unloaded not 50 yards away, from the fishing vessels, moored along the harbour and taken straight into the kitchens and served immediately. It was this village that we endeavoured to reach for our overnight stay.

Alas, time was not with us and John and I had started to make a conscious decision not to drive through the night as the roads were becoming more and more crowded with local traffic and only rarely lit. In any case we both felt that the point of this expedition was not only to complete the project but also to enjoy the experience in the process, as financially we stood to gain very little from it. Eventually we became so tired that we decided

The Journey begins - The first faltering steps

Kavalla would have to wait till the following day and at an opportune time we pulled over into a small copse that offered some privacy. It was well away from the main road and in the quiet of the evening sunset, we gratefully sat on a grass bank, in peaceful reflection of the day's events, whilst a few feet away the lapping waves of the light blue Mediterranean sea provided a most spectacular view.

John and I had our first warm, relaxing night of the journey and were able to enjoy our meal of sausage and pancakes outdoors in the tranquillity of the beach. We talked about diving in the Red Sea and of possibly going for a swim the next morning. After another exhausting day we drained our beers to settle for the night, bathed in the soothing caress of the sounds from the shore line.

We awoke at 8 am to a glorious day and I can remember the feelings we had of throwing off the initial worries and tiredness that had beset us from weeks of preparation. The trials and tribulations of simply organising such an expedition and its logistics, together with the frustrating bureaucracy that had us swearing in frustration, now gave way to a more relaxed daily routine. We were coping with immediate problems, such as route planning, obtaining food, fuel, information and of course developing the photographs. All this became a welcome change of activity with as yet, unknown destinations, developing within us an eager awaiting. No longer the baggage of worry and the many "what if" discussions that John and I had played out so carefully during our planning.

We were roadies and thoroughly enjoying it. Simply to be part of this experience was now in itself our reward and our destiny awaited, unfettered by bad news from radio, television or newspaper. With this freedom we naturally became more optimistic in our abilities to cope with whatever lay ahead. This belief was to be sorely tested! Next morning, after a wash in the flat calm sea, too cold for a swim, I took my first medium format shots around our camp site that had become invaded by some sheep. This was a milestone in the expedition and the first of many hundreds of rolls of film that were to be taken. We also

checked our other camera gear and the vehicle engine before driving onto the beautiful fishing village of Kavalla for supplies. Wandering through the narrow alleyways of the market, we bought fresh vegetables, some wonderful bread, a pot of freshly made taramasalata, and a bottle of wine for our meal later on. On the way back to the van, I couldn't resist the smiles of two bronzed young girls who, in the early months of March, were quite curious about our two anaemic looking figures but who quite happily but shyly, allowed me to photograph them.

Later we walked down to the quayside where the early morning catches were being unloaded which provided some further shots for the start of our journey. Once back on the road we passed through *Alexandroupoli* where we intended to spend the last of our Greek money on provisions. The place was entirely closed and so we pushed on to pass quickly through the Greek customs and arrived at the Turkish boarder at about 5 pm. Plenty of time to reach Istanbul, or so we thought!

Chapter 3

Turkey

In the late 1970's the political regime in Turkey, like that of Yugoslavia was still a fairly closed and rather isolated one. Although tourism was well established the presence of military personnel and machinery was all pervading, together with an attitude more of sufferance than encouragement as far as foreign visitors went. I always adhere to the rule that you can tell the politics and general demeanour of a country by the state of the building and attitude of staff in its foreign embassies and likewise at the entry points along its borders with its neighbours.

Turkey was no exception. We were anxious to press on from Greece, across the border and on to Istanbul, the celebrated "gateway" to the Orient where one passes from the familiarities of Europe, to the quite distinct changes both geographically and socially that one finds in the Middle East. This begins once you have crossed over the Galata Bridge from West to East, spanning the Bosporous which bisects this ancient city of Constantinople, the former capital of the mighty Ottoman Empire and now called Istanbul. The famous Orient Express steam train, the setting for many films, used to stop here on its way East to the steppes of Russia.

Our brief elation at reaching the border became immediately thwarted as the Turkish customs official had other ideas.

The official not so much greeted us as sneered in our direction, and was dressed in a black leather trench coat, (I swear I could see the dim outlines of SS patches) jack boots and a black uniform, complete with high peaked cap, which resembled a truly awesome replica of a Gestapo officer.

Ever hopeful, we asked for our passports to be stamped but no, he couldn't stamp them just yet as we must wait for him to sort out the relevant paperwork. Unfortunately the paperwork probably included filling in the football pools in triplicate, since we returned at the designated time to find him with feet on table and leaning back in his chair just at the end of a sports special on his TV.

We were furious, especially when he simply stamped our passports in front of us. We quickly grabbed our papers, only to be asked for them again just 40 yards down the road by more, rather slovenly dressed and unsavoury military guards. Again keeping our feelings to ourselves we obliged these militia but I floored the accelerator in a pique of rage once the formalities were complete. I had travelled only yards when another soldier skulking around in deep shadow loomed out of the black night air. On the unlit bridge there was no room for manoeuvre and as I passed him with fractions of an inch to spare, I spun him around in angry surprise.

We crouched low in our seats, quite expecting a hale of bullets but were soon lost to the pitch black of the night, along a road which we hoped would eventually take us to Istanbul. Sheepishly we drove through the night wondering if the next bend would reveal a road block but with ever rising confidence we arrived at our destination and parked with other travellers, next to the Blue Mosque in the centre of the city. With a bottle of wine inside us, followed by a cup of Kenco's best coffee, we felt exhausted, as much from fear of the Turkish army as the arduous driving, as we had only covered a mere 600 Kms since that morning. With a little food inside us but already starting to miss friends and loved ones, we were happy just to sleep the day's experiences away. We had enjoyed one delightful meeting in Yugoslavia but this was overshadowed by a rather traumatic one in Turkey.

We awoke on the 17th March, still feeling tired from our efforts of the last few days and decided to stop for a little rest and relaxation. We decided to visit the city and take some representative photographs of the market and some of the world's most famous mosques. The market in Istanbul is quite extraordinary. The sun bleached shades overhanging the shop fronts, almost meeting in the middle, covered an already narrow street. Only the smallest crack of brilliant sun could penetrate the cool darkness, alive with the throng of shoppers. The mysteries of the Orient truly unfolded here, in a wealth of goods of all descriptions as the heated, yet friendly voices, bargained for the last discount.

Eventually we reached the *Galata* Bridge in the centre of Istanbul and indulged ourselves with freshly caught and exquisitely grilled fish. Already tired, we then returned to the van to pick up soap and towels to take advantage of refreshing showers at the youth hostel nearby. For two days we plied the city streets, sometimes together but also alone, taking photographs of the people, tradesmen and of course the areas in and around the Blue Mosque which is the predominant feature of Istanbul.. The change in religious outlook as well as the obvious mannerisms of the Turkish peoples really impinged upon the mind.

We felt that walking through Istanbul would be a preparation for the journey to come, for what lay beyond this city would be new to us. I had tried not to let past experiences of the year before flavour my view of Turkey and other foreign lands. Then, as a tourist and still a green traveller , getting used to "their ways" was to be a baptism by fire, by recognising the pitfalls of travel and adapting to an awareness and avoidance of tricky situations as they arise.

Now back at the van I was waiting for my curry to cook. All the freshly bought ingredients were feverishly bubbling away and reducing to a rich and succulent meal. At that moment two ingrained memories of Turkey came back to me.

The first occurred on a ferry cruising across the Black Sea from Istanbul to *Trabzon* on the southern coast. I had discovered that my treasured 35 mm SLR Pentax Spotmatic II had been stolen, by being cut from around my neck whilst sleeping on deck. The culprit was caught but only after the ship's captain and I discovered one of my lenses, clearly marked "Royal College of Art" in his knapsack.

The traumatic part was to follow in the local police station, when I was sat down to a meal I really didn't want, with the prison cell of the accused, at the far end of the corridor directly ahead of me. I was able to observe, between hesitant mouthfuls of food, an interrogation in which he was slapped about (probably for my benefit), generally berated and I dare say later, beaten, before being released. I tried to intervene but the police clearly did not want me to interrupt and I would probably make it worse for him and more importantly, for myself. In the end I decided I really couldn't care a damn about any of them. I had got my one and only camera back, as well as an irreplaceable wide angle lens. I wanted to get out of the developing situation, so with a courteous and very English goodbye, I parted company with my hosts and their captive.

I stirred the curry whilst I mulled over the second event. This concerned my foolhardy wish to live native. During my previous visit I was trying to get used to the custom of using my left hand for basic toilette functions. The memory of trying this only the year before, (1977) in a hotel nearby, still left me with embarrassed feelings. With no precious loo roll or paper in sight and alas the water jug and tap just above completely dry, it was highly alarming! Having to approach the manager at the reception desk in the lobby was much worse.

I don't think I need words here to describe my predicament but I eventually managed to induce him to turn on the water allowing me to complete my first...and last abortive attempt at going local in so far as ablutions are concerned. Whatever else I may adopt as native, I certainly was not going to be trying that again, wherever I happened to be at the time, no thank you very much!

Back at the van my thoughts drifted back to food. We ate our curry with gusto, sitting in the still warm evening air and once replete we walked along the pavement to meet several other fellow travellers who were also parked up near by. One of them called Skip from his resemblance to a seagoing mariner, was travelling alone but with a little Scottish Terrier for company. Skip had been married but his children were now grown up back in England. He had spent his time travelling in his little box van, living off the land so to speak, but had made friends and acquaintances everywhere he went. This seemed to bode well for John and I, and seemed to set our minds towards more positive experiences.

The following day we said our goodbyes to everyone and walk down to the post office in the city centre to sort out our mail. I received my first two letters from home. One was from Hanna in the Netherlands and the other from my father. On the way back we passed a sign for a Turkish baths. John instantly wanted to go and try it out as the thought of a genuine steam bath would be something new and a great line to put in his letters home. Aware of our valuable time going by I convinced him that we should press on but to have one when we passed by on the return leg.

We packed up and fuelled, then headed off to the hinterland of Turkey in the hope of reaching the Syrian border by nightfall.

Following the main *Aleppo* road across the *Galata Bridge* we were officially on our way into the Middle East, leaving behind our homeland but full of joy for the adventure that lay ahead. That is until we passed a rather terrible road accident that people were starting to gather round. Was fate trying to tell us something again, or were we just over sensitive? We decided to err on the side of caution and kept a watchful eye on the road.

The rest of the day was spent travelling through glorious mountain scenery, still blessed with a covering of winter snow that was thawing in the spring sunshine.

The main roads were still very rough at the time and provided very little leeway for passing traffic. They were highways for all kinds of vehicles but also stray animals that wandered without a care into the stream of traffic. Lorries, vans and cars abounded, whose suicidal attempts at blind overtaking left one quite breathless and after several near misses with lorries, we were "bounced" off the road into the "rough" by a maniac driving a van full of adults and children. Soon afterwards we nearly beheaded a cow that wandered aimlessly into our path. At 70 mph, a stationary cow can do a lot of damage to a vehicle and it was only with the utmost luck that we swerved, just in time to save all our necks.

Inshallah

Finally, after only a few more bends we passed two "duellist" lorries that had overturned on opposite sides of the dusty gravel road and at that we decided enough was enough. We stopped soon after this culmination of "brown trouser episodes" and simply had to have a cigarette. This was to be our first taste of the type of driving that became familiar to us and moreover, one of many packets of cigarettes to calm already strained nerves.

The rest of the day was relatively uneventful, passing through *Ankara* (several times as we got lost on the many unsigned roads and diversions there) and thence along the main road towards *Adana*. We finally rested up in a lay-by, next to a lorry driver who was trying to mend a puncture with the biggest set of tyre levers I had ever seen!

After covering a rather traumatic 559 kms from Istanbul we were safely parked up by 9 pm. We tucked into what was to become our staple diet. Namely, baked beans with bread, sausage, egg, chips, bread and butter. There was also plenty to write up in the diaries that night and spurred on by events we felt our letters home might possibly represent our last! We decided to break open a few bottles of beer to celebrate our continued survival

The following day was bitterly cold. During breakfast an elderly shepherd tapped on the window and when we slid back the side door he put his head round and gave us a wonderful toothless smile and with that was on his way. Now wasn't that nice to wake up to? He demonstrated the natural inquisitiveness that people had for us on the road and we took it as a sign of goodwill and concern rather than the gate crashing or scrounging that we had expected.

On the open road we passed some magnificent but rather bare mountain scenery looking for all the world like a science fiction movie set, complete with, we think, extinct volcano vents. We stopped to photograph the landscape, including a derelict car with a cat and dog ensconced inside it, before making our way joyously along the mountain passes. We passed through high mountain valleys on the way to *Adana* and realised that we were not going to make it to the Syrian border that day. We eventually stopped at the top of a narrow pass some 2,460 ft above sea level and managed to get well away from the main stream of traffic by pulling into a secluded area on top of a large heap of broken rocks and rubble.

The view the next morning was spectacular. Before us were the rolling and very fertile plains of the richest red soil forming the "bread basket" of the Middle East. We packed up the van and with a little difficulty I managed to back the vehicle off the rock boulders, being careful not to damage the engine sump on the way since getting stranded here would be a disaster! Ahead lay *Adana* which was to be a surprise for us as it turned out to be extremely well kept and picturesque, providing John and I with a wealth of photography of all sorts of buildings mosques and people. Much of the traffic was horse drawn with the carriage and pony a typical means of transport. These changes in life style became more prominent as we drew closer to the flat plains of Syria.

The Turkish border loomed ahead and with our hearts in our mouths in case we had been reported by the unsavoury character at the last customs, we presented our carnet and passports for stamping and surprisingly had only minor delays. This border crossing then seemed to enter a kind of no-mans-land, before reaching Syria, on the other side. The stretch of road before us looked like a battle ground as it was littered with the hulks of cars on either side. It was a creepy area, and like something out of a horror movie.

We felt some one or some thing was going to jump out at us at any moment and so we kept going. All around were the ruins of ancient and modern buildings which I was able to hurriedly photograph as we were sure that we were being observed. A little way on we came across a make shift wooden office where we stopped again. This time the guard was a lone, very overweight but squat woman dressed in a khaki army uniform that was far too tight for her. She wore the mandatory leather black jack boots and came out to greet us. She looked as though she meant business. We both wondered if at this late stage she and goodness knows who else may be laying in wait for us, having been tipped off about our near miss with the guard at the border when we entered Turkey. At this point we held our breath.

Chapter 4

Syria

Our hearts stopped for a few beats as we felt this must surely be the coup de grace. Letting us think we have got away with it before swinging into action with an AK47..... but no, we were waved on by this rather malicious looking woman and negotiated our way through the surreal junk yard, pressing on to the Syrian border.

Our passage here was swift and efficient and after the usual formalities we were issued with a pink entry card that we had to get stamped within 24 hours at a police station. For the first time our carnet for all the film we carried was stamped and we were "encouraged", to take out a special car insurance for third party injury for sixteen Syrian Rials. The customs officials then volunteered us to take a Yugoslavian hitch-hiker with us. His passport had expired and therefore he was to be sent back to Damascus to book a plane ticket before being allowed to leave the country.

We set off once more, along the road to the next major city on our itinerary, *Aleppo*. It wasn't until we had to negotiate some extremely bad road surfaces that threatened to wreck our vehicle, that we started to ask for directions. Eventually found the correct road at a small village near *Reyhanli*, situated at the intersection with the main road. All the time we were crossing extremely fertile land with ochre red fields and I was struck by the avenues of tall trees which lined the straight and narrow roads. Spring was in the air and the land was abuzz with all manner of machinery, as the growing season was starting in earnest before the warmth of March arrived.

The land we were crossing, was part of the so-called bread basket of the Middle East. It was irrigated by the plentiful supply of water from a well developed irrigation scheme fed by the relatively heavy rain-fall from the mountains in the north. It was to compare so starkly with the rest of the Arab continent to the south. Despite advances in agriculture the donkey or pony and cart was still used for many tasks around the villages that we passed through.

Finally, we arrived in *Aleppo* and dropped the hiker off. We looked around for a suitable police station to have our own driving permits and passports stamped but everywhere seemed closed. At this time we were in unfamilier countryside and for safety, felt obliged to go to a local campsite to stop over.

We were directed by the local traffic police, in broken English and sign language to a site just 1.5 km back down the road we had come in on that lead straight out of Aleppo. We eventually found a small, hand written sign, nailed to a wooden telegraph post that said "camp" and an arrow indicated the direction to follow. We drove onto a narrow track and above an entrance found an Arabic inscription made from wrought iron, in the shape of a crescent and placed between two pillars of roughly cast concrete, which we took to be our campsite.

We continued down a very rough track and looking for the keeper of the "camp site" we eventually passed into an inner "sanctum" through another set of open gates and it was then I turned to John and asked "was that an armed guard we just passed?"

John didn't have time to reply for at that moment we became caught in the cross glare of intense light, bringing us to a screeching halt with dust from our wake being blown about and covering all and sundry. The engine, quietly ticking over, was now the only noise we could hear.

Peering out through the windscreen, eyes adapting from inky blackness to the stupefying brilliance of several million candle power, it began to dawn on us that what we thought was a campsite was actually a Syrian Army barracks. Before us were several hastily clad and rather bleary eyed and anxious looking soldiers, machine guns at the ready. The commander was shouting some thing with the anger of one disturbed from much needed sleep. Wiping the dust from his eyes, he ordered us, in Arabic, which needed no translation, out of our vehicle at the point of a barrel. I am sure he really wanted an excuse to use his AK47 but we eventually convinced him we meant no harm.

For just such an event as this, Miz Rhaman had drafted a letter in Arabic explaining the nature of our business. Using the guide book to Islam, we pointed to phrases, which satisfied the senior rank as to our intentions, and who now seemed to be humoured by the whole event and our state of shock. He directed us down the road after explaining " La, la, (no, no), this Army Camp, you no camp here, must go out of city."

Ah, ok, sorry, sorry! "Shukran" (thank you) we said humbly and returned to our search for the illusive campsite.

By now we seemed to be making great advances in winning over armies and influencing them! Lawrence (of Arabia Fame) would have been turning in his grave! As it was late, we decided we could not press our luck again and so headed out of the city to find a piece of ground to camp on. Discovering a patch of grass next to some rather tall cypress trees we made camp and settled down to a warm meal of boiled eggs, baked beans, chips and tomatoes.

The following day I woke early to find it pouring hard with rain and simply drifted off to sleep again. I re-awoke at about 9am to an altogether different day. The air was fresh from the recent rain but it was gloriously sunny and after a hearty breakfast of fried potatoes and beans we set off to explore the Crusader castle in the city centre. Wanting to photograph as much as we could, we stopped mid morning, to have a cup of rich black Turkish coffee. Very hot and quite exhausted we found a café opposite the castle, deep in the shade of some gnarled but leafy trees and here we sat to recover from the mornings exertions. We decided to try smoking the Arab way and for a little extra cash, were presented with a beautifully hand finished *hookah*, or hubbly bubbly, as they are known locally. The tobacco was somewhat pungent but I felt like an emperor, sitting in the shade, trying to look "cool", complete with sun glasses but rather dishevelled hair (see photograph). I think the locals thought otherwise of us, since we stood out like a sore thumb amongst the clean and brilliant white dress of the obviously wealthy locals and merchants who sat at the other tables.

We planned the rest of the shoot to take in the cooler parts of the monument. Unaccustomed yet to the rising temperature which had reached the upper 20's Centigrade, we found the sharp morning sunlight had disappeared to be replaced by a dusty, rather diffuse glare, that seemed overbearing to us at this early stage of the journey. These conditions were mild compared to the 40-50 degrees Celsius and 90% humidity we were to endure later in the journey.

Now, refreshed by the break, we crossed the road and made our way to the market or souk which was a magnificent example of a traditional Arabic centre of commerce. The *souk Elzerb* was enclosed in the underground vaults of the crusader castle itself, and was every bit as busy as the market in Istanbul. Many shops were selling exotic carpets which can take several months to weave and command a hefty price. Alas we had no room in the vehicle with us and little enough money for food, let alone souvenirs, so we decided to revisit the city on our return passage. For now we had to settle for some photographs and a little window shopping.

Passing down a passageway we eventually entered a mosque and were taken (literally) in hand by *Abdulla Maktabi,* the Imam or chief priest. Individual travellers like us, were still uncommon in these parts, but fortunately we had befriended perhaps the one person who could grant permission to areas normally barred to "unbelievers".

We were allowed to photograph literally everything. The mosque itself, call to prayers and even the sacred tomb of *Sheik Alshikh Marouf.* Over a cup of hot sweet black tea with a refreshing sliver of lime in it, we talked at some length about the politics in the west, Islamic culture and also about our project, in which the Imam was deeply interested. Especially so, as we Christians were helping in the education of the growing Muslim community in the west.

Syria

All too soon we had to part, but with offers to return to talk further with the Imam we headed back to our rather impromptu site outside the city. As we passed the small sign to the "camp site" which had carefully guided us into the army camp the night before, we were curious to see if there really was a public campsite. It turned out to be a bit of waste ground behind a garage and the owner wanted an exorbitant fee for just one night.

"What's the point of this" we thought and so we returned to our original site to cook food. By this stage we were beginning to feel that we were much happier being as independent as possible on our overnight stops and from that point on we generally avoided areas close to major cities when setting up camp.

We had just finished our meal when a head popped round the side door, making John and I jump almost out of our skins. He introduced himself as *Abdalrheen Khaled*. He was dressed in immaculately pressed western clothes and we offered him some chi (tea) which he gratefully accepted. In conversation he, in no uncertain terms indicated that we were camped in a rather dangerous spot.

"Did we know there was an Army barracks not far away?" he asked, as he explained that some of the incumbents were a little nervous of strange peoples, especially as the Israelis were reported to have spies everywhere! He suggested we return to his village to stay the night as we would be safe enough there.

Keeping quiet about our nocturnal wanderings and "interview" with representatives of the Syrian Army the previous night, we packed up the van and followed a little apprehensively behind him to his village. We sped along mostly narrow and very dusty tracks, all the time wondering if this were to be the end of our journey. Ambushes and God knows what were going through our minds, but after the steadying influence of a cigarette, we calmed ourselves and decided to let fate take its course.

After a harrowing and rather dizzy 30 km drive we stopped at dusk in his village. The buildings were typical for the area as the roofs were strangely domed, atop four square walls but all freshly white washed. This was a prosperous farming village with an abundance of tractors and other agricultural implements left in surrounding fields, as well as dusty new cars that we could see parked close by. It was obviously a hard working and proud community and this revelation somewhat eased the tension that had been troubling us since leaving the outskirts of *Aleppo*.

As the honoured guests we were ushered inside to meet the elders in their "conference" room. With warm greetings we were introduced to *Abdalrheen's* brothers and the other elders of the village who were sitting on heavy cushions placed around the thick, cool, whitewashed walls. There was not a table or a chair in sight, just a free and open space. The centrepiece was a highly decorative, charcoal burning hearth, in which glowing embers heated metal jugs from which the aroma of fresh coffee pervaded the smoke laden air. The warm atmosphere was congenial and welcoming and pulsated with the hum of heated conversation, only becoming subdued on our entry. With the cordial welcomes over we accepted our host's offer and took part in the ritual drinking of coffee which provided the signal for discussions to resume.

Small talk does not exist in the Middle East in the sense that it does in England where we deliberately and frustratingly, discuss anything non-controversial. The inquisitive mind is too literal in the Middle East and in assessing us, the first part of our "interview" comprised several basic questions. "Where have you come from?", "Where are you going?", "What are you doing?", "Are you married?", "Have you children?", "What is England like?" And so on until they were happy that we were genuine travellers. It then came as a stark shock to be asked "and what do you think of the Israeli conflict. Do you think they or the Arabs are right?" To which John and I both gulped, the sweat now starting to run freely under my shirt.

Taking the middle path, with some inane though very English and compromised diplomacy, John and I explained something along the lines that, " It was really a shame that war has broken the two great nations apart but that Arabs and Jews should live together in peace as they have done for hundreds of years, as life is surely hard enough as it is."

Although rather patronising, this seemed to satisfy all those gathered, as a philosophical and pragmatic answer and we were astonished to find that they felt the same way, openly talking of the conflict as basically bad, a waste of money, resources and most of all, good lives.

"This is Syria?" we thought, taken off balance by their reply. It was supposedly one of the more aggressive nations in the Middle East but as the evening drew on, we were able to talk with more confidence about politics, ourselves and our aspirations.

The discussion finished, the room finally began to empty and we were shown our sleeping quarters, complete with floor mattress, quilted eiderdown (for the nights are still very chilly), and nightgowns (*kaftahns*) for us to sleep in.

The hospitality continued the next morning, when we were sat at a communal table to eat a breakfast of fresh yoghurt, goats cheese, hot milk, tea, a rich and very creamy rice pudding, unleavened bread and olives. A very filling working meal indeed.

The family insisted that we take several photographs of the village, its peoples and a group shot with the entire clan, (see photo).

I remember lining up the picture, when one of the elder brothers picked up his very young daughter to pose with her. Into her hand he placed from his shoulder holster, a colt 45. for show! Guns are still part of the culture in the Middle East, from years of family feuds or national conflict. This the little girl held but with such difficulty that she flopped the damn thing in all directions. Knowing my luck, I could imagine it being dropped and firing off a round in my direction.

I very quickly took a couple of pictures and then we said our goodbyes. The conversation still continued (as happens after a party in England) and whilst attempting to extricate ourselves, "humbly" talking to the elders, we could not help but keep one very troubled eye, firmly on the little girl. She had now been placed on the ground, and was preoccupied in dragging the gun along the earth and fiddling with its various parts. "Don't be alarmed, the safety catch is on " somebody said as we looked on. " Good God, so it was loaded with amunition!", I thought and much to our relief, they took the gun away. Waving goodby, we got back onto the main road and after passing more vehicle wrecks along the way our host asked to drive the VW himself back to Aleppo. We obliged, but held our breath until we arrived once more outside the citadel and parted company. Whilst John returned to the mosque, I took some further shots of the crusader castle. By mid day we had covered as much ground as we could and decided to head on south to *Homs* which we hoped would bring us to the famous crusader castle known as the *Krak de Chevalier*.

Eventually nearing Homs, we found ourselves driving along a bumpy track but as it was getting late we decided to leave the castle till the next day and pulled in for the night onto a hard standing. This was full of empty oil drums, under the watchful eye of two rather despotic looking security men who allowed us to park up. It was however on firm ground which was just as well, as that night we experienced one of the most ferocious storms I have ever witnessed. The thunder and lightning continued through the night, lighting up the interior of the van as well as the sky with tremendous flashes. This was accompanied by hail, rain and wind which hammered on our roof as well as the hundreds of empty fuel drums that surrounded us. Before turning in to sleep, we ate our meal and wrote letters to the accompaniment of the very atmospheric Vangellis album, "Heaven and Hell" which seemed appropriate music for the storm raging outside.

We awoke on 24th March, Good Friday, to a troubled sky. The front wind screen above the wiper blades, was covered in hail, so I emerged into the grey cold damp of the morning to clear away the screen and to check the side door which was sticking somewhat. No wonder I thought, that the land is so fertile with this amount of water. I did not know it at the time but this was to be the last real rain we would see until our return to Europe six months later.

Stopping only to pick up two French hitchhikers, we made our way along a further 50 km of road until we entered the village of *Al Huwayz*. This surmounted a hill some 250 metres above sea level, and up behind it, in clear relief against the sky were the huge walls of the castle ruins themselves.

Krak de Chevalier must be one of the best preserved examples of crusader architecture in the world. From the guided tour, we could see that the whole structure had extensive renovations, courtesy of the French government and close by was the Christian settlement, inhabited by the direct descendants of the soldiers who came there around 1150 AD.

This town demonstrated a tolerance to other cultures within the predominantly Muslim country, where all creeds go about their daily life in harmony, distanced as they were from the political strife of Palestine and Lebanon. From the town of *Al Huwayz* were splendid views of the castle and the surrounding countryside. It was identical to the rolling landscape of Yorkshire with which I was so familiar, having spent many hours exploring the ruins and moors of the Dales.

Later it was explained in a chance meeting with a local English teacher that the castle was occupied for 170 years but eventually the crusaders were starved out after 70 days by a sultan from Egypt who came to sack the citadel. A discussion over a further delicious cup of, we think alcoholic coffee, the inevitable conversation was struck about the Arab-Israeli conflict. The teacher *Michael Bazah*, who apparently worked with the UN forces during the "Six Day", Arab Israeli war, described the basic contention between the two opposing sides. Land, or rather, lack of it, is the cause of all the problems. Israeli settlers were aggressively intent on divesting the Palestinians of all but the least fertile earth. This was quite a different view point from that which the media in general cared to emphasise in the West.

The following day, I woke early, and from our campsite just under the towering walls and drawbridge of the castle, I climbed a hill nearby to take some dramatic dawn shots of the huge walled ruin. Spring blooms of the many delicate meadow flowers abounded, some of which I picked to press and send back home. Returning to the van I once more played Vangellis under the daunting presence of the castle walls whilst preparing breakfast and pondered on the history of the place.

"Imagine the crusaders, banners streaming in the wind, on their horses bred for one purpose alone. They majestically gallop over the baulks of the cedar drawbridge, leading out from the castle, carrying their masters on tasks to be fulfilled. The early morning mists part and swirl about the galloping legs of their mounts. From above, the bright sun glistens on polished armour, whilst the heavy drumming of shod hooves, beat out a prelude to the deadly force they bring".

"Come on Kev!" shouts John, jogging me into the present, "give it a rest, there are some other tapes you know!"

Thus with the spell of my reverie broken we sup the last drops from our cups of tea and head out towards Damascus. This is "The" holy city of Syria but for the most part it is not barred to non-Moslems like the city of Mecca in Saudi Arabia.

The next morning was Easter Sunday but a normal work day in Syria. We spent an energetic few hours photographing the buildings, students and other aspects of the University close by. By chance we met a biology lecturer who I got on with exceedingly well due to my background in the natural sciences. He gave us an account of the struggles that Syria had been through in the past and detailed areas in the city we must visit. After an abortive attempt to park up and in the process, getting unceremoniously thrown out of a disused quarry, we returned to photograph the "old" city centre, posting urgent mail to friends and family on the way.

The heat was building up in the afternoon and the cool and quiet interior of the two main holy centres, the *Mosque des Omiaad* and the *Mosque Jaameh el Oumawy* beckoned. The buildings were stunning with marbled courtyards, minarets and a roof bristling with fine detail, a rich taking in photographs but the best was yet to come. We were ushered into the *Covenant of John the Baptist*, which was once the site of a Christian church. We witnessed much praying in a holy shrine of supreme importance to these people. The ancient well of this site is now covered by a font, carved in a most exquisite way and with the stone work clearly showing fossils embedded within it.

I returned to the mosque itself to find John, deeply in conversation with the Imam of Damascus, who offered to give us an audience to talk about Islam, his country and, of course, us.

For the moment the Imam briefly invited us for coffee to have a discussion with him as he was about to leave for a meeting in Beirut, so we arranged to return to his house in a few days. Having met people with power and influence, and it is clear the clerics have both, they did not fill us with trepidation any longer and informal talks became a more natural way of finding out and gaining access to important cultural features to photograph. To fit in more with the hosts we met on the way we learnt as much Arabic as possible, which was no mean feat as so many people speak very good English.

After our parting, we talked with some of the Imam's assistants at length. One of them, *Al Sayad Hassan* gave us an expert tour of some important historical sights, which included the ancient and sacred tomb of *Hussein's* daughter, *Zeinab.*

Hussein himself was a revered warrior who became overwhelmed in battle along with his generals and was slain. The custom at the time was for those defeated to have their heads paraded throughout the city on wooden pikes. As the story goes, his daughter on seeing her father's head displayed thus, cried and died of a broken heart and was buried here. Though normally closed to western eyes we were honoured by being able to photograph the small tomb full of worshipers.

After our photographic tour we arrange to meet with Sayad, on our return from Lebanon and to talk further with him and the Imam. The day turned out to be most productive as it was laced with all manner of interesting meetings and venues which no background research could have unearthed. Contact with the people we so much wanted to understand, made the experience highly worth while and productive.

Exhausted, we decided not to cook but celebrated the eventful day and our Easter Sunday, with a supper of barbequed chicken bought from one of the shops near where we were parked. This was the life!

Thoughts now turned to Beirut and to what we might discover there. We of course knew that fighting had ravaged the city but at this time reported instances of military action were far and few between. We calmly planned the route we were to take the next day, quite oblivious to the explosive political situation developing on the borders surrounding Lebanon which threatened to ignite once more into an all out conflict!

Chapter 5

Lebanon

The next day, 27th March, was also to be eventful but in quite another way. After visiting the main post office for mail, we made our way to the Syrian / Lebanese border along the main road to *Rachaya.*

On the way we passed slow moving convoys of military vehicles of all descriptions which we thought were simply taking part in training exercises. The truth, we were to discover later, was more disturbing. On arrival at the Syrian side we were greeted by several boy runners, who were the recognised helpers in what seemed a sea of utter chaos. Deciding against just handing over our most valuable papers, passports and carnet that covered the importing of our film stock, I followed one rather enthusiastic ragamuffin from official to official. It seemed that the paying of these lads greatly accelerated the speed with which the many official stamps could be obtained.

More importantly, these young boys often spoke fluent English and therefore became the crucial link between us and the Arab speaking customs officials. Without this help, non-commercial traffic would most definitely be left to languish at the back of the queue. For foreigners these delay tactics would be extended in the hope that a little baksheesh might change hands. For example I spent 20 minutes queuing for visa stamps at the entry office but for a few coins, the young boy smoothed the way in minutes!

As far as the Syrian customs went, after what seemed a mere moment compared to our recent experience at the Turkish customs, I successfully gained the necessary clearance from the passport control and we were waved on our way. We followed the main road up through the mountains beyond, with spectacular views between the borders, spoilt only by the many wrecks of abandoned cars and lorries along the way. At the Lebanese border, a shanty town of tin shacks had grown up but we could clearly see a military build up taking place. Something was brewing.

Ignoring the money changers who charge extortionate prices to convert the eagerly awaited hard currency, we attempted our most diplomatic request for passage through but the customs officials obstinately refused us entry. We again decided to bring out the letter from Miz about our mission to photograph Islam for educational publications. This eventually satisfied the border guards although they would only give a 14 days pass. This was more than enough for our needs and one which we were told could be renewed in Beirut!

A little further on we obtained some local currency for immediate purchases and against our better judgement we went over to a money changer to exchange a SR100 Syrian note, getting ripped off in the process. Seven kilometres down the road we stopped in *Rachaya* to buy some onions, sausage and tomatoes. I walked across the road to purchase a few potatoes but the shopkeeper at first would only sell us a whole sack. I only wanted a few as they would go bad so quickly in the heat and to my surprise and delight, the sack was opened and I was given, probably out of pity, several of them free.

The shopping done, we carried on along the winding mountain roads and at the site of a burnt out, shell blasted building, the first of many we were to see, we stopped to take some photographs. Getting the wheels of our VW bogged down in some deep mud, I attempted to extract the vehicle, placing some discarded planks under the rear wheels, whilst John walked back to the building from which smoke was emanating to see if help was at hand. He returned to say that he had found some rough looking but friendly people there who had invited us for tea.

We entered the building, or rather what remained of it, to find a shepherd and his very grubby looking eight year old son, as well as a Syrian soldier sitting over the warming flicker of a wood fire that threw shadows upon the dank walls. We were invited to sit and share tea, bread, yoghurt and cream with them, a ritual

Lebanon

Bedouin greeting for travellers no matter how poor the hosts. Of course we in turn obliged when they asked excitedly for us to take their photograph. They reciprocated by allowing John and I to have our portraits taken, with loaded AK47 on hip looking for all the world like macho and rather rough looking terrorists.

For myself this consisted of a rather muddy pair of (flared) jeans, bomber jacket, shades, and tousled, curly, unbrushed and dusty hair. John was similarly dressed but with his Palestinian head dress (à la terrorist), purchased in *Aleppo*. If the security forces in England had got hold of these pictures I am sure we would now have been detained at Her Majesty's pleasure, somewhere on Dartmoor no doubt!

With the meeting over we were about to return to the task of extricating the bogged down VW, when I discovered my Pentax camera missing. At this I asked the group where it was and after a heated argument directed by the soldier in Arabic to the shepherd family, the small boy returned it with a sheepish grin. The ravages of war obviously equipped people from an early age for survival. The soldier whose Kalashnikov we had used as a film prop, asked for a lift to his barracks. We agreed since we saw this as extra security for us because of the military build up. So with shepherd, soldier, and John pushing I managed to drive the VW out of the mire and onto firmer ground.

It then dawned on me that we had left the vehicle open and I discovered my fathers watch which I had removed when placing the planks underneath the van, was now missing. This was a family treasure to me, as it was the only momento remaining from his time with the RAF during WWII. The Syrian soldier spontaineously offered to sort this out on the condition that we did not get involved. In typical Arab fashion it was eventually "found" in the mud. This saving of face for the Arab shepherds was an important issue for the soldier and the rogue of a son, who we were sure was the culprit and who also handed over our Arab phrase book. For the soldier, the family represented his countryfolk whilst we were their guests, and so by careful negotiation, decorum was finally restored with no accusations laid. Stopping on the way to drop the soldier off we arrived in Beirut at about 4.30 pm. We looked around for a secure place to park for the night as the city showed obvious signs of past military action, looking like something out of the London Blitz

In stark contrast to the Arab world we had seen so far, Beirut we noted was far more westernised, denoted by the complete freedom of dress and abundance of the many beautiful women in public, compared to other areas of the Middle East.

We pulled up opposite a hospital and to the amusement of the nurses and female receptionists there, we engaged them in conversation explaining our need for a camp site for the evening. Over a cup of coffee they confirmed there was no official site but pointed us in the direction of the British Embassy who may be able to help after assurances from us that we would return and visit them later, WOW!

After many re-directions, we chanced upon the United States embassy. This was an imposing building with a frontage akin to a Las Vagas Hotel. It had an immaculate front porch to which was attached a stripped awning. This covered the entrance to two massive brass and wood panelled doors. We pulled the filthy and mud caked VW up outside where an armed marine in full dress uniform was standing, to full attention. A real home grown apple pie sort of bloke according to my diary.

After our usual explanations and rantings about what we were doing and how we got there, the marine who so far seemed very wary, eventually took on our explanation with a look, somewhat of bewilderment. He eventually relaxed somewhat, surprised at having met two, now apparently rather hippy looking dudes in the middle of the war-ravaged city that was Beirut. He turned out to be very congenial but fired off several questions of concern to us. "How on earth did you get here as the borders are supposed to be closed since there is a military build up."

"Ah ..um.. we... er... just sort of crossed over, seemed alright to us," was the sheepish reply we gave.

He explained that this was still a dangerous city and to take good care as fighting still erupted and the militia still guard some areas with a rule of iron. He did oblige when we ask for directions to our British embassy which had us following roads along the shell cratered streets to pull up outside a terribly mutilated structure.

Well, it seemed not so much an embassy as a building for target practice!

The structure was all shot up and had only one massive main door. No fancy panels, awning or guard on sentry duty here, just a slab-like, steel reinforced door. This it appeared was built like that of a bank vault, as it had a six inch diameter steel bar door stop, firmly cemented into the floor. This had been a security measure against being rushed by terrorists as it allowed the passage of only one person through at a time.

Now it appeared deserted inside and so we wasted no further time in our hopeless search since dusk was rapidly approaching in this rather irksome part of the city. Returning to those lovely nurses for a coffee and a chat, they suggested the football stadium by the sea front might be worth a try for overnight camping. With blown kisses and fond farewells we drove down to the promenade area to find the stadium rather uninviting and full of refugees, with other displaced persons camping out rough and a hubbub of mean looking cuthroats watching us nearby.

We decided to lock ourselves in the van. Sitting there, whilst pondering our next move, the unsavoury looking people seemed to be taking a rather unhealthy interest in us. It was then that a white Range Rover came up to the VW. This type of vehicle usually signified either the secret police or worse, possibly the PLO militia.

As it turned out the people in the vehicle were friendly and speaking across to each other through our open windows, a very friendly face enquired who we were and what we were doing. We explained our "mission" for Islamic Information and our immediate need to find a camp site. At this he whispered that this was an area teeming with bandits, looters and just about anybody with a grudge. In other words not safe at all. It was the infamous football stadium where the PLO had a stronghold at one time.

Inshallah

So we followed the man in the Range Rover back to his "house" through the Parisian style streets of this ex colonial French city until we arrived at the gate of a beautiful mansion. "*The Cornish Manora*" we now entered was in a more selubrious part of the city, but was looking rather sad and desperately in need of some repairs.

Our hosts, the *Tabaris* family, were positioned high up in the pro-western, "*Christian Philangist*" movement and had been resident in Beirut for many years. They were, however, aghast at the project we had undertaken, especially since we had no local contacts to speak of. They went to great lengths to put us in the picture about Beirut and the conflict affecting much of Lebanon.

Although no active warfare was happening at the time, just a year before things were very different. Street fighting and terrible scenes of carnage were everywhere. Their house, they explained, wasn't suffering from neglect. The apparent dilapidation was a premature ageing brought on by the malicious intents of the various factions. Bullet holes and the splashes from mortar fragments abounded. We sat and talked to the younger of the Tabaris family and his charming wife, over a whisky and soft music, which by contrast to the potential danger we now found ourselves in, provided quite a relaxing, almost holiday atmosphere.

We were, it seemed, just over the dividing sector between east and west Beirut, inside the Christian demarcation line, hence the damage that the mansion had suffered in the past as a front line target.

We realised just how lucky we had been, since word travels very fast in this city. This sad conflict had produced a mêlée of warring armies hell-bent on protecting their interests and producing a conflict with far more complexity than Northern Ireland. The roots of the conflict, as ever, were over politics, religion and land. For the moment John and I were ensconced in as safe an area as you could find in this city, finding time after a luxurious shower to write troubled letters back home, whilst in the background there was the frequent crack of threatening gunfire.

The next day, March 31st, we decided to take a trip about 25 km north, up the coastal road to photograph the historical site of "*Biblos*", the oldest known city in the area. John was driving at the time and we were almost two thirds of the way there, when one of the shock absorbers failed. The steering suddenly became impossible to handle, slewing the campervan into almost uncontrollable oscillations when encountering some of the more rougher sections of road. We decided the vehicle needed immediate attention and so decided to head cautiously back to "*Chez Tabaris*". They kindly organised Edward, their chauffeur, to lead us to the local VW agent for replacement parts.

This was a particularly hazardous journey for not only was the steering attempting to roll us over at every turn, but following the chauffeur through the myriad of traffic lights and playing "chicken" with other traffic was not our idea of a restful day. We were about to be given a frightening lesson in Middle East traffic management. The traffic lights similar to our own in Britain, go through a sequence designed to alert drivers to either stop or be prepared to go. Here however drivers simply ignored the lights altogether. This state of affairs was only rectified for legal reasons by the police setting all lights to flashing amber (be prepared to stop/go) to save face, since pulling over an offending driver could often result in a shoot-out.

Having several near misses on the way, we arrived rather flustered at the VW agents and parted company with Edward to duly await our turn to be seen. We lit up cigarettes to calm stressed nerves and watched the mechanics at work on their vehicles. Just by the very heavy double doors at which we stood was a VW Beetle getting some urgent attention to an engine problem.

This Beetle was a custom job. Apparently, caught in crossfire, it had become riddled with bullets looking like a proverbial tea strainer. Only the glass has been replaced and with the rest of the car repaired, it looked like a moving target from an action movie.

Inshallah

The mechanic was draining the sump of this curiosity only to discover that the idiot driving the vehicle had poured petrol into the oil filler, instead of into the fuel tank. With the reek of petrol fumes pervading the whole area and the exasperated mechanic standing under a potential bomb, he not surprisingly yelled at us to put out our cigarettes. We hastily obliged. In frustration the Beetle was rolled off the ramps and the poor driver told in no uncertain terms that he had to leave it there for further inspection which by the look on the mechanics face wasn't going to come cheap!

The mechanic now turned his attention to our problem. Whilst trying to convince us that the shock absorber needed replacing, it was obvious to us however that it was ok and that it had simply lost the two washers holding the assembly in place on the chassis. So grudgingly he replaced the missing washers on the bracket and locked it together with a new split pin, having the whole job fixed in no time.

Amazingly, after the troubles that had hit the city, the shops were still full of people, eager to spend what monies they had, and we were no exception. Stopping by the waterfront, John and I split up to look around the busy streets. I eventually ended up browsing through a book store where by chance John and I met up once more. We returned to "*Chez Tabaris*" where *Jack*, one of their sons, offered to take us on an "unofficial" tour of the city, or rather, what was left of it in the main battle zone.

We left the rather ponderous VW behind and ended up cramped together in a small BMW, with four, heavily armed minders in a Mercedes following closely behind us. We had a Colt .45 in the glove compartment, just in front of me, in case of an emergency but I hoped it would not be put to the test as I was the nearest to it! The crew in the large Mercedes kept a watchful eye on us throughout our "tour", seemingly stuck like glue to our rear bumper whilst Jack, using his rear view mirror never let them out of his sight.

The tour took us past some very sorry sights including a block of flats scorched up one side. Jack explained this was a terrorist stronghold at the height of the conflict. At the top was sighted a rather troublesome RPG (rocket propelled grenade) crew, who eventually blew themselves up with a faulty launch.

On the floor below had been snipers, picking off men, women and children indiscriminately. Outraged, some phalangalists had commandeered a fire wagon and converted it to a makeshift flame thrower. They filled it with a very combustible concoction of fuel and then casually sprayed the outside and much of the contents of the building with the pressure jet … and then set the building alight, all ten or so stories of it. We were given examples of other accounts where women, of their own volition, had strapped on explosives and turned themselves into human suicide bombs at check-points and other military targets. This had become a fairly common hazard at the time.

We could see the city was gradually turning itself round with market stalls being set up in the basement of otherwise destroyed buildings. The ravages of war were still evident and displaced people of all ages could be seen eking out their wretched lives amongst the rubble and broken buildings that were once a beautiful French resort. With skiing in the mountains or a swim in the Mediterranean close by, it was now hard to imagine that this was once the holiday playground to which the rich and famous would flock.

Seeing an elderly couple pushing a pram, full of their worldly possessions, picking their way through the desolated streets, left me saddened at what had happened here. I admired the resoluteness of the human will, enabling people to start over and scrape a living from what little remained of a once proud city. I was abruptly brought out of my musings when static on the walkie-talkie, indicated the Mercedes was calling us, urgently it seemed!

They had spotted some other suspicious vehicles moving in on us, which could signify a potential hold up. I had the feeling that events were starting to overtake us now. The PLO would be only too glad to capture us and more especially Jack, for bargaining purposes and so in a screech of tyres both cars quickly performed a "U" turn and raced at full throttle back to the safe haven of the Christian area.

After negotiating our way out of trouble several times, aided of course by the letter from Miz, I could see that in Beirut we could not afford to "take" sides in any conflict if our passage were to be completed. We were becoming embroiled against our will, in a struggle that at best could end up severely delaying our journey or at worst, result in imprisonment or, being shot up. We thankfully arrived back at *Cornish Manora* where our hosts that evening provided abundant hospitality in the form of a delicious meal at their French restaurant. Apparently they flew in much of the produce, especially meat and wine from France, to satisfy even the most discerning palate.

We talked at length about Beirut and a possible solution to the problems. Syria had at one time annexed the state of Lebanon and were still negotiating a mandate to patrol the area. The build up of military hardware along the border, testified to their recent intentions. It seemed that Syria was hotching for a fight and should diplomatic methods fail, a full scale invasion was imminent which at present was setting the city abuzz with rumour. I believe though, that apart from a small minority, most people in Lebanon were fed up with this continual strife and would welcome the return of peace, almost at any price. The *Tabaris* family, however had prepared for all eventualities should Lebanon suffer a full scale invasion by Syria with the city erupting into yet another round of violence. A surprise awaited us.

The following day with the vehicle mended, we set off once more to explore the ruins at Biblos and driving through torrential rain arrived to take some rather atmospheric photographs with clouds just lifting from the sea behind the ruins. This provided a theatrical backdrop to the standing columns that are all that is left above ground of this great city.

We were invited back by *Hussein Ebrahim,* a local "seller of antiquities", to view some ancient treasures which although looking the part, were probably fakes. Over coffee we negotiated

Lebanon

a reasonable price for a few items including some earthenware oil lamps and exquisite pearled glassware that glistened an iridescent green. We bade our farewells and returned to Beirut reaching the Tabaris's by early nightfall.

They had apparently become quite worried after the previous days events and were becoming concerned for our safety. On the other hand, John and I had become more knowledgeable about Lebanon by then but still didn't fully realise the seriousness of the hostile situation, indicated by the continuing build up of military material in Syria. Any invasion would immediately start an uprising in the city, one for which our hosts had to be prepared. After a welcoming cup of coffee over which we discussed the feelings which were running high in the city, we were to be given a lesson, in no uncertain way, as what could soon be unleashed on the city.

Jack ushered us upstairs into one of the bedrooms and gave a quick lesson "just in case" for our self defence should the house be attacked. This turned out to be a run down on the inner workings of a Colt .45 side arm and yes ... an AK47. We were shown different fire modes, single, burst, cyclic (full automatic) as well as a description of the ammunition. Different colours for the mixture of ammunition in the magazine, Armour piercing we were told would penetrate the 2ft thick wall at the end of the garden, tracer to see where the shots went and for others to converge fire to, hollow nose (strictly against Geneva convention) that would instantly incapacitate anyone it hit and all this mixed in with standard rounds.

We nodded in the kind of stunned silence of understanding and complete submission, as the real danger around us was emphasised. I still wasn't sure if this was for real or whether they were showing off the cache for John, (an avid collector of arms) amusement. This was immediately put aside when on opening a wardrobe we were further instructed on the use of a 2 inch mortar. John and I both looked at each other briefly and with a knowing raise of the eyebrows, we knew it was time to be on our way. Hospitable though the family were, we still had so much more to see and photograph. We talked through the situation over a few drinks but everybody agreed that we should get out of this steadily worsening situation and reluctantly John and I decided to return to Damascus the next day.

Chapter 6

Return to Syria

We awoke the next morning in the grounds of the *Cornish Manora*, 31st March, to a pleasantly bright and warm day. *Helen Tabaris*, Jack's mother, had made a beautiful food hamper, as good as any from Fortnum and Masons and full of luxury items such as Belgium chocolate, freshly baked croissants and even a bottle of wine. In the morning sunshine she was already in her beloved garden having got up early to prepare food for us and she was now busy weeding the flowerbeds close to the shrapnel marked walls of the house. Helen, like many others in the city, was a determined woman and the war had encouraged in her a defiance especially towards the danger she and her family were exposed to. Here in the garden, under the canopies of the palms that even in this early hour were drenched in the already warming rays of the sun, the tranquillity belied the encroaching danger the family were steeling against, which threatened just a few blocks away.

It was here in her treasured sanctuary that I took several photographs of her. One especially beautiful feature, a marble statue of a water nymph, was so serene in this setting that the hostilities seemed just too distant to contemplate. To see us on our way we discovered that another son *Peter*, had just returned from Biblos in a shiny new Mercedes and together with Helen and his father invited us to have a drink, "for the road" from a rapidly depleting bottle of Black Label whisky.

After a few drinks John, who was staggering about somewhat, in an alcoholic daze, and I, said our goodbyes and handing a letter to *Helen* for posting to *Peter Lang* in London, I couldn't help wondering what would become of their world in Beirut, surrounded as they were with constant danger, every day of their lives.

Inshallah

Driving for the last time through the burnt out and blitzed streets of Beirut we were off once again, to our great relief, on our adventures. Taking some shots of wrecked buildings and cars in the suburbs, we eventually drove clear of the madness of Beirut and continued on up into the clean mountain air, reaching the Lebanese border at a refreshing and much cooler altitude, some 1500 metres above the city.

Gone were the little ragamuffins who proved so helpful before. The atmosphere at the border, after just a few days had become decidedly icy and considerably more hostile. Our carnet and passports received the usual detailed inspection and to our surprise were immediately stamped. However, our presence at the border at this sensitive time did not go down well and they gave us looks that suggested we were mad travellers and definitely up to no good. Before we could be on our way, two guards decided to search our vehicle for drugs and the possibility that we may be carrying guns.

I knew then, that the decision not to carry arms was most certainly a good one. The search was very thorough, with the guards taking everything out and placing it all on the concrete road next to the van for anyone to pilfer. They even crawled underneath the van to strip off the insulation foam from around the heater pipe running from the exhaust manifold at the back of the vehicle to the front cab, a favourite spot for would be dope smugglers. The small chipboard eating table inside also got a similar treatment, with bayonets being hammered into the wood to reveal any secret caches of hashish. The sink was treated with contempt and dismantled or rather, ripped out whilst the side door was taken off its hinges so that they could feel around inside the metal frame. They knew all the hiding places and were very thorough.

By then my alarm at being searched, turned to annoyance as I knew we had nothing to hide but for the time being decided to let it go assuming that this is a ritual to which all people, especially foreign travellers are subjected to. The present situation had of course been exacerbated by the deteriorating political climate at the time with the Syrian forces poised for battle just across these hills. Whilst this ordeal was going on, one of the guards took me to the rear of the vehicle, away from John so that we could not corroborate our stories and started to interrogate me.

"Ok, if you tell me where you have hidden the drugs we will be more lenient on you, but you must tell me now!" he said in a quiet but very assertive voice. His cold black eyes stared into mine trying to burn a hole between my eyes and trying to decipher any hint of guilt from me.

My mind started to race as I frantically assessed the strategy I should adopt to deflect a rapidly worsening situation. If I told the truth that we had no drugs will they plant them instead or if I make up a story to satisfy them, that will surely make it worse?

I decided to play it straight since under pressure the truth will come out any way and also I did not want to mention who we had stayed with in Beirut for fear this might raise suspicions of spying and God knows what. I explained that we had a breakdown in Beirut (the shock absorber) and stayed only to get it fixed to enable us to take some documentary photographs for the "firm" back in England, at which point Miz's letter in Arabic came to the rescue yet again. This was of course the truth but not the whole truth.

The guard persisted saying I looked frightened and must have something to hide, which in a sense I had. I was also petrified as their body language reeked of hostility towards us. I started to get somewhat angry which probably covered any fears I had and was able to counter this accusation saying that I was getting fed up and cold, suffering this indignity with only a thin shirt on.

The fact we were only in Beirut for a few days and that we were two photographers travelling overland was almost unheard of at the time and must have made us look very suspicious to say the least. After failing to illicit any guilty pleas from us they eventually became bored and we were, to our great relief eventually cleared to drive on.

Hastily replacing all our goods and chattels, repacking them neatly to emphasise our annoyance, we continued on our way through to the "no mans land" leading to Syria. Like the Turkish border this was a small road about 5 km in length, on the way to the Syrian border and was similarly lined with the burnt out wrecks of cars either side, a constant reminder of danger. Occasionally we passed the odd car, full to the brim with people, belongings and no doubt booty, that had pulled over to transfer belongings or contraband to other vehicles. A very peculiar carry-on we thought, and no wonder the customs search had been thorough. But we drove on pretending not to notice, in case we were being observed.

Once at the Syrian side we were stopped. To our joy the familiar melee of small boys offering to sort out our passports and carnet, came to greet us. Out of the guardroom close by came a very British looking army captain, dressed in regulation green wool jersey and lightweight dress trousers but sporting Syrian insignia. He was also wearing a highly polished Sam Brown and holster set from which protruded the but of a well handled gun.

With a smile he very courteously and in a perfect English accent (he was Sandhurst trained) asked where we had come from. Holding back our desire to joke and saying something like "Disneyland", we explained the dire search we had just been through, carefully over emphasising the trauma this had caused and which had left us devastated, yet pleased to be back in Syria.

Apologising for our problems he stunned us when he said, "ah yes, we know!" leaving John and I in no doubt that the two borders either "talk" to each other, have very good spies or more probably had been observing us through powerful binoculars. He went on to explain the situation on the border was "very tense", but apologising and in a very nice manner asked us to remove all the contents of the van once again as he also wanted to search for drugs, guns and explosives. Having re-emphasised that this had just been done on the Lebanese side not half an hour ago, he reposted "Oh but we are much more thorough here".

By now John and I were so fed up with this impenetrable burocracy that we left them to it. We decided to hand round some cigarettes to the other security staff and have a chat, which went down extremely well as it was obvious they really didn't want to be bothered with this. Having a smoke ourselves, we were eventually allowed on our way again with further, sincere apologies and a wave from the captain. Returning his wave, we headed on back to Damascus once again, lucky in the thought that we had got through to Beirut and taken some great photographs there. However we were still happy and thankful to be away from what seemed to be a daily worsening state of affairs in Lebanon.

The drive back to Damascus was marked by several road blocks, most of them erected as a result of the military build up. We were stopped at only two of them and with only the briefest of contact. In such situations we felt it important under the circumstances to be as relaxed and cordial as possible. Whilst sharing out cigarettes, we hoped to convey just how pleased we were to be back once more on Syrian soil and that we were (genuinely) glad to be out of Beirut. In return the militia guarding the road blocks had to agree that it was all a very bad business, since they were probably afraid for their own families and friends should the conflict spread. With firm handshakes and parting words of good wishes for our onward journey, we were waved on. The journey continued past more military convoys until we arrived in the centre of Damascus, thankful to be out of harms way, and amazed that this familiar yet foreign land could seemingly become an old friend.

Whilst sitting in our van and cooking an evening meal, a head popped itself round the door and turned out to be a Palestinian clothes merchant who was returning to Kuwait from Europe where he had recently been buying goods.

He was looking for a place to stay for the night and obviously with very little spare money on him, we offered him the space in the front seat of the van to sleep. The conversation soon turned round to the now familiar exchange of personal information. It turned out that his family came originally from a Bedouin tribe, based in *Jordan* but that they moved to *Kuwait* to find a better living and to get away from the fighting.

Inshallah

We talked at length about our journey south through Saudi and across the mountains to what was then the northern territory of Yemen. We talked about etiquette in the Middle East. He advised us that whilst in the company of Bedouin, or other travellers, it is the custom to offer something to your fellow and that one should never refuse water or food, even if only to take just a small piece, as to do so would be considered extremely bad manners. We seemed to have already adopted this mode of conduct such as offering border guards a cigarette or just a friendly conversation, not so much as a bribe but to try and allay fears that we were subversives or dishonourable people.

Our guest turned out to be an organic chemist and so we struck up the most extraordinary conversation, (parked up as we were in the middle of Damascus), about pesticides, or rather the abuse of them, the dumping of potentially lethal products on an unsuspecting developing world and the consequences this was having in the build up of resistance in stored-product pests. My concerns about the abuse of the so-called "green revolution" and the over use of monoculture for cash crops, were also shared by him.

The following day John and I walked down to meet *Haj Hassan,* the Imam of Damascus, and at last had our audience with him. The clerics were all seated around the now, familiar, open white washed room on cushions and once seated we conversed about many things. He asked us what we had accomplished so far, what we wanted to do and where we were going.

Listening intently and with respect, over snacks of dates and coffee, we were fascinated by the words being spoken to us on all manner of things. During the conversation the Imam, through his interpreter, recounted the *Ten Basic Ways of Islam.*

We were later offered the exceptional gift of being allowed to be some of the first westerners to enter *Mecca*, and to photograph the *Haj* or pilgrimage. We, of course, in stumbled Arabic, confirmed this would be most welcome, whereupon we were told "it shall be so, but first you must become Muslim".

"Ah. And how long for this we enquired"?

Return to Syria

"About six months of prayer and learning." he replied!

Politely (but not trying to sound patronising) we thanked the Imam for this truly wonderful offer but explained our "mission" was ostensibly for three months and that we must pass this offer up but will give some thought to it for the future. At the time we were actually sincere and meant it!

And so this fascinating meeting eventually drew to a close. True friendship had been shown to us recently in both Beirut and Syria from people whose opposing cultural differences and religions at war with each other. But to the traveller they displayed the universal hand of friendship for which we were thankful. It is a tragedy that twenty four years on, these cultural struggles are still causing so much suffering for these wonderful people.

Maybe we had been lucky, for I am sure our feelings would have been quite different had we been caught up in any conflict during those few days. However this universal wish to help a fellow traveller is part and parcel of a culture steeped in the traditions of the nomad. We were grateful for this experience and we were to have many such meetings along the way. Parting company we said our farewells in Arabic fashion, *shokran* (thank you) and in return they bade us safe passage, Inshallah.

On our drive south towards Jordan we passed convoy after convoy of military vehicles, tanks, artillery pieces and anti-aircraft weapons. In the desert, a few hundred metres off the road and behind barbed wire, we could see the hardened tops of underground bunkers and radar installations, with their plethora of slowly rotating aerials. They contained not just personnel but also huge hangers for other aircraft and military hardware, safe from aerial attack from the Syrians arch enemy, Israel.

We reached the border, with only the minor incident of a crash between a military and civilian lorry to hold us up. During the three quarters of an hour it took to clear the road we struck up an animated conversation with a family whose daughter was on leave from the army but who was still dressed in military uniform. The girl had exceptionally good looks and spoke broken

Inshallah

English in a very sexy, husky voice as John and I talked with her family to while away the time.

We had an interesting experience in Damascus but were glad to be leaving the heavily militarised Syrian countryside, which had blossomed with so much war-like activity in recent days that we were happier to be moving away from potential conflict to the more sedate and rolling plains of Jordan.

Chapter 7

Jordan

The Jordanian border was to be our overnight stop as the delays in getting through meant that we couldn't reach the capital Amman, by nightfall and we were desperately tired after the slow crossing.

We awoke next morning to a warm and sunny day with a cool breeze blowing. One of the benefits of stopping over at this rather busy check point was that I was able to enjoy the luxury of a cool but refreshing shower in the facilities block. Outside, whilst I took in the scenery and had a cup of freshly brewed coffee, in the background our cassette machine was playing the atmospheric Fleetwood Mac music "Albatross" from our growing collection. The crossing itself was relatively hassle free but for some reason we were only given one week on our carnet. We argued to no avail, as this was far too little time for the photography we had to cover, and so we decided to sort this out later.

We met some Greek lorry drivers who were a mine of information, giving us tips on where to stay and places to visit. This was to include the ancient ruins of *Jerash* and the Nabatian caves of *Petra*, as well as a drive into the desert to photograph the stunning colours of *Wadi Rum*. Here the sandstone rocks take on a deep purple colour during the day and at sun set glow an iridescent red, due to the minerals they contain.

We diverted to the Roman monument at *Jarash* which is a magnificent site and we spent a long time photographing the ruins from all angles. Most of the site was gradually being restored. From the Triumphal arch to the Amphitheatre and Hippodrome, wooden scaffolding abounded on many of the pieces of masonry still standing. Whilst we were working our way methodically through the ruins, we met up with *Charlie and Kathy*, who were looking for a lift back to Amman. They were living in North Yemen but at the time were taking a well earned vacation. Charlie taught agriculture whilst his wife Kathy was teaching English as a foreign language.

I was able to talk at great length to Charlie who had recently been to *Nepal* as part of his PhD and knew the people attached to *Tribuvan* university where I had worked when I was collecting specimens for the natural history museum there only a year before.

Pointing out that we would be driving to Yemen over the next few weeks and asking for information on road conditions, they both looked very worried as they said we would have to drive through dangerous bandit country, along very poor dirt roads. Undaunted, if not a little excited, we put these worries away and having shot plenty of film, continued on to Amman with our hitch hikers.

Deciding to spend the next day photographing some of the more interesting places in the city we awoke to a hot and sultry day but with renewed vigour, set off once more to the city centre. The Amphitheatre was still used for plays but looked very impressive in its own right. The Museum also had a lot to offer as I was able to photograph some of the better preserved examples of local Bedouin costume, which vary considerably from tribe to tribe. This included close up detail of *Yashmaks* (female head dress), which to my western eyes were a most attractive piece of adornment for women.

After a hard day shooting in the dry and dusty heat of the city, we befriended yet another ex-pat called *Archie*. He worked as a bursar for British Airways and after eating our meal at a local restaurant, we crashed a small drinks party (courtesy of British Airways), at the Hotel Intercontinental. The night was spent talking to the aircrew amongst whom were some stunningly attractive yet seemingly unapproachable stewardesses. With his kind offer to drop any mail off for us on his next trip to England, we said our good night's and returned to our camper van to sit and write about our tales from the Middle East. On our return early the next morning, and still under the influence, we quietly slipped the letters under Archie's door as there was no response from within and made our way back to the van. We hoped these would eventually arrive safely at their destination and provide an update as to our whereabouts to the folk back home.

We headed to the ancient ruins of the *Nabatian* capital at *Petra,* still far to the south. The drive took us through the towns of *Madaba, Karak, Taifila,* and *Wadi Musa,* the gateway to the spectacular man-made carvings and caves which created the monuments that abound the city of Petra..

Taking many photographs on the way we managed to get as far as *Karak,* a distance of only 139 kms and stopped amidst an enclosure of fir trees. By this time the temperature had dropped considerably. However, it seemed that some of the restaurant food must have been suspect as I had developed "the trots" once again but decided not to take anything for it just yet and sit it out. After the tenth visit to the trees, preceded by severe cramping of my stomach, I had decided that sleep was off for the night, and pondered on the symptoms and the gradual onset of the next wave of cramps.

I reflected on the similar cramps that I had endured the year before when in Istanbul. I had caught Amoebic dysentery which is a hard infection to eliminate and facing this discomfort, had to endure a train journey to Tehran at the same time.

I had been very pleased to arrive at the American Hospital there, as I was by then, doubled up with severe cramps and in extreme pain. I was hospitalised for three days during which time I was given heavenly shots of torpor-inducing morphine, together with a saline and dextrose drip in each arm to replace the depleted body fluids and electrolytes.The only good thing to come out of this experience were the extra shots of morphine that I conned out of the talkative and pretty Iranian nurse. This provided a very pleasant and very deep rest but disturbingly, her hero turned out to be the infamous "Carlos", alias "The Jackel", who she worshiped as an ikon since he was seen to be fighting the capitalist corruption of the west, represented by the *Shah of Persia* in Iran.

Inshallah

My speedy recovery was eventually brought about by the drug chloromycetine or chloramphenocol, a broad spectrum but very potent antibiotic that will kill any nasty beastie lurking in one's abdomen. The cost of the two days hospitalisation was an astronomical £2,500, paid for fortunately by Endsleigh travel insurance, whilst the cost of a back up supply of antibiotics came to just four pounds. I therefore vowed that any future travels must include a supply of this medicine.

In my current predicament in the van I was fearing that I had picked up some form of dysentery again and so I decided to break open the chloromycetin which by the morning had eliminated the cramps, I felt that I was well on the way to recovery. We set off once more to *Karak* to photograph the Crusader castle there. It was not as impressive as *Krak de Chevalier* in Syria but it was nevertheless very photogenic and provided a good start to the day that I badly needed.

Later we decided to visit the Dead Sea only a few miles away but were stopped on our way at a police check point where they insisted that we should first obtained a pass from the police back in *Karak*. Returning to the police station we found a make-shift and flimsy hut where we sorted the passes required. With the paperwork completed and the passes rubber stamped, we picked up some provisions. These included 10 eggs, a couple of wonderful Mars bars and some fresh bread and milk. The latter was obtained only after John provided a rather amusing impression of milking a cow's teats and someone breaking bread.

The bakers shop consisted of a ramshackle, mud walled house, enclosing a huge earthenware oven into which dough was placed using long wooded spatulas, to come out some minutes later as unleavened bread. We watched as boys of about 10 years avidly scooped fresh bread into baskets waiting to be delivered about the town. We bought two of these and I consumed one of the still warm loaves with much relish, after the previous night spent fasting and evacuating the contents of my stomach.

With my stomach now almost free from any hint of trouble we set off replete, to the shores of the Dead Sea. The police at the road block were very friendly but for some reason now asked that we leave our cameras behind. Rather reluctantly we left a sample (John's old Canon 35 mm) and drove down the winding road which passed through a narrow gorge, until eventually reaching the very hot and dusty plain that surrounds the sea. Unbelievably we passed some palm trees bordering a little oasis with white adobe walls, all that remains from a community that thrived there about 200 years ago.

Still feeling a little the worse for wear, I decided to give swimming a miss but watched as John attempted to launch himself into the sea. In the process he had to wade up to his knees through sticky and rather smelly black mud and so I left him to the raptures of the warm (40 degrees Centigrade) and hyper saline water they call the Dead Sea. This is so saturated with salt as to be treacly or greasy to the touch but the mud is supposed to have a beneficial effect on skin and people come from afar for its supposidly medicinal properties. Quite frankly it seemed so scummy and polluted that I classed it as a natural biohazard.

On our return to *Karak* we collected the camera from the police who good as gold, had not even opened the back, since the frame counter had not been re-set. We then passed on through a landscape interspersed with gnarled white limestone outcrops seeded with grasses of the palest green. Through the town of *Moza* we drove on past a paler, more rocky landscape until by the evening we eventually reached a flat open plain. This was bisected by a deep canyon at the base of which we could see the tops of *Aleppo* pine trees. Having such a splendid view, we set up camp for the night, writing letters home and later, sat back to chat whilst gazing at the valley below, which was awash with the balmy evening breezes.

The next morning I felt a lot better and we hoped to reach Petra, our destination for the day with plenty of time to spare. On the way we were to traverse valleys, gorges and canyons that were quite unexpected and which gave a relief from the flat plains that we had passed further north. We finally broached the crest of one last hill to see down before us, spread in all its glory, the valley of

Inshallah

Petra. We could see the majestic rocks that marked the presence of this ancient Nabatian site, glistening with hues of red, cinnamon and burgundy in the afternoon sun. Passing through the approaches to the desert citadel, along a dried river bed, we stopped at the tourist office to obtain information and the possibility of a cold beer or a coke.

Ensconced in the relative cool of the lobby, we were just enjoying our cool drink when a coach load of American tourists turned up with cameras blazing. The thought dawned on us that to get caught up in this group would not be good for us or the photography and with drinks swiftly gulped down, we headed off to the ticket office to book our passage and stroll through a geological fissure to the rocky citadel within.

"Would we care to go by horse?" the keeper inquired, but we could see all manner of vendors peddling goods displayed on Persian carpets now insistently hassling for business. We declined the offer of a horse with protestations on the keeper's part and walked the gravel path down to the entrance.The vendors were selling "genuine" artefacts including, jambias or ceremonial knives, wood carvings and even Roman coins. All are, of course, fake but it is amazing the livelihoods they support.

We decided that we would make this a quick recce with the main photography waiting till the following day. We were able to look at and photograph some of the many splendid sites in the rapidly setting sunlight and once into the interior found some restoration work going on to the caves there.

By this time the crimson sunset cast a truly magnificent light onto the red, iron rich sandstone with the cobalt blue sky contrasting so starkly with the ruby red foreground of the ruins. Some of the Beduin still lived in the caves with their horses, scratching a living but today, 25 years later, they have been moved into prefabricated accomodation elsewhere by the Jordanian interior ministry as the site has now become a preserved national monument.

On Sunday, 9th April, we woke to a clear and bright morning, with not a soul stirring, save for the muted sounds of goats nearby. Feeling fully recovered, I prepared a simple breakfast of banana which we washed down with several cups of tea. Our diet we noted, was becoming very much more simple as we acclimatised to the increasing heat. At this time of the morning, about 7 am the sun's rays were warming but not too sharp. By 10 am it would be a different story.

We made our way once more along the gravel path through the rock fissure, eroded over the years by lashings of water. The light at this time was superb and slanting through the top of the chasm, we were presented with the classic shot of the "Treasury". This was a monument carved out of the face of the sandstone directly in front of us and was framed by the diagonal fissure of the chasm through which we were passing. The atmosphere was electric and we felt like treasure hunters out of a film such as "Raiders of the Lost Ark". The monument before us had a huge carved bowl on top, which was alleged to contain treasure. The many bullet marks bore witness to the attempts by people to make it reveal its contents.

From here one walks down the paved Roman road to the *Tomb of the Lion*, quite small but with rock carvings of lions either side. The path then opens into a large uncovered atrium, the heart of the site at Petra which is surrounded by cliffs to the left and right. Hewn from the sandstone cliffs are caves still inhabited by the last descendants of the Nabatians, whilst hitched outside on a wooden corral post were the horses, used later in the day for carrying tourists along the trail. In the still air the horses' tails swished away the troublesome flies and to all intents looked the part of a classic adventure movie about Arabia.

About 30 metres above, was the *Monastery*. Like the other monuments this too has been hewn out of the solid sandstone, complete with pillars, archways and detailed relief. The weather had been kind to the stonework since much of the water falling from the heavens is relatively unpolluted, so the curse of acidified rain had not taken a hold there yet. Most of the damage to the carvings was through natural sand weathering or human hand. Working my way to the *Monastery* I took a wrong turning to find myself at the house of the local doctor. We sat and talked for a while in the deep shade. His supplies were very basic for the needs of this community and he re-directed me past the *Tomb of the Lion* to the plateau above. I eventually skirted the base of the cliff and came to a well marked staircase cut into the rock. After a 45 minute climb in the rapidly increasing heat, I found myself on the plateau at the top of the site. As I crested the final set of steps there in front of me was a kind of amphitheatre of rock and sand, in the centre of which was the remarkably preserved *Monastery* itself.

Within the amphitheatre was a young shepherd boy and girl, no older than eight or nine years, tending their goats. I gratefully accepted some refreshing tea which tasted exceptionally good. However being tainted by the western tourist trap that Petra had become, they asked for *baksheesh* (money) in return. This open demand for bribe money, I felt was unwarranted but I grudgingly obliged with a few dinars. They appeared to be rather disgruntled by the small amount but offering to take their photograph seemed to satisfy them.

From the top of this plateau were the cliffs of this massif, not 300 metres from the Monastery itself. It provided a magnificent view across a sea of rock and sand. The colours of distant hills through the mid morning haze were full of deep purples and blues above which hung the high pure white, brushed-cotton cirrus clouds.

Back at the café I met John, who had not long returned himself. By chance we met a resident archaeologist from England called Colin. He turned out to be a mine of information and was there to record and translate some of the Nabatean inscriptions. Colin gave us a late evening guided tour of the main site at Petra. We were fortunate that the sun had by now turned the sandstone rock face into the deepest shades of colour from light orange to rich ochre. With the most perfect lighting possible we took many more photographs of the site and especially of the particular area on which Colin was working. Enhanced by a polarising filter these shots are amongst my most favourite of the whole project (see photograph).

Jordan

We stayed till dusk, which at this latitude fell suddenly and during the walk back we were treated to the most splendid view of the valley by starlight. Without the pollution from street lamps, one of the curses of modern civilisation, they shone brighter and sharper and with so much more detail than I had ever seen them back home.

That evening we struck up a friendship with a fellow traveller, *Dave*, from England, who had been on the road for about five years. We met the following morning for breakfast and over coffee he recounted his travels and recent experiences. Apparently he had sustained his wanderlust from selling British Jubilee crowns, costing him 50 pence each in England, to the German market where he received around ten Deutch Marks in return. This gave him a tidy profit of about £4 per coin!

Dave's stamping ground were the Austrian Alps where he obtained holiday work during the skiing season. He was a remarkable fellow looking like a hippy version of John Lennon, complete with national health specs. He seemed to be permanently dressed in green parka, jeans and sandals which I found extraordinary in this heat! This eccentric picture can further be enhanced for the reader since his only means of capturing photographs of his unique experiences was through the lens of a very old and battered, Kodak box brownie made in the 1950's!

From the deep recesses of his parka he pulled out a wad of rather curled but remarkable black and white photographs of stunning quality in both composition and lighting. These included pictures from ski slopes in Austria, to scenes from Lebanon full of militia and rather mean looking and well armed and masked street gangs. That Dave managed to journey through all these areas by hitching was in itself a tribute. The story that unfolded however, brought home the luck with which John and I had been blessed whilst touring Lebanon.

Dave had wanted to make a trip to Israel via Jordan but journeyed first through Syria and Lebanon. He was in Lebanon about the time that we were there and had just visited *Poseidon* when he was captured by some militia. His hands were tied and he was questioned and beaten to reveal the "true" nature of his presence. After all they had not seen a camera quite like a box brownie and the photographs could be those of a spy. Dave reassured them that he was a "Press Photographer" (the mind boggles at the thought), and just wanted news stories. In the late 70's there was still some respect for the news media and so his interrogation didn't necessarily mean an instant trial and execution as it can today.

We all tried to suppress an urge to burst out laughing at this point as the thought of the interrogation of a "cool dude hippy" in war torn Beirut was at odds with the seriousness of the situation.

Dave was released by the militia, either they believed his story (unlikely) or they thought he was mentally defective (more likely) and out of sheer pity decided to let him go. At this point any sane person would be happy to get away, just as fast as possible but not Dave. He discovered that in being searched the militia had stolen *100 Deutchmarks* (£45) from him and so he turned around and demanded his money back.This brought an instant rain of blows down on him again but this time they turned the "heat" up and asked where he was going. On mentioning the Golan Heights, a P.L.O. stronghold to the south of the city, they made clear in no uncertain way that they would shoot him on sight if he tried to go there!

Eventually he made his way to the hills in the north of Lebanon where he was taken in or rather "adopted" by a Christian village. When told of his "near death" experience at the hands of the militia, they clothed and fed him, gave him shelter for a few days and when continuing on with his journey they presented him with some travelling money. He was now able to hitch to Israel encountering no further problems and always with generosity from the many drivers on the way. He had returned to Jordan where we had now met, leaving John and I stunned as we could see how close we had come to being involved in a similar event ourselves.

Jordan

Experiences like this demonstrate the uniqueness of travel. Great moments of kindness and danger often go hand in hand, emphasising the absurdity of communities, steeped in strict moral codes themselves but which are destined to annihilate each other in power struggles that seem to have no end.

Whilst Dave left to see Petra, we decide to pack up and leave as well but a severe dust storm meant another overnight stay, as driving was impossible and sand would probably have clogged the engine. The storm continued for some hours and with it came an appalling heat. For the first time John and I donned our Arab head gear which helped to stave off the waves of fine grit. Relaxing in the cool of the café, another chance meeting this time with a fellow photographer called *Maurice*, soon had us talking "shop."

Maurice gave me some hints on disguising cameras as he reckoned that a shiny silver jobbie like mine was simply an invitation to theft. He had taped his Leica MIII and Pentax 6X7 with black canvas floor tape and I repeated the procedure on my Pentax. It now looked extremely rough and battered but underneath was perfectly functional.

John and I planned the next day to drive to Wadi Rum and return to pick up *Maurice* before heading down to Aquaba, a coastal resort near to the Saudi border. After setting off quite early we realised that our estimate of 60 Kms to *Rum* was optimistic and was more like 130 km as we had to wind through some very tortuous roads to get there. We eventually decided to postpone our visit for a day and returned to Petra for an overnight stop and to refuel.

The following day we set off once more, this time accompanied by Maurice who decided to come along to take photographs. We stopped at *Maan* to take on some fuel, thinking it prudent to have at least one spare jerry can with us at all times as garages were becoming fewer and further between. Unfortunately we reached the massif surrounding *Wadi Rum* too late to record the sun setting but nevertheless I still managed to capture the glow of the twilight by climbing to the top of a hill nearby, borrowing *Maurice's* rather battered *Velbon* tripod for a time exposure.

We set up camp in the desert, built a fire from brush wood and spent the evening talking, over beer and a bottle of whisky, that Maurice had in his knapsack. Maurice's story unfolded whilst we sat by the fire and listened intently with just the crackle of the glowing embers to break the silence of an otherwise still night. Maurice still carries out photo shoots but his main income was from lecturing at the Royal College of Art in London. He got his first break as a photographer whilst in *Cyprus*, a country deeply divided between the Greek and Turkish communities, when he witnessed the invasion by the Turkish army to take a hold of the northern territory. Maurice had been caught just under the air drop, recording shot after shot of the landings, safely ensconced or so he thought, behind the stone walls of a deserted farmhouse.

After being taken prisoner by the Turks he had managed to extricate himself with film and camera intact and with the help of the British consulate escaped to the Greek sector. The consulate then arranged to fly him out to England as he was fast becoming an embarrassment as the only British citizen to be taken prisoner!

Astutely Maurice had asked a British pilot at the Airport to post his unexposed film of the events of the landings (to his own address) in England for him. When Maurice himself arrived at Heathrow, a reception committee from Special Branch was waiting for him. He was searched thoroughly and very fully debriefed about his experiences on the island but was eventually allowed to leave.

After processing the film he was able to auction them through Sotheby's to the world media who awaited. Each frame from just one film, fetched enough for him to live comfortably for some time and basically set Maurice up for life.

Whilst he obtained work at the Royal Collage of Art he had also become intrigued by the Moony cult, (now a discredited organisation fund raising, it is alleged, on the back of the very profitable Ginseng market). At the time, the sect had become notorious for luring away all manner of people to become militant followers.

Maurice, in his capacity as a photojournalist had taken part in one of their meetings in London and was immediately asked to join. Contemplating this for a few days he returned (against his better judgement) to a further meeting as an observer.

This turned out to be a large congregation but he was singled out to come to the front rostrum, he thought to be introduced as a guest. Here the speaker talked at length about the benefits of the Moony "ways" and when asked if he were satisfied to become a member replied in the negative. Immediately he was verbally "set upon" by the entire congregation, and to Maurice, a well seasoned and street wise hardened traveller this came as a severe shock. Never had he felt so threatened and with so little control over his destiny. It was all he could do to walk down the centre aisle, voices screaming at him, fists of the crowd clenched, hitting his face and back as he walked out into the daylight a thoroughly shaken man. He was never to attend a further meeting but subsequently wrote at length on the subject in the press warning about the cult.

In turn John and I recounted our own life stories, slowly becoming more and more mellow as the alcohol took effect. We turned in, feeling all the better for good company, soul searching conversation and excellent whisky.

We awoke to a scorching day, and by 8.30 am it was already almost too hot in the direct sun. With breakfast finished, John and I decided to treat ourselves to a camel trek from one of the local Bedouin encampments in the desert. Sitting atop our mounts with Arab head dress on, we photographed each other for the record, whilst learning the subtleties of holding on to the saddle at the same time. Riding on the back of a camel is an experience in itself and one I felt could not be sustained for any length of time.

Finally after only 30 minutes but what seemed a lifetime, we stopped and settled by the shade of a tree. The young boys leading our mounts quickly had them hobbled with ropes around their legs, whereupon the camels chewed on the poor and inedible looking scrub with alacrity.

On our return I decided to photograph the Bedouin camp and their camels in more detail. The one I had recently ridden was lying down looking very sedate, around which a chicken was scavenging, clucking and pecking at the ground for scraps of food at which the camel took great exception. I was about to click the shutter of my camera when with perfect timing and just as the chicken reached its rear end, the camel gave out an almighty fart, which sent the squawking chicken, wings flapping for all its worth, about twenty feet in the air. I hastily withdrew and rejoined Maurice and John in fresher air for a game of frisbee on some mud flats nearby.

With the coming sunset we experimented with shots taken through Maurice's diffraction filter, attached to his fish eye adapter. I took these close to the cracked mud forming a strong foreground image with the sand and mountains in the background developing into a very dramatic shot. We packed up in the cool of the early evening and travelled once more back across the sandy wadi to reach the main highway and Aqaba beyond.

In the dark we negotiated the many sharp dips and inclines of the rough road which almost proved our undoing but we eventually reached the main road, only to be flagged down by two Arabs having trouble with their car. We offered them a lift to Aqaba but they later insisted on being let out in what appeared to be the middle of nowhere. Did they know something we didn't, or were they perhaps a little afraid of the company of three Westerners, (or possibly Israelis)?

We eventually arrived at a checkpoint, guarded by militia a few kilometres before our destination, who though curious about us turned out to be British trained Jordanian soldiers, with an excellent knowledge of pubs in the English countryside! A few minutes were passed smoking cigarettes and talking of England. More we think to determine our true origin, as much as friendship. With offers of good luck but with looks of concern for our future journey through Saudi and Yemen, we were waved on our way.

At Aqaba, we pulled into the exotic sounding "Coral Beach Hotel" for directions and a place to eat as we were by then feeling very tired. We eventually ate at the *Ali Baba* restaurant. John and I had spent the equivalent of £8 a piece on a slap up meal, exorbitant luxury indeed in 1978 and by today's prices probably around £30-£40 each but we felt justified due to the amount of work accomplished.

We set off towards the beach to camp but were stopped again at yet another check post and again had to get a pass from the local police station. This was another shanty hut within a small enclosure, filled to brimming (behind solid metal bars) with drunks, thugs and other unsavoury looking people. The policeman at the table was eating his meal but broke off to radio the guard post to let us through.

We continued in our quest to find the long awaited "Yemeni" beach, that we had been told offered the best bathing and diving on the Red Sea coral reefs. Driving blindly past it during the night, we found ourselves suddenly coming to the Saudi border. The police, a mixture of Jordanian and Saudis on guard duty were very nice about having disturbed them and even offered a jeep escort back to the beach at Aquaba.

Apparently Israeli commandos regularly swim across at this point, then go to Petra, take a photograph for proof and return incognito to their base in Israel having proved their abilities at concealment. I with my fair hair looked decidedly foreign, possibly Israeli and indeed in the escort jeep on the way back (John drove the VW) I was asked in an unfamiliar language all manner of things, only to be told later that the guards were speaking Israeli to try and catch me out.

On arrival at the beach we settled down, lit a camp fire and into the early hours sang, danced and got thoroughly drunk along with our Jordanian friends from the border post.... what a barmy army!

Inshallah

The last days heavy photographic work in the searing sun now got the better of me and turning to bed, I crawled up close to the VW, warm in my sleeping bag. With a freshening breeze drifting off the sea I quickly succumbed to the weariness from the day and drifted off to sleep to the melody of John's inebriated rendition of the Lonny Donnigan song, *"Putting on the Agony"* wafting across the still warm sands.

The following days were spent on this stretch of Yemeni beach which was situated only a few kilometres from Aquaba. We had started to acclimatise to the sun, by this time which was scorching during the day but left the beach pleasantly radiating heat during the night. I slept out under the stars every night as the cooling sea breezes gave a balmy restorative and much needed rest after our hectic schedule so far.

By now it was becoming very clear that to keep to the current pace of travel would not only exhaust us, but that we would now need to aquire more local information by taking a little more time over our research on the way.

John, being an avid sub aqua diver and instructor, was keen to get into the water with fins and mask on. He was ecstatic about the wealth of marine life that abounded the reef. Initially borrowing his equipment, I made my mind up to buy my own as John offered help with my training. So I went back to Aqua to purchase some fins, a mask and snorkel, all one really needs initially, since most marine life and the best colour photography can be taken within the first three metres depth. Going deeper however requires flash to bring out the best colour rendition.

The easy living soon took over and the routine life of a beach bum became irresistible. We organised a great party, inviting all the people with whom we had quickly made friends to bring plenty to drink to the beach for the meal. Alcohol consumption is fortunately tolerated far more in Jordan, due to its traditional openness to tourists but we were careful nevertheless that we should not arouse undue resentment by the local muslim population as we contented ourselves by imbibing only in hotels, cafés and the beach areas.

Jordan

For the party I cooked one of my now famous curries. The fresh provisions were easily purchased at the many shops in Aquaba, as most western palates are catered for there. The meat especially looked fresh compared to the scraggy ends we saw in other parts of Arabia, so we had no worries about the "trots", which was a great relief as I had not been able to purchase another supply of antibiotics.

We had made great friends of the *Blooms*, a recently retired Dutch couple. He had been a commander from NATO and she a dutiful and much loved wife, who had been living for some months in a home-made "Robinson Crusoe" style, on the beach and were generally enjoying life to the full.

Other characters included *Jan* a Peace Corps worker, also from Holland (a great nation of explorers). He had recently crossed through Saudi from Iraq where he had been studying and had helped re-develop the irrigation systems there. Apparently the older system in *Basra* is built so accurately and with such fine inclines that they allow water to run unassisted over great distances. The Nabatians of Petra had similar systems and to this day cannot be improved on. After all this time the cisterns and water conduits are still watertight!

After several days of this rather relaxed life my mind started to yearn for adventures anew and I tried to talk John round to moving on. We drew a compromise and decide to give it just a few more days. After all there would be a disco on in town soon.

Lying on the beach the sun-induced torpor left me relaxed but introspective, thinking of the recent days and the worries I had left far behind me. I also became very conscious of the physical state of my body, as any little open cut or wound from the coral took ages to heal and many swimmers were suffering with their feet and hands at that moment.

I had now lost weight and with the regular exercise through diving and snorkelling, I was beginning to feel a high level of physical fitness all too easily lost back home. Though not as saline as the Dead Sea, the Red Sea is however far more salty than the open oceans. For this reason and because of my fair skin

Inshallah

I fastidiously washed regularly in fresh water in a jerry-built shower close by. Luckily I therefore escaped the rash of tropical sores that seem to be prevalent amongst others.

We had not put work aside altogether and managed to obtain an underwater camera, a Nikonus Mk IV from *Conner*, a British naval aid to King Hussein who had borrowed it from the King to take photographs at *Aqaba*. He astonished us by saying that the king had built an underwater playboy den "*à la James Bond*" in a secret location on the bottom of the Red Sea near Aquaba but would not reveal its location. This came complete with cocktail cabinet, living and sleeping quarters and plexi-dome roof, through which the fish could be viewed at leisure.

I had tried taking several frames of the coral on the Nikonus but unfortunately just as I had the shot lined up, the buoyancy of my own body would lift me up and away from the subject which I knew would throw the shots out of focus. I decided to borrow a weight belt from John, adjusted it for neutral buoyancy and to my delight solved the problem. I cautiously edged over the reef to photograph a deep gully full of goldfish and parrot fish preoccupied in playing among the technicolor carpet of anemones. Diving down to about 18 feet I set the speed and aperture, wound on the film, framed up the shot, focussed, then released the shutter taking several exquisite photographs through the turquoise blue water. My lungs started to complain so I kicked away to make a speedy ascent to the surface.....nothing. I seemed to be glued to the spot.

"It must be the weight belt", I thought which had reduced my usual speedy upward ascent to a crawl. I daren't drop the weight belt as it was not mine so with lungs now bursting I kicked out for all my worth, finally breaking the surface very winded but having learn't an important lesson!

John and I took on a more relaxed approach to our journey. Perhaps too relaxed, for we still had a long way to go. However the border patrols and police by now were very familiar with our VW and by driving slowly, would wave us through automatically. Even the loss of our beach pass in the strong winds one night presented no problem. That particular night saw everything filled with sand, and as I was sleeping outside I had to re-arrange my bedding about five times until in the early morning the winds subdued and I was finally able to drift off into a deep, deep sleep.

A coach had recently arrived, the infamous *Magic Bus*, fresh from *Kathmandu*. Many of the travellers camped out in the grounds of the hotel and it was here, during one of my shopping expeditions that I met a very animated American girl. We chatted about our travels and without a seconds thought she accepted my invitation to Yemeni beach for a swim.

On passing the check post to the beach area the engine of the VW spluttered, made an almighty rattle and quickly died. This immediately put paid to any romantic notions I may have had. Eventually we hitched our way to the beach and I got *Otto*, a fellow traveller, to give me a tow with his camper van.

Otto it turned out, along with his French wife, *Lillian,* led a charmed existence. He was a fully qualified Mercedes mechanic, also handy at mending sewing machines, whilst his wife was a nurse. With these skills they had been able to travel all over the world, sustaining themselves from the casual work they were able to pick up. They traveled in a magnificently equipped Mercedes long wheel based box van, converted to a lounge area at the back and with cooking and ablution area just behind the driving cab.

This was true luxury compared to our humble abode and I took detailed notes of its lay out for future travels. We eventually towed the VW back to the beech and Otto explained that the problem was probably a broken (No 1), exhaust valve that had overheated and "dropped" into its cylinder. This is a common fault on the earlier VW and as an engineer and former driver of one of these vehicles Otto had written to VW suggesting a modification to the engine cowling to improve the air cooling properties. With no acknowledgement, payment or word of thank you VW adopted his modification but provided no retrospective fitting, which should have been carried out back in England!

Inshallah

With little to do Otto and I decided to set about stripping the engine from the vehicle the next morning.

Meanwhile at the disco in the evening, I began to get acquainted once more with the American lass and we talked at great length about Nepal, our lives and what we wished to do next. We soon found an empathy growing but with a longing kiss we all too soon had to part as a lift back to the beach was beckoning. We parted company with a firm view to meeting again after my trip was over and the next day her coach returned her to Europe whilst a rather broken engine beckoned for me to carry out some desperate repairs.

Anxious to discover the extent of the damage, Otto and I eagerly set about stripping the engine. We unscrewed four locating bolts on the gearbox bell housing, removed ancillary equipment, cables, fuel lines and cowling. Then supporting the engine on wooden blocks, the motley crew on the beach all heaved the VW van forward leaving the engine extracted and free to work on. What a brilliant German design! How come they lost the war?

By morning tea we had stripped the engine completely and Otto had been right all along. The number one exhaust valve had indeed dropped into the cylinder, severely damaging the piston as well as bending the con rod and scoring the cylinder bore.

There was nothing for it and with no VW agent nearby I would have to return to *Amman* to purchase new parts.

Fortunately Otto came to the rescue once more as he was able to determine the wear and tear on the rest of the engine with one of his micrometer sets. He concluded that many of the parts were all still original specification and wouldn't need replacing. The cylinder bores were another matter and the pistons all looked rather worn! Otto advised me not to renew just one piston and cylinder as this would leave the rest of the worn engine out of balance.

We decided to replace all four sets of pistons and cylinders, one con rod, one cylinder head complete and new big end shells. As the expedition mechanic I now had the unenviable task of lugging this lot through Jordan to Amman and back in my ruck sack!

Jordan

Seeing us all struggling with the engine and VW body, Ray, an Australian ex-pat drove his Chevy pick up onto the beach and offers a hand. As luck would have it he apparently lived in Amman, and would be driving back early the following Saturday, after installing some radio telephones nearby. We arranged to meet at the top of the beach at 7.30 am on the appointed day.

Phoning the VW agents in Amman, they assured me they would be able to get all the parts, pistons, cylinders, cylinder head, valves, con rod, new big end shells and gasket set by Saturday. The cost was somewhat pricy and John and I were forced to contact Miz for further funds.

At the time mobile phones of the kind today did not exist and so to send a clear request to Islamic Information we went to the cable and wireless office in Aquaba to send a very expensive Telex. This was complicated by the fact that due to faulty equipment incoming messages could only be received on a machine in the basement unit but only sent by another on the first floor. Consequently our requests and their replies required several mad dashes up and down the stairs of the building to complete a basic converstaion over the wire. Whilst waiting for further communications to arrive, Otto and I set about cleaning and de-coking the engine parts ready for reassembly on my return from Amman.

I also spent time diving the reef in the relative cool of the early morning with only a little sunbathing afterwards to dry off. Having been so careful with the sun so far, the morning before my departure I overslept. I was uncovered and this was enough to burn my arms, legs and chest to a cherry red. With my rucksack packed full of engine components to be refurbished, I met Ray at the designated time and through the early morning we traveled back towards Amman. Becoming more uncomfortable in the heat of the day, I had no choice but to hold my light shirt away from burnt skin, cursing myself for being so stupid, especially at this time.

Ray was working for the Jordanian government, installing solar powered radio-telephone links so that the local administrators and sheiks could have instant access to the people in power. One installation took about 3-4 hours being just one of many that Ray had installed all over Jordan.

We talked at some length about the journey we were making around the Middle East and as he became reassured that we were indeed bone-fide photographers, he opened up a bit more. In his line of work he comes across all sorts of people but many of them are Americans. He is always cautious as the CIA have payrolled many civilians to return basic information to the United States or local contact. This in itself is not usually hard intelligence but more about developments such as his, or road, rail networks and the like. In itself perhaps not significant but an analyst would be able to draw some interesting conclusions when plugged into the big picture. Jordan was then and still is a key diplomatic buffer between the West and other more militant Muslim countries such as Syria, Iraq and Saudi which it borders.

Ray eventually contacted a "friend" in the border mountains, about 200 km away, to see how he was getting on with installations, warning me to move along the bench seat of the *Chevy* as he had a "burner", or linear amplifier behind it to boost the transmitted signal. So powerful was it that the Microwave radiation could cause damage to tissue nearby, i.e. my kidneys!

Back at his house in *Amman* we transfered over to his Renault and now together with his wife Elizabeth and their children we finally arrived at the VW agents late in the afternoon. I organised the purchase of the spare parts which included valves and springs and for the agents to re-condition the old cylinder heads.

Using the phone from the Intercontinental Hotel, I contacted Miz at his home to check that our funds were on their way. To my relief he confirmed that they were telexed two days ago and that we should receive them any time. He had also written to our families to let them know that we were alright but experiencing some technical problems with the vehicle. What an understatement!

Spending some of the afternoon sight-seeing I became lost in the city and finally ended up at the sports arena to have a drink and a sit down in air conditioned luxury. Here I struck up a conversation with a taxi driver who bought another round of soft drinks and eventually offered to take me back to Ray's place, or at least to the address on the piece of paper that I had.

Setting off we quickly seemed to be deviating from any area I could recollect and the driver simply replied "every thing OK". As my eyes became accustomed to the darkness outside, I could see the outline of a house we were making for. I tried to convince myself that he was just taking me back to his family for a coffee. Any doubts about this were dispelled when on entering the house, there in the centre was an unmade double bed to which he motioned! In his urgent haste he immediately started undressing on the far side.

At this I grabbed my jacket and satchel, made some inane remark and ran outside and across the open ground as fast as possible. Thinking that I would be pursued by a taxi driving maniac, I wasted no time in finding sanctuary in the darkened streets beyond, any thought of finding Ray's place gone.

Eventually I came to the *Hotel Maryland*. A rather basic hostel with modest cuisine. I stopped to eat a chicken sandwich and have a coffee before I turned in for the night, heart still beating, shocked at the experience. As I lay on top of the bed I turned over the events in my mind. Should I have opened the door and rolled out of the taxi to find my way back on foot? More importantly what, I kept thinking, is Ray going to make of my overnight absence and what possible excuse could I use. I am sure he thought I had got laid, or much worse that I was a spy! My imagination ran riot that night but I eventually drifted off to sleep reading the only book available in the room, the Gideon's Bible.

As the VW agents closed early in Amman, I quickly went from the hotel to the bank the next day, where the money had finally arrived. I then walked to the VW agents and was delighted that all the parts were restored and new items booked out. With a very full rucksack this time but in brilliant daylight, I easily managed to find Ray's house, giving the part truth that I got lost and decided to stay in a hotel overnight. In the warming sun we sat and talked about Elizabeth and their family over a welcome cup of tea. They had also travelled extensively showing me photographs of their diesel mobile home in which they explored the length and breadth of Iran. Now, the work Ray had with the Tele-Com service brought in an impressive (for 1978), $40,000 per year and was too profitable to miss.

After packing up for the journey back to Aqaba, we spent a happy evening with friends at a Chinese restaurant aptly called "*The Chine Restaurant.*" Back at Ray's, I drifted off to sleep, mentally re-building the VW engine in my mind to see if I had forgotten anything as these critical parts represented our passport to ventures new. Suddenly I was woken out of my slumber by a commotion outside my room. On further investigation it turned out to be Ray who is apt to sleepwalk once in a while. Elizabeth and I quickly returned him to his bed. I was soon deeply asleep once more, safe between the clean bed sheets, assured the repairs could be completed!

The next day Ray apologised that he could only take me half way to *Aqaba* and that we would have to make a stop to install another radio set. This turned out to be in a sheik's house which was a beautiful building, set in a high enclosure and built with thick walls, with traditional cushions surrounding the cool interior for guests to sit on. The main reception room had a semi circular atrium opening onto a veranda. From here there was a clear view of the approach to the building. In the centre of the atrium was an ancient looking but very serviceable, First World War water cooled machine gun, with its ammunition belt already loaded.

We were told that one can never be too sure of the intent of visitors since the region is infamous for tribal feuds. Our guess was that it was more for show than for real use but I wouldn't like to be around if it had to be put to the test. We were offered tea and a talk with the sheik and afterwards bade our farewell. Having thanked Ray for all his kind help, I walked to the main road to hitch a lift on one of the many lorries going down to *Aqaba.*

Jordan

In no time an Arab had stopped to pick me up and we drove as far as the turn off to Wadi Rum where we paused for a tea break. On a small primus stove the driver boiled water and we sat in the shade of the vehicle, silently drinking the sweet black tea that in the enveloping heat was so refreshing. We had little conversation throughout the whole trip but were both happy just for the company and as we sat I tried to explain what I was doing and about our breakdown in Aquaba by showing him some of the spare parts. On seeing them he tutted and in Arabic which I could not understand but indicated that it was indeed one "mother" of a breakdown!

On arrival at the first road block outside Aquaba, the lorry had to stop for a thorough checking by the military inspectors who were looking for illegal arms shipments that were being made at the time. We were delayed by two hours and having no means of mobile communication could not phone ahead to John and so I had to stick it out until told I could leave. I just couldn't believe it! Eventually I was let through on foot to hitch once again and arrive in Aqaba for 7.30 pm, too late to get a pass to reach the others at Yemeni beach. In the *Palm Beach Hotel* a Swedish guy kindly offered to put me up and we spent the rest of the evening getting slowly drunk on a mixture of beer and Arak. The next day, having obtained my pass, I bumped into *Bloom* who offered me a lift back to the beach. Here I was greeted with open arms as the long lost traveller and learnt that John had also been suffering from stomach pains but was now on the mend.

It was not long before Otto and I started the careful work of rebuilding the engine. Nearby, I noticed, was a disused military bunker which fullfilled the function of a garage admirably as it kept any wind blown sand out of the engine parts. Otto and I continued rebuilding the engine with a break for lunch over a cool beer and cheese. We needed a torque wrench to properly retighten all the important nuts of the big end bolts, as well as those of the cylinder head if we wanted trouble free performance and so we scouted around for tools to improvise with.

Inshallah

We set about using Otto's socket set with a piece of tubing to extend the leverage and a spring balance for weighing fish to measure the force. The pull was calculated as a function of fulcrum length (distance from socket to spring balance) to the poundage measured on the balance and then using my pocket calculator, I worked out the force to match the specification required in the workshop manual, hoping they were within acceptable limits.

All went well with no parts broken or missed out and by late afternoon we all gathered around to lift the completed engine out of the bunker and back onto the wooden blocks to position it behind the van. This done, we reversed the process we adopted before and gently eased the van back towards the rebuilt engine.

After several abortive attempts with pinched fingers and liberal doses of swearing, we finally "jiggered" the engine into place within the body of the van and scurrying madly about like a demented crab, I was able to quickly locate all four mounting bolts to their respective housings and had the engine support replaced in no time. We could now relax and with the wooden blocks removed, the engine was once more ready to have its ancillary components re-connected. I filled the engine with oil as one last task, allowing it to thoroughly soak the internal engine parts overnight. We decided to leave the other, rather minor details of re-assembly till the following morning.

By now it had dawned on me that *Victor and Jan* had departed to make their way back home, which left our little group sadly diminished. Soon we were to part company which felt sad after such a welcoming stay within our adopted and extended family, but nevertheless we would both be glad to be continuing on the road once more.

Now though, my thought was to get the vehicle roadworthy once more. Impatiently I awoke early and continued replacing the parts on the engine. Try as we might though, the engine just refused to start. I checked the timing of the distributor as well as electrical connections. Finally checking to see if there was a fuel blockage, I discovered to my embarrassment, that in my haste I hadn't reconnected the fuel line from the tank to the carburettor and the end was hanging down with its cloth bung staring me in the face. I soon had this connected and with that the engine fired up on the first turn of the ignition. With only some minor adjustment to the clutch cable which I had also decided to replace, we left the engine to tick over while we enjoyed a well earned cigarette.

John and I decided to stay a couple of more days to run the engine in and indulge in yet another disco at the Palm Beach Hotel. My diary recalls that now we had sorted out our VW, people who had kindly stayed to help, started to drift off. First of all *Conner*, the naval attaché who had lent us the *Nikonus,* visited us to say his goodbyes and now *Otto and Lillian* were to leave the next day. We sat around a last great campfire, a sort of respect for those about to leave and had a rather subdued and moody evening, singing songs that blew away on the rising wind. How quickly close companionships were made and like the Bedouin we realised the importance of company and the empathy towards one's fellow traveller.

The next day I adjusted the engine tappets since we had given the engine enough time to settle down and later in the morning sadly bade our fond farewells to *Otto and Lillian.* It is *Otto* who had saved the day for us with his engineering experience as well as his indispensable set of tools. We were so grateful for his help and company. In parting Otto and Lillian gave both John and I some light Indian pyjamas to wear since we were told the heat we would face in the mid summer months, was going to be far more intense than anything we had experienced so far. With final kisses and hugs all round they waved their farewells and drove carefully over the soft sand and were soon lost from sight, but not from mind.

We made a last journey into Aqaba to stock up on provisions and to mend the patch on one of the inner tubes. We returned later to the beach to spend the rest of the day talking about *Bloom's* life with his wife, *Anke.* They had known each other as children and whilst separated during the war, Bloom in German occupied Holland, Anke in Japanese Occupied Indonesia, they re-met after the fighting was all over, married and had children. With Bloom working as a pilot for the RAF and later as a commander in N.A.T.O., they had began to explore the Middle East as a celebration of their recent retirement. After remaining on Yemeni beach for several months, they too were wanting to move on and began packing up their belongings. The little beach cabin had now become a lonely and forlorne place, without the hubbub of activity and voices that had become so much a part of our lives over the last few weeks.

As the the 2nd of May came round, my mothers birthday, we were finally ready to set off once more, satisfied that the engine, now purring reliably away, would take us towards our southerly destination in Yemen.

Chapter 8

Saudi Arabia

After such a laid back existence the border crossing proved to be a bit of a trial. The Jordanian side were concerned at our considerably overdue stay. We had been allocated a week's permit but the carnet was now well out of date. Fortunately we were not turned back, to go through endless days of bureaucracy since the customs seemed satisfied with a bribe of just 8 Dinars. The sea close by looked so inviting whilst we waited for the carnet to be sorted and we were tempted to go for a swim but thought better of it. Once cleared we quickly made our way to the Saudi side, wondering what was in store for us there.

Initially we were refused entry as they insisted our visas would soon expire. This was probably more from the fact that only commercial vehicles or people with work permits were allowed into the Kingdom and we looked highly unusual and rather hippy looking travellers to say the least.

As it happened our visas wouldn't expire till 14th May, a few days hence. We should have been well into the tour by that date according to the original itinerary but with all the delays because of the vehicle problems, we had arrived at the border just in time. We held our breath since to be turned back would also mean a return journey all the way back north to Amman to renew the visas. We also impressed on them the commercial work we would be doing for Dolphin Construction and showed them their letter of introduction for just such an occasion as this.

We were searched very thoroughly as they were looking for alcohol and girlie magazines. They were opening all sorts of containers to sniff the contents but once satisfied there was no contraband, we were waved through. The roads were becoming more and more deserted and we thought it prudent to stock up on fuel and water. At *Hagle* we obtained 10 gallons for the van itself and filled up all 5 Jerry cans, a total of 35 gallons for just 28 Saudi Rials or about £4.00. The Saudis seemed a lot more detached but still friendly towards us, having been a more closed society and therefore less exploited by western tourism. The main influence and driving force has come from the massive influx of oil money which sustained a huge importation of goods and services from all over the world. The revenue from the oil has obviously been diverted to very specific areas such as defense and communications, with road quality varying from excellent to quickly made strips, often no more than a thin veneer of tarmac over the rubble strewn ground.

We started to pass through spectacular countryside, similar to that of Wadi Rum with high sand dunes, interspersed with monoliths of sand weathered rock on the hilly plateaux. We knew we had really left behind the greener lands of the north and were starting our journey into true desert country. We wound our way through deep valleys and gorges, totally barren save for the scrub bushes that were able to exist in this arid land.

With the engine still bedding itself in we made occasional stops to allow it to cool down. At one of these breaks we noticed a phenomenal weathering of the sandstone. The scouring of wind blown sand had left large boulders balanced on impossibly thin pedicles of rock. It was a weird, almost science fiction landscape, so surreal that we spent considerable time photographing them.

The heat was becoming almost unbearable and when towards the mid afternoon, temperatures were reaching into the high nineties, we stopped to rest up once more in the relative shade of a concrete bridge. We both lay down to sleep and when two wonderful hours later we awoke, the sun was already much lower in the sky. We pushed on through some rather flat and uninteresting terrain, stopping to buy two ice cold Pepsis and a chocolate bar. The cost for this luxury was an exorbitant 5 Saudi Rials or about two pounds stirling, a small fortune but consumed eagerly nevertheless.

Saudi Arabia

The next day we headed for the famous Nabatian city, similar to the one at Petra and situated at a remote site called *Madane Sallih*. The report that Lawrence's' famous railway engine is still there encouraged us further. Again it was an exceptionally hot day and in the heat our tempers began to flare.

Probably a little over protective of the vehicle at the time as one engine rebuild was quite enough, I had been reminding John not to over rev the engine in the heat as the thought of a seized piston in this wilderness didn't bare thinking about. I was becoming more and more agitated as John seemingly missed or crashed gears and gunned the motor to breaking point. As we swapped drivers, John now had his turn to express doubts about my driving abilities. The situation got more heated first through swearing at each other and then by John grabbing my shirt. With me brushing his arm away with my right hand, whilst the left still kept control of the steering. Eventually I had had enough and in anger I pulled the VW up in a screech of brakes, dust and locked wheels. "That's it", I said, and with that we both jumped down from the vehicle, and lined up for a head to head confrontation. Staring each other out we argued at the top of our voices in the wilderness.

Here we were in the middle of nowhere, completely on our own, with an engine that, "Inshalla", would keep going, having an argument about...... gear changing. We could both see the absurdity of the situation and finally broke the now deafening silence by talking things through, over a cigarette.

This had the instant effect of breaking the stressed and distinctly icy atmosphere so that we both burst out laughing. This was a soul searching experience for both of us and was to be the only heated argument we were to have on the whole journey. Although this experience brought us much closer together as a team, it would be put to the test during our journey ahead.

We returned to the van and settled down to drive on to the *Al Ullah* junction. On the way we could see evidence of the now defunct *Haj Railway*. This was built by the Turks and fiercely disrupted by T.E. Lawrence. During the second world war it was partially restored by the Germans only to be blown up and dismantled by the British because it could provide a vital rail link to the oil fields for invading armies. It was at one of the old water towers that we found a pile of rails, heaped en mass, by the remains of what had once been a major strategic link. Excitedly we took photographs inside and out, whetting our appetite for our hope to find some original rolling stock at the *Madain Salih* terminal.

By this time the light was almost gone but we found a beautifully green oasis to park up by. The lush vegetation however held its own secret. Attracted to the abundance of water, the place was a Mecca (no pun intended) for every crawling, biting, beastie, that found our arrival to be irresistible. Over our meal of egg and chips, we stared out of the van to see the ground teeming with ants and beetles that were making their way towards us and seemed to infest any crevice or food container left unattended, whilst the air above was abuzz with moths and mosquitoes.

We had just backed the vehicle to a clearer patch of land when a stranger came over and started gesticulating, first at us, then at a building close by which we realised was the local prison. Indicating in no uncertain way that we would have our throats cut if we stayed around the place we were too tired to carry on, and decided to stay put. We slept restlessly in the VW, mosquito nets covering the open, rear and side entrance, and lay there with selected weapons hidden within close range in case of marauders. Mine was the centre leg from our very flimsy table that with luck would possible knock out a mouse but it was comforting to have close by nevertheless. The heat was appalling and neither of us got much sleep that night and were relieved when the dawn broke so that we could move on in search of *Lawrence's* lost train.

The drive to the site at *Madain Salih* was extraordinary. We drove for several kilometres along sand rutted tracks at the bottom of a deep gorge. The cliffs either side were sheer and above this was a plateau that seemed completely flat on top. Only the scrub bushes and the occasional tree, broke the otherwise barren and distinctly orange, desert sand. The road eventually straightened out into more open country carrying on as far as the eye could see. This whole region like an Arabian version of Death Valley, seemed to be hotter than anything experienced so far. Approaching the outskirts to *Madain Salih*, we twisted around great red sandstone outcrops, driving through softer and softer sand.

Eventually we arrived at the Nabatian tombs themselves. They were far better preserved than their counterparts in Petra as they were kept well out of harms way having been buried for many centuries by the surrounding sea of sand. Only a fairly recent French expedition revealed the extent and exquisite detail that still remained. Sadly, as the inscriptions above the tombs pre-dated those of the Prophet Mohammed, much of the intricate work has been deliberately defaced over the years by militant religious extremists.

We spent the whole morning photographing this wonderful and ancient site but were finally stopped dead in our enthusiastic endeavours when the VW got bogged in the soft sand. Our first of many encounters.

Unloading the sand ladders, we dug out the sunken rear wheels, placed the ladders in front and slowly, foot by foot were able to extricate ourselves from this difficult situation. Exhausted we pulled off the dirt track onto some solid ground, just underneath the sparse but welcoming shade of a nearby tree.

Immediately we were surrounded by insects but this didn't stop us enjoying some well earned refreshment. Our musings of the morning were broken suddenly by the arrival of a military Jeep. The driver dressed in army fatigues came across to us to ask what we were doing there. We explained about our project which helped in part but he insisted that we should have a special permit which could only be issued from the capital, *Riyadh* for this. He asked us to follow him back to a disused railway station and his headquarters, for an interview with his commander as it seemed we had trespassed into yet another Army camp. Oh no, we thought, not again!

First Turkey, then Syria, and now Saudi.

Inshallah

We decided we had to obey his instructions not knowing what was in store and following behind we drove at a cautious but obedient distance and whilst on the short drive, John and I heatedly talked about our strategy. Should we own up and say that we were photographing in the area or make out that we are just visiting on our way to Yemen.

We were still deciding on whether to keep the photography quiet when we arrived at the remarkably well preserved *Haj* station within the rocky embrace of the massif. We were ushered into a large room and beckoned to sit on some cushions by the Saudi commander, who was immaculately dressed in a clean, traditional white gown, (*thobe*) and corresponding white headcloth, (*ghutra*). On top of his headwear sat his *ogal*, the dress version of the circular rope, once used to hobble a camel's front legs but now adopted as head adornment. He looked every part a proud commander and turned to us indicating with a glass in one hand, Chi….(tea)?

Awah (yes) we replied in our best Arabic.

John and I whispered further about our photography hoping he could not hear our conversation when to our complete and utter surprise the commander turned once again from the side board where he was preparing the tea and asked in perfect Oxbridge English,

"Would you like some sugar?"

Aghast that we may have been found out and with lumps in our throats we gasped a throttled "yes please"

We settled with our teas, not daring to speak first and the commander apologised, "I'm awfully sorry about this but did you know you are in a guarded Army camp?"

We stayed silent

"I'm afraid I must ask you to leave but first can I ask have you been taking any photographs?"

I started to crawl into the stone work.

"Um er oh no ," I said with Pentax slung over my shoulder!

"We were about to when your guard called us over," John chipped in.

"That's probably confirmed that we are outright liars and should be shot," I thought to myself.

We decide not to pull out our ace, Miz's letter of introduction as this very firmly stated that we were photographers, not a good idea to offer proof of what we were doing! We had to let it go this time.

I prayed they had not witnessed our earlier wanderings over the tombs.

Seemingly with his curiosity and honour satisfied, he explained that the site was officially closed to all but the army and that we should have asked for a pass from the police at *Al Ullah.* He went on to explain that this station was indeed the one where Lawrence based himself for a while and the train and railway carriages outside do date from that period.

What a scoop! If only we could get just one good photograph. This was too much of an opportunity and so on the way out, John drove the VW, whilst I attempted to sneak a photo of the train. Through the view finder the shot was lined up, fast shutter speed to counter the bumpy ride, camera slammed hard against my head for stability, I leaned across John's right shoulder when in the corner of the frame I could see a car nudge closer to our vehicle and from the drivers window, a hand extended towards me clutching a Colt .45 automatic, pointing straight at my head and waving frantically, motioning us forward and out of the area and most definitely "*not*" to take any photographs! Oops!

We returned to *Al Ula* and there met up with the school master from the village, who was also the regional headmaster for the Medina district and worked for the museum there. We hoped he could organise a permit for us to return to the *Nabatian* site. He offered us a welcoming shower and said he would attempt to get a pass for us to return to the tombs but held out little hope as it was now closed off to almost everybody. Also, did we know?

"There is an army base there!"

Inshallah

The drive to the site in the morning as well as digging the van out of the sand had left the VW filthy and on examining the air filter it was choked with dust. Whilst I replenished the oil bath and cleaned the grit from the bowl, the headmaster, amazed at the sight of our decrepit looking vehicle, walked over and invited us to look at his fully equipped mobile home whilst offering us a snack of cheese and tea in the meantime.

His pride and joy turned out to be an air conditioned Toyota land cruiser, complete with a bed, refrigerator and TV, more a luxury boat on four wheels than a converted van like ours. We were very impressed as it represented the travelling style we could only dream of.

It was still oppressively hot, even though the night was closing in and so we had little thought for a hot meal and just ate some oranges, the only refreshing thing at the moment, as all our water was by now a tepid stew, tainted with the aroma of polythene from their containers. Turning in for sleep we watched from the van as huge humped back spiders, some almost four inches long, came crawling across the sand, which soon put paid to any thought of sleeping outside on the ground.

The van had turned into a kind of storage radiator and at fist we slept in fits and starts but by midnight it had eventually cooled off enough for us to drift off into a much needed slumber.

The next day we again awoke at about 6.30am. At this time the morning was still fresh and in the sharp sun light I took many photographs of the palms and irrigation systems making up the oasis. The oasis itself was also filled with inhospitable insects, whilst the valley retained an appalling heat that we had endured enough of. Without further delay we decide to push on.

In one of the fields further down the road and on the border of the oasis we saw *Abdullah*, the headmaster's assistant, working in the fields. The scene looked so picturesque that I pursuaded John to stop, whilst I become engrossed photographing *Abdullah* tending the irrigation system. This provided the all essential water that makes this area so verdant, a jewel of sparkling amethyst in the midst of an otherwise barren landscape. With some urging from

Saudi Arabia

John I noticed that an hour had passed and we headed south to *Al Matran* where there was yet another splendid oasis, but on an even grander scale. We passed kilometre after kilometre of palm trees, standing sometimes next to open expanses of fresh cool water. It was truly a magnificent sight.

Driving further into the desert towards Medina the air had become so dry that John and I sat with a bucket of water between us, soaking our *shumaghs* (Palestinian head cloths) and swathing our heads in rapidly evaporating water to cool parched and over heating bodies. In Medina, we negotiated the dirty streets and countless road blocks of the city to head once again into the cooler hills above the desert plain. Though extremely tired, we decided against our better judgement to carry on. After another 80 km we found ourselves well clear of habitation, and just past *Al Musayjid*, we turned onto a track leading from a bridge down to a dried river bed.

Pulling up onto a sand pan we got the rear wheels bogged down straight away. We dug ourselves out and John walked ahead of the vehicle this time, to test the sand in front. We eventually pulled up next to the river bank itself and were completely screened from the road above, a cosy place to settle for the night.

After writing letters to family we settled down to sleep and in the absence of biting insects I decided to lay outside on the sand bar whilst John opted for the van.

I awoke the next day at 6.30am and made tea. John got out for his morning ablutions and saw a disturbing sight. There were footprints around where my head had been, clearly embedded in the sand. On closer inspection John and I agreed that they looked familiar. They looked like pussy cat prints that one finds on the car some days, except this print was about four times as large. We were told later that they had probably been left by a jaguar on the prowl for any food we had left out. I had been lucky even if it was only scavenging. We therefore decided that it was becoming too risky to sleep out in the open and that we must get hold of a strong, full length roof rack to sleep on, safely out of reach of ground dwelling animals, whilst open to the cool of the night air.

Inshallah

We made our way to the coastal city of *Jeddah*, where after a few hours driving, we were to rendezvous with our contact, *Joe Neville* at Dolphin Construction Company. Here we were to photograph the prestigious sites they currently had in operation. Jeddah looked to all intents and purposes like a typical American town, as one passed a plethora of billboards on the approaches to the centre of the city. Our first task was to visit the main post office. John for a change found mail awaiting but unusually there was nothing for me. I was crestfallen.

We spent a rather restless night in the VW, with mosquitoes biting despite netting and smoke coils that we now started to use. The next day, 7th May and Hanna's birthday, we met Joe who took us to some of the construction sites. It turned out to be a busy and very productive shoot as I alone shot 15 rolls of film on the Rollieflex. During the shoot we talked to many of Joe's colleagues about their work in *Jeddah* and one of them, *Bob,* offered to put us up if we ran into trouble.

The rest of the day was spent researching the route through to Yemen as well as visiting some of the very Western shops in the new market area. The food malls were especially well stocked, better in fact than many at home since they catered for international tastes with some products unobtainable in England. We also visited the old souk (market), as we were told that the real souvenir bargains could be picked up there. I decided to buy a little transistor radio which boasted not only AM but FM as well. This I felt would give us contact with home, as well as giving news updates about the Middle East on the BBC World Service since we had become very aware that the stability in some regions could change from day to day.

We also bought the lighter, Saudi, *ghutra* head cloth, made from a much thinner white muslin and offered a more comfortable choice for our onward journey. They were plainer but far less bulky than their heavier *shumagh,* the Palestinian counterpart (synonymous with Arrafat and terrorism) which we had been wearing and offered a cooler, more comfortable material to shade our heads and keep out the dust which blew in through the open

Saudi Arabia

windows. We were still not sure of the viability of the overland route from Saudi to Yemen and so we explored the possibility of putting the VW on a ship via the Red Sea, to the Yemeni port of *Hodeida*. Finding an Arab import/export business we asked about prices but it quickly became obvious that it was going to cost a great deal and also that there could be a long delay waiting for a suitable ship.

We asked about the overland route and the owner was able to help by introducing us to some Arab drivers loading up their lorries close by. Lorries apparently made the journey overland all the time but for individuals, especially foreigners, there were other difficulties to overcome. There are tarmac roads to within about 30 Kms of the official Saudi border but it continued south of the town of *Najran* through desert. There were patches of very soft sand and for people unfamiliar with the crossing such as us, a guide would be essential, especially for a two wheel drive vehicle like ours. After the desert crossing, which would take about 2-3 hrs (about 40 Kms) we would then ascend into the mountains. These areas were known to have occasional problems with bandits but the tracks, although rough in places were clearly marked with little soft sand to be negotiated. He omitted to tell us of the flooded wadis to be negotiated. The lorries had a high enough wheelbase to clear these but we were much lower and later on they were to nearly be our undoing. We talked at length with the drivers and from this we obtained a written guide from them for the most difficult leg of our journey:

SAUDI : by road to *Abha* then onto *Najran*. We then had to take a further rough road to *Al Khadra* where our passports would be stamped for exit. If we made it there we must then cross soft sand to a shanty town in no man's land called *Al Bogeh* where we could rest, re-fuel and take on water for the onward journey. From there the soft sand gives way to mountain ranges that we must cross (some 200 Km) before we reach the official Yemeni border

YEMEN : We would drop down to the plains around *Sadah* and from there is a good road to the northern capital *Sanaa*.

103

Inshallah

We spent two days at *Jeddah*, photographing more sites for the Dolphin Construction company and also visiting some of the more interesting areas of the city. One of these is the harbour since it is always busy and full of *dhows*. They may be many years old and are handed down from generation to generation. Whilst very photogenic, Joe warned us not be too open about taking photographs, especially since the Saudis are paranoid about spies and so have designated all harbours and airports off-limits for photographers. If caught, there is automatic imprisonment and a heavy fine.

This was a great pity as we were driven to the far side of Jeddah airport to find five World War II Mitchell bombers, disused and collecting dust on the concrete. Over the other side of the road was a heap of aircraft scrap including the remains of a Douglas Dakota DC 3, worth a small fortune in Europe. Joe told us of one person he knew that couldn't resist the temptation to take an instrument from this aircraft but who had been caught and imprisoned now for several months.

However we did obtain some beautiful shots of the harbour, late in the evening. Then after a rather exhausting day, we returned to *Joe* and his wife *Brenda's* house for our last dinner with them before continuing with our journey to Yemen. In appreciation of their wonderful hospitality we bought chocolates for *Brenda* and cigars for *Joe*. We talked a good part of the evening away over a delicious supper of steak, baked potatoes and salad, the last substantial meal of this kind until we reached Yemen. This ecstatic change to our diet was followed by a magnificent bread and butter pudding and cup after cup of English tea. Music had become our travelling companion for the long drive south but with very little to chose from, I set about recording some more of my favourite tracks from Joe and Brenda's record collection.

The next day we first picked up supplies from a supermarket, and then said our goodbyes to *Brenda* and *Joe*, setting off on our way via the *Mecca* road, pointing ever southwards. Along the main road we came to the junction for *Mecca* on our left and *Taif* which we followed straight ahead. We then started to enter the foothills of these unexpectedly high mountains. The tarmac roads were already sticky with melted bitumen when suddenly the asphalt about a hundred feet in front seemed to be moving in a kaleidoscope of colour.

We did not realise until too late that we had hit a massive swarm of ground hopping locusts, still in their immature "hopper" non flying stage. I tried to brake to avoid them but the wheels had already become caked in the crushed and greasy remains of hundreds of these insects. We slithered to a halt in a sideways, four wheel drift, as if on ice. Once we regained some degree of composure we moved out more slowly, crunching our way across this moving carpet of crop pests.

Once clear of the swarm which was concentrated into a narrow band, I opened up the throttle and climbing for several hours up a gradient, we ascended the massif surrounding Taif, which is the cool summer resort for the better-off Saudis. Just outside Taif we had to make our way through a maze of small dirt tracks, along which goats were being herded whilst all about seemed to be in utter chaos since in every direction there was a new road or building under construction.

We awoke to a rapidly warming day, having overslept despite the insects. The mosquito net had done its job and with a liberal dose of fly spray had kept out all but the most determined individuals. Even my wealth of bumps were beginning to recede with no new ones in sight.

John made tea, whilst I changed the oil bath in the air filter that had become choked with grit. We set off down the road to our next destination, *Abha.* Our speedo by this time was registering that we had travelled a total of about 8000 kilometres since we had left England. The van had been once, if not several times, "around the clock" but still seemed to be providing sterling service since the engine overhaul.

The landscape made a dramatic change at this altitude, some six thousand feet above sea level. Gone were the desolate rocks and deserts of the lowlands. These had been replaced by fertile terraces, cultivated with a variety of crops and making full use of

Inshallah

all available growing space which is at a premium in these rugged mountainous parts. Cattle too were kept, along with oxen, used for ploughing the fertile rich earth we now passed.

The houses too were very different to those in the plains as the weather brings more rain and strong winds. The houses were built mainly of stone with concrete and brick for the more modern ones. At regular intervals there were old stone towers, once used for the storage and milling of maize grown throughout this area. The men wore more traditional Saudi dress while the women had much more brightly coloured clothes compared to the bleak attire worn elsewhere. They tended to dress in traditional patterned top, black pyjama trousers over which was usually a skirt or apron. On their heads they wore straw hats, similar to those of Mexico, wide brimmed but with a curiously tall conical centre piece.

I managed to obtain several photographs of the communities as we passed by, as well as several of the wide varieties of vegetation, such as the cacti with its brilliant yellow flowers and sometimes even large stands of trees, reminding me of Spain. From our vantage point we could look from the summit at about 2000 meters to the plains below. This was a wonderful sight, with patches of green among the deep red colour of the rocks, beyond which was the Red Sea, the source of rain for the area.

We pulled off the road and stopped for a break. Over a dinner of chicken legs and bread we chatted to a fellow traveller who was in the process of mending a puncture. He was English and had made the journey in an official capacity from Yemen once before. To our relief he confirmed that the crossing was passable for our two wheel drive VW but only just, as there were some very bad stretches of soft sand and rock strewn road in parts. So with hearts lifted, I took over the wheel, to drive with renewed optimism, whilst John had a nap in the back.

The VW drove like a bird, down through *Abha* and beyond. Taking a short cut along a dirt road the Englishman had suggested, we stopped outside the town of *Khamis Mushayt*, a distance that day of 600 km.

Saudi Arabia

Next morning we were again up early to another cobalt blue sky with cirrus clouds, so high they seemed to be in orbit. They gave a feeling of openness and space that is all too rare in England where the closeness of the cloud base seems, by comparison, very claustrophobic. Once again we discovered that we had inadvertently parked outside an army barracks but fortunately were not disturbed, with not even an inquisitive face present.

We set off at 9 o'clock, spending some time obtaining only a little Saudi money for basic needs in *Khamis Mushayt* as we would soon be in Yemen. We then negotiated our way through the busy traffic onto the main road to *Wadi Najran*, the southern most town, down in the plains and last major stop for fuel before the desert crossing. The highways were of reasonable quality and even had road markings from time to time but the town of *Najran* itself was an enormous lorry refuelling depot. The sand was littered with the detritus from thousands of passing lorry drivers and travellers. Tin cans flattened and scoured under the huge weight of passing lorries glistened in the sun, whilst the sand itself was not the pure clean crystal yellow from the open desert but a grubby and rather discoloured earth-brown, oil-soaked crust from the many spillages that had taken place.

We topped up the main fuel tank as well as the jerry cans for the desert crossing as there would be no fuel for 200 km or so. We were also concerned as to whether the roof rack would hold all the weight now loaded on it and which made the slats bow alarmingly. We drove on and met some Korean workmen who were building an extension of the road that would eventually run to the Yemen border itself. It was several years away from completion as there was competition between Italy and China for the contract to build it. The construction had only just begun and in no time at all the road petered out and we found ourselves in the desert proper. The sand track led to a shanty town called *Al Khadra* which we reached after about 30 minutes drive. Once there we joined a long queue waiting to get visas issued and passports stamped. John and I became concerned that we would become unduly delayed and were just not going to have the time to make the desert crossing to *Al Bogeh* on the other side of this desert which was our destination for the day. Any further delay for the start of the mountain passage would eat further into our rapidly approaching deadline to enter Yemen itself, as the visas expired four days hence and to be turned back having crossed the mountain range would be disastrous.

I decided to jump the queue and walking up to the Saudi passport officer, I was assured that they would expedite our stamps for us. Ushering us to take a seat close by, the customs official explained for our benefit, that it was vital for us to obtain a further visa in Yemen itself, (ours was just single entry and exit for Saudi) to enable us to come back this way and re-enter Saudi territory. Without it we would be refused entry to Saudi, no matter what our circumstances.

Unaccustomed to this friendly help from border staff, John and I sat close by, watching the other applicants plead in all manner of ways to be let through. Some clearly were regular visitors and passed through on the nod, while others entered into an animated yet friendly conversation with the inspector. Casually he demonstrated his complete authority over all around him, our host turned and with a wave of his hand, asked if we would like an ice cold drink. By this time we were both thirsting from the mid day heat and gratefully accepted. He leaned over to a chest freezer powered by a portable generator, as the mains from *Najran* had not yet come as far as this remote outpost.

He opened the top of the freezer and reached in, moving aside what appeared to be official papers, since the fridge was also acting as a filing cabinet. He extracted two bottles which we sipped, whilst waiting for our passports to be returned. We were obviously unusual visitors and many of the staff made an almost embarrassing fuss over us. One of them, the medical officer by the name of *Mosbash Kawamolleh*, brought us hot, sweetened tea which we drank along with the other refreshments.

When we explained that we were to cross the desert that afternoon, they tried to talk us into delaying our journey until the cool of the next morning. We insisted however that we wanted to cross immediately and so they organised a guide to take us through the worst parts. We followed a black saloon car, never letting it out of our sight. With us was a young Arab boy who gave additional hints on driving technique as well as directions in broken English which he reinforced with the rapid gesticulation of his hands.

First, he said, we had to let some air out of the tyres to give extra floatation on the sand. Second, we must not under any circumstances stop, as to do so would invite disaster since we would become bogged down in the very soft sand. Third, when we hit soft sand it was essential to waggle the steering wheel left and right. This has the effect of tossing aside the "bow wave" of sand which tends to accumulate under the front wheels and can rapidly reduce the speed. Feeling like an entrant into the Paris to Dacca rally we set out, thanking the officials which they responded to with many hand shakes but with more than a hint of incredulity in their eyes.

It was enough that we should be driving through the soft sand in our two wheel drive but at least the VW had a good ground clearance. Goodness knows how the much lower car guiding us was going to cope. The Bedouin however, are much respected for their ability to effortlessly drive ordinary cars and navigate through the most hostile deserts without the benefit of four wheel drive, or the plethora of gizmos now available these days. They have simply substituted, and mastered one form of transport, the camel, for another one, the motor vehicle.

No sooner had we started than we were waved to a halt at yet another guard post. This time it was to check papers, presumably to counter (or more likely tariff) any contraband that smugglers were trying to sneak across. Again we went through the ritual tea drinking and then we were allowed to push once more into the desert. The car in front threw up clouds of fine dust that started to choke ears, eyes and noses and was rapidly finding its way into every crevice, leaving a fine covering over everything in the van. "Go on, go on!" the boy said with a flick of his hand, indicating that we were driving too slowly. The track was heavily used by commercial lorries, evident by the deep tyre ruts that we were now driving down. Too wide for our vehicle to straddle, I was driving with one wheel on the centre mound and one in a tyre rut.

We occasionally drifted too far one way or the other and would feel the dreaded sluggishness of the van which was rapidly beginning to stall. More power was needed from the straining engine to allow the steering and tyres to re-mount the centre hump left by the lorries but which miraculously the car in front seemed to negotiate with ease. We very much respected the person for his driving abilities and the ease with which he negotiated the seemingly impossible slopes of sand. Three times, we became so bogged down that we stalled and stopped, having to dig ourselves out with the help of our guide. As the light was fading by this time, we needed to urgently press on to make the truck stop at *Al Bogeh*.

With the thought that I must keep going we careered along the deep lorry ruts that made the van wallow from side to side, John shouting "soft sand, soft sand" at appropriate moments. One memorable occasion came as we hit a sandy switch back. This consisted of a series of hard gravel ridges interspersed every ten feet or so by very soft sand. Like a ship in the Atlantic, the van lifted, then in the next moment, plummeted to pan out on the soft sand. Each time there was a resounding thud from underneath. On one particularly bad stretch, the front of the van dug in to just above the front bumper, the weight of the sand loading up the over strained shock absorbers and suspension. The forward speed however overcame the resistance and with an almighty heave the van recovered, throwing several hundredweight of sand and powdered dust high in the air and over the windscreen. All forward vision was obscured so I just held the steering straight and prayed, while the sand cascaded down through the open side windows, to be sucked into the driving compartment covering myself, John and the young boy in a fine gritty veil.

"This good driving," the young boy said with a beaming smile on his face. John and I could only hold on for dear life, wishing for a hasty end to this drive. We stopped only once about half way, on an open stretch of gravel to let the over taxed engine cool down (see photo). Here we met the desert taxi for the first time. This was invariably a Toyota Land Cruiser, whilst the better known Land Rover was conspicuously absent due, we heared, to poor marketing. The taxis were full with people whilst on top was a mountain of luggage but nevertheless these taxis would cruise through the sand all day without any trouble, much to our envy. The mistake we made at not insisting on a 4X4 vehicle now became all too apparent. We just had to make the most of it and Inshallah, we would get through.

Eventually the sand became firmer, indicating our approach to the outskirts of *Al Bogeh*. Mercifully the desert crossing had been accomplished. We had been driving for several hours through the sand but it had only seemed like minutes. No wonder the dark was closing in as it was now already 7.15 pm.

Resting for a short while, John and I cleaned out as much of the sand as we could and refilled the tyres with air as from now on we were almost clear of the soft sand and into rocky mountains. We pressed on to catch up (so we thought) with our guide vehicle, only to get bogged down yet again. We extricated ourselves with a final effort of will and energy but decided to return to *Al Bogeh* for some much needed rest and with a view to start afresh the next day. It was not to be!

Chapter 9

Yemen

No sooner had we arrived back at *Al Bogeh,* when to our surprise we met up with our guides who, it turned out, were still sitting in one of the cafes drinking tea! Once finished they indicated for us to follow them and in the rapidly failing light we knew the mountain crags could easily wreck our vehicle, should we drive off the main track. We therefore had no choice and despite our weary state decided to fall in behind, noting that they had now ominously transferred to a Toyota Land Cruiser. Was this a sign of things to come?

Aprehensively we followed them in convoy with other 4 wheel drive vehicles and lorries, also on their way to Yemen. A short distance from *Al Bogeh* we started to climb into the mountains, along a heavily used but rough single track, that released fine clouds of billowing dust at the slightest disturbance. With head lights on full beam there was just enough illumination in the rapidly approaching dusk to cut through the dust laden air, allowing us to negotiate the many boulders in our way. We travelled on like this for several hours, passing between crags on unseen ridges and then dropping down into the soft sand of dried wadis until climbing out to traverse the next ridge. All the time we were climbing imperceptibly higher into the rugged frontier mountains separating Saudi from north Yemen.

One particular wadi still contained pools of water which we noted were coming well up the side of the vehicle in front. We were able to push through the first of many but with the rear wheels spinning in the mud beneath the surface we could only extricate ourselves with difficulty. We then encountered a further, much larger and deeper pool than the rest, which flooded the entire width of the Wadi. Lorries and Land Cruisers had gone through with water well above their axles indicating the pool to be about two to three feet deep in the centre, higher than our engine bay but hopefully not as high as the air intake.

With steep rocky outcrops either side, we had no option but to return or go through. Turning back was now impossible as a convoy of all types of vehicles, a sort of midnight safari, had now built up behind us and as we blocked the only road, were becoming impatient to move on.

I revved the engine hard to keep the exhaust system pressurised and prevent ingress of water, slipping the clutch to reduce our forward speed which allowed plenty of spare torque to pull ourselves out. We were undecided how to drive through the water, should it be fast or slow? In the event we decided to move off at a modest pace to prevent a bow wave from washing over the vehicle. It was a mistake as our speed proved too slow to push through to the other side of the mini lake. The water must have flooded up from below and soaked the electrics in the engine. The motor started to splutter and we were rapidly losing all forward momentum, vital to push out of the pool.

Finally the engine cut altogether leaving us stranded with only the front wheels on the furthest bank of the pool. Whilst the drivers cab was out of the water, the back wheels were firmly embedded in sand and with it the engine which was now almost covered in water! Clearly the cylinders had filled with water and to attempt to turn the engine over could cause severe damage. We were being urged on by the irate drivers behind and so it was not long before we had attached our polyester "tow rope" (that came with the emergency kit from the Royal Automobile Club) to the vehicle in front who offered help.

The rope snapped immediately as if it were wrapping twine. The driver of our tow vehicle took one look at our miserable efforts and tutting to himself, returned to collect and attach his steel tow rope. We were pulled clear after a few heaves and a help from a multitude of drivers and passengers, now desperate to clear the way and who were now leaning on the back of our van. They had now been delayed for half an hour and were impatient to resume their drive through to Yemen.

Inshallah

The Toyota pulled us a little further down the track to where it opened out allowing lorries to pass us by while we tried to get the engine going. Thanking the Toyota driver with a few of our cigarettes, he went on his way whilst I began the task of drying out the engine.

Unscrewing the spark plugs by torch light I asked John to turn the engine over to blow out any water from the cylinders. However, I had forgotten to take my head out of the engine bay and in true "Laurel and Hardy" fashion the high pressure spurts of compressed water from the cylinder bores squirted straight into my face. This had the immediate effect of making me jerk my head upwards and out of the way. Unfortunately the top of the engine enclosure was only three inches from the back of my head which I now smacked with some considerable force.

Nursing a developing bruise on my head I squirted a liberal dose of WD 40 water repellent in and around the engine, then cleaned and re set the spark plug gaps and replaced them. I replaced the HT leads, distributor rotor arm and cap and then wiped and checked everything else. John turned the engine over which began in coughs and splutters to start. Finally it burst into life but left me surrounded by a cloud of heavy, oily smoke from the residues of the WD40 squirted down the bores.

We let the engine tick over happily for a few minutes to get warm, then set off once more. We eventually hit more soft sand again getting bogged down. John by this time had had enough and wanted to stop. However the track was quite narrow at this point winding between pools of water and the banks of the wadi and so I persuaded him to go on. With the help of a lorry driver who pushed from behind, we got our vehicle up a slope and off the main track. We soon hit deep gravel and on becoming bogged down once more, decided enough was enough and gave things a rest for the night.

By this time I had developed a greater faith in the endurance of our vehicle and had become more confident in our abilities, compared to the early days in France where, with several punctures already impeding our progress I had become quite dejected. Now it seemed, was John's turn. This was probably because he had become more of an observer in the continuing problems we were encountering over our transport and had become, quite rightly, more concerned at the risks we were taking rather than being absorbed on mechanical problems as I was. John at this point was for turning around and going back to Saudi the next day which I couldn't blame him for. I was able to convince him that we were now so close to our objective, the higher and wadi free mountain road to Yemen, that to turn round now would not only mean losing the chance to fulfil this part of the journey but also having to re-cross the desert immediately. This was a prospect I hoped to delay as I had had enough adrenalin coursing round my body over the last few hours. I wanted to put the desert crossing out of my mind for another few weeks. At that moment I preferred to chance the unknown than to go through our recent ordeal again so soon. I took a pragmatic view of things and was quite enjoying the challenge of crossing the mountain range!

I was at least happy that the engine still worked after the gruelling crossing of the desert and now the soaking the vehicle had just been through in the wadi. Tomorrow was another day, there would be plenty of people passing by to help. I made a resolution that has kept me going through life sustaining me in difficult times. That is to "follow your heart and inner conscience. If it feels right, then go on and never turn back along a path once taken." So with renewed hope we decided to press on and not go back.

The lorry convoy had finally passed and all was perfectly quiet. We were finally able to settle down to a deep sleep at about 3.30am. When we awoke a few hours later, I was able to flag down a kind driver who stopped to help push us out of the gravel and back down the small bank of the wadi onto the main track.

We drove for a while but did not encounter any great hazards as we had the night before, since in full daylight it was easy to spot the jagged boulders, some of them knee high, that all too easily could slash our tyres. I was, however, becoming more unhappy about the performance of the engine which was showing a distinct loss of power. I hoped that we hadn't bent a valve or blown one of the four cylinder head gaskets. Finally I decided to check the engine out and so pulled onto a piece of gravel where we had a break, a cigarette and photographed a shepherd girl and boy who were very curious at our presence. I discovered the air filter bath was completely clogged with damp sand. The dust from the desert crossing had mixed with the water from the wadi to form a slurry that was almost impervious to air.

No wonder the engine was complaining! I set about cleaning the oil bowl and gauze filter liberally with petrol, and also replenished it with new oil. I hoped the cleaning had sorted things and that *Inshallah*, the engine should run a little smoother now! We cautiously moved off and it was immediately evident that the engine power had been restored and we both breathed a heavy sigh of relief.

We enjoyed some magnificent views across the rocky outcrops of the mountains we were traversing which were about seven thousand feet above sea level. The wadi bed turned into a tortuous rocky track that wound its way over shale strewn plains, once fertile and with past evidence of terracing and storage towers like those in Saudi but which were now barren and untended (see photo). The track across this Martian landscape ranged from difficult to diabolical, not from sand hazards but from the rocky outcrops over which we had to pass. These must be so easy for four wheel drive vehicles or lorries with a high wheelbase but the track now presented fissures and steps about one foot deep, down which the tyres bumped and the engine support would crash, with bone jarring thuds. We tried to be so careful, with shoulders braced for the inevitable crashing of the chassis against hard rock, which would be followed by the wild rocking of the van on the suspension. The inside of the cab soon became strewn with all our possessions like a sail boat in a storm. We were only too well aware that neither the vehicle or ourselves could take much more of this punishment.

Yemen

We eventually arrived at the mud citadel of *Al Kataf,* (see photo) that nestled in a valley and we were glad of a break from the tortuous mountain passes. The buildings were typical of Yemen with beautiful square towers and very thick walls. They were ornately painted a brilliant white, surrounding the deeply recessed windows which were framed in wood and gaily painted with reds and deep blues. In the midday glare of the sun these dwellings blossomed out of the otherwise stark landscape, whilst surrounding these buildings were signs of life giving water which encouraged the growth of palm trees and scrub.

Little children suddenly appeared from nowhere and came to see who we were. With shouts and smiles that seemed to drift over the shimmering heat of the day their enthusiasm on seeing us would invariably be followed by shy laughter as we waved back to them in greeting.

One of the children, only thirteen or fourteen, was, like many, carrying a Kalashnikov sub machine gun and beckoned us to stop. He was curious as to who we were and in exceedingly good English, asked if we would like a "go" of his AK47. John jumped at the chance and whilst wanting to get a move on I also decided to "go with the flow" and had some target practice myself.

I am not an expert but the weapon seemed well balanced and not too heavy as the only other one I can remember handling was an old and heavy Lee Enfield .303, belonging to the Army Cadets of a public school near home. I remember how loud the gun was but more importantly getting a finger pinched in the damnable bolt action.

In Yemen the boy who was about shoulder high to me, now demonstrated that I must pull the stock of the AK 47 into my shoulder, aim along the two sights and try to hit a large boulder about 30 meters away. I loosed off a round but God knows where it went as I heard it ringing out from its ricochet off an unseen rock. This was rapidly followed by a single bleat from a goat, also hidden from sight and I hoped just startled and not injured. I needed a lot more practice I thought, and at that the boy, now smiling at my poor marksmanship, shouldered the machine gun himself and effortlessly sent off a round to land slap bang in the middle of the boulder!

John and I both took pictures of each other and the boy to capture the moment, after which he offered us some Quat, a mild narcotic leaf that the Yemenis chew all day. To me they tasted bitter and once on our way again, I spat my portion out. John meanwhile persevered with the amusing result that he became mildly intoxicated so that for the time being I had to do all the driving. By 1.30pm we needed a break and stopped at what appeared to be the highest point of our crossing, to cook some scrambled eggs. Although seemingly barren, when one looks carefully at the ground one can find hidden in the crevices really beautiful flowers. We photographed these in the high altitude, pin sharp sunlight, as they represented the last vestiges of life, clinging to an otherwise inhospitable landscape. We could see from this high plain a landscape that descended through a blue haze to the lowlands far below. The air temperature, further reduced by the chill of the freshening winds, really was starting to bite at exposed flesh since at this altitude it could have been no more than ten to fifteen degrees Celsius. A huge change from the temperature we encountered in the desert crossing.

The throttle now began to stick intermittently, so we thought there might perhaps be a broken return spring in the mechanism. We had to continue on our way, flipping the accelerator peddle with a right foot once in a while to return it to the idle position. This had to be accomplished whilst holding the clutch down with the other foot to prevent the van from surging forward and crashing down over the boulders on the track. Our progress was somewhat erratic consisting of a series of "Kangaroo" hops before the cable became unstuck. I inspected it as far as possible but could find nothing unduly wrong and so we continued on our way, becoming more adept at the temporary remedy, intending to sort the problem out later.

We passed still more villages with their own *oasis*, that made welcome breaks between mountain peaks. On the highest, "*Jabel Mar*", which we estimated at 3000 meters, we found that even in

Yemen

the direct sunlight, it was distinctly cooler than the high summer resort of Taif in Saudi, even though we had come 600 kms further south towards the equator.

Interspersed along the journey and signifying the proximity of a village were *Bedouin* camps. Frequently they consisted entirely of corrugated iron sheets, nailed to ancient dried timbers. The build up of heat inside was unbearable, unlike the cool shade of the traditional thick walled buildings we had passed earlier. We stopped at one "shack" in the afternoon where the track intersected several others, to have tea and a well earned cigarette. In this culture it is the young children who excitedly prepare the boiling water whist the mother kept a watchful eye over her brood and guests. The man of the house at this time of day was invariably taking part in a Quat session, akin to our going down to the pub.

Using basic sign language we confirmed the direction to take, and set off once again across the rugged mountains. Slowly we found ourselves descending towards the heat of the lower plateau and after another bumpy and gruelling ride of several hours we came upon the official Yemeni border, signified by a line of blackened and very battered oil barrels. Guarding this prestigious place was a boy, no more than twelve years of age, dressed in the customary black *dishdash* and also gripping a sand polished Kalashnikov machine gun, looking absurdly large across his chest.

Missing were the usual belts of ammunition traditionally worn by border police but if the previous day's encounter with the other gun toting boy was anything to go by, this "child" was probably a dead shot. Children learn to grow up very quickly in this harsh and bandit ridden country. We were motioned out of the VW van and directed with great solemnity to see the "Chief" who was a few yards away in a traditional Bedouin tent.

We explained our project for the umpteenth time but by now we got the distinct feeling he must have known of our journey from fellow drivers who had left us behind the day before. He kept nodding in acknowledgement, quite matter of factly but perfectly able to understand our English. With little ado we had our

Inshallah

passports stamped and were led out to our van and motioned through. My last sight was of the little boy having an AK47 slung over his shoulder, the butt of which was almost dragging on the road. As he disappeared from sight, I could see him struggling with all his might to roll the sand weighted oil barrels back into place.

"What a country!" I said to myself, whilst turning over in my mind the thought of the return journey and making it back along this same route! Relieved that we were now almost through to the tarmac surfaced road which lay just 20 kms further on, our hearts began to lift once more.

Again we encountered the wadi country of the lowlands but by now had a much better idea of the sand driving required.

".....just keep going, don't drop gear otherwise you lose traction through wheel spin," I kept saying to myself.

Passing more and more buildings we negotiated one last piece of flowing water, only about 2ft deep but we decided to take no chances. John "walked" the road first and the river bed seemed hard enough to support the vehicle. This time I determined not to stall in the middle and with my foot down on the accelerator, I shot across, almost too easily in fact. John, meanwhile, was taken unawares by my enthusiastic crossing and had to dive out of the way to prevent being hit by the VW as it clambered up the bank on the other side.

Soon we found a place to rest under the shade of some nearby palms, as we had descended several thousand feet with a corresponding increase in temperature. We were parked next to a modest hill, about 100 metres high, which we climbed to photograph the surrounding valley. This was now lit by the deepening sunset, with hues of pinks, deep cinnabar orange and buttercup yellows. All around us the tranquil scene was untouched by 20th century civilisation and we were suspended in time for a moment. Looking up above the surrounding mountains, the contrails from jet aircraft, high up in the cobalt blue sky brought us out of our reverie, back to thoughts of our daily routine once more. Returning to the van we took stock of our

1. A dramatic start to the journey. Our first bit of trouble when one of the new tyres developed a puncture in the Marylebone road outside the offices of Capital Radio. As the expedition mechanic I set about changing the wheel whilst John stands guard!

2. The *souk* or market place below the citadel in Aleppo. We spent hours looking at the carpets which were considerably cheaper than in England, but with little cash to spare, we had to make do with window shopping.

3. Puffing on a hookah during a break in a café, outside the citadel of Aleppo in Syria. My hair at this stage relatively short and tidy.

4. An Arab's pride and joy: his horse. This classic photograph presented itself whilst we were drinking coffee by the VW on the side of the road.

5. A Syrian family who took us into their home and who were so hospitable. The little girl in the middle is playing with a Colt .45 hand gun. Guns are a way of life here!

6. This rather sorry looking street scene was typical of Beirut, that had suffered years of military conflict but where the resilient inhabitants still thrived regardless.

7. Posing in my official capacity as photographer whilst John lined up this shot. The scenery across the Jordanian highlands was spectacular but more was yet to come.

8. This shot was taken at the museum in Amman showing the beautiful and highly decorative head dress for women of one Bedouin tribe.

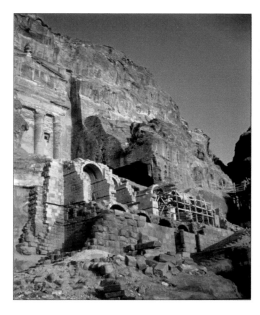

9. The famous Nabatian ruins at Petra in Jordan. Archaeologists have now established the site as one of national interest and in need of preservation.

10. Whilst visiting Wadi Rum in Jordan this rather chic looking specimen was my mount in a camel trek.

This is the camel that farted, frightening a chicken close by which took off vertically into the air just as I snapped this shot.

11. Arriving back in Aqaba from Amman where I had hitched to collect the parts to mend the van engine. I was extremely hot and tired but anxious to get on with repairs.

12. One of the compensations at Aqaba was the superb diving in the Red Sea that gave me my first taste of underwater photography using King Hussein's own camera.

13. View within Wadi Rum with spectacular cloud formations as a backdrop to one of the imposing and unspoilt cliff faces, now used by tourists for rock climbing.

14. With the heat and humidity building up in Saudi Arabia, our stopover at Al Ula revealed a beautiful oasis within an otherwise barren landscape, where date palms were thriving as well as other food crops.

15. Not far from the oasis at Al Ula is this track leading to the Nabatian site at Madain Salih where only sparsely growing scrub broke an otherwise barren yet spectacularly surreal landscape.

16. The tombs at Madain Salih were considerably better preserved than those at Petra in Jordan. At the time we were totally ignorant of the presence of soldiers not very far away, who took us to be questioned by the commander over our trespassing on the site.

17. A welcome break and a chance to talk to other travellers about the road ahead, during the desert crossing between Saudi and Yemen. John (far right) and myself were dumbstruck but envious of the 4X4 Toyota and the load it was able to carry!

18. One of the market stalls in the *souk* at Sana, where fresh spices and foods of all kinds were easily available. I had just negotiated with the seller for the ingredients to make a curry for Paddy and Rosemary that night.

19. View across the fertile plains of Yemen.

20. One of our overnight stops in the mountains between Saudi and Yemen.

21. Two of the towers we passed on our way over the mountains in Yemen which were used for the storage of crops and for irrigation, though we saw absolutely no one or any activity on the walled terraces.

22. One of the villages we passed on our way into Yemen. Typically they nestled between the higher peaks along the main levelled track and close to life sustaining water as indicated by the relatively lush growth.

23. Beaching a Dhow for repairs near Hodeida in Yemen. Some of these fishing vessels are very old, being handed down from generation to generation as the timbers they are made from have a high value.

24. Looking back along the road we have just taken in Yemen, that winds its way steadily uphill from the coast at Hodeida towards the capital Sana.

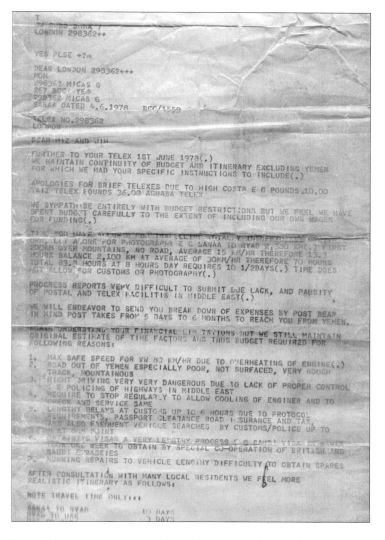

LONDON 298362++

YES PLSE +?a

DEAR LONDON 298362+++
MON
298362 MICAS G
267 BCC: YES
298362 MICAS G
SANAA DATED 4.6.1978   BCC/1559

TELEX NO.298362
LONDON

DEAR MIZ AND JIM

FURTHER TO YOUR TELEX 1ST JUNE 1978(.)
WE MAINTAIN CONTINUITY OF BUDGET AND ITINERARY EXCLUDING YEMEN
FOR WHICH WE HAD YOUR SPECIFIC INSTRUCTIONS TO INCLUDE(.)

APOLOGIES FOR BRIEF TELEXES DUE TO HIGH COSTS E G POUNDS 10.00
TAIZ TELEX POUNDS 36.00 AQUABA TELEX

WE SYMPATHISE ENTIRELY WITH BUDGET RESTRICTIONS BUT WE FEEL WE HAVE
SPENT BUDGET CAREFULLY TO THE EXTENT OF INCLUDING OUR OWN WAGES
FOR FUNDING(.)

THAT YOU HAVE SHOWN OF THE TRAVELLING TOTALLY INSUFFICIENT ROAD
OWN, LET ALONE FOR PHOTOGRAPHY E G SANAA TO RYAD 2,300 KMC.) FIRST
200KM OVER MOUNTAINS, NO ROAD, AVERAGE 15 KM/HR THEREFORE 13.3
HOURS BALANCE 2,100 KM AT AVERAGE OF 30KM/HR THEREFORE 70 HOURS
TOTAL 83.3 HOURS AT 8 HOURS DAY REQUIRES 10 1/2DAYS(.) TIME DOES
NOT ALLOW FOR CUSTOMS OR PHOTOGRAPHY(.)

PROGRESS REPORTS VERY DIFFICULT TO SUBMIT DUE LACK, AND PAUSITY
OF POSTAL AND TELEX FACILITIS IN MIDDLE EAST(.)

WE WILL ENDEAVOR TO SEND YOU BREAK DOWN OF EXPENSES BY POST BEAR
IN MIND POST TAKES FROM 5 DAYS TO 6 MONTHS TO REACH YOU FROM YEMEN.

AGAIN UNDERSTAND YOUR FINANCIAL LIMITATIONS BUT WE STILL MAINTAIN
ORIGINAL ESTIMATE OF TIME FACTORS AND THUS BUDGET REQUIRED FOR
FOLLOWING REASONS:

1. MAX SAFE SPEED FOR VW 80 KM/HR DUE TO OVERHEATING OF ENGINE(.)
2. ROAD OUT OF YEMEN ESPECIALLY POOR, NOT SURFACED, VERY ROUGH
    TRACK, MOUNTAINOUS
3. NIGHT DRIVING VERY VERY DANGEROUS DUE TO LACK OF PROPER CONTROL
    E POLICING OF HIGHWAYS IN MIDDLE EAST
4. REQUIRE TO STOP REGULARLY TO ALLOW COOLING OF ENGINER AND TO
    CHECK AND SERVICE SAME
5. LENGTHY DELAYS AT CUSTOMS UP TO 6 HOURS DUE TO PROTOCOL
    REQUIREMENTS, PASSPORT CLEARANCE ROAD INSURANCE AND TAX
    AND ALSO FREQUENT VEHICLE SEARCHES BY CUSTOMS/POLICE UP TO
    AT ONE POINT
6. OBTAINING VISAS A VERY LENGTHY PROCESS E G SAUDI VISA OF OTHER
    TOOK ONE WEEK TO OBTAIN BY SPECIAL CO-OPERATION OF BRITISH AND
    SAUDI EMBASSIES
7. RUNNING REPAIRS TO VEHICLE LENGTHY DIFFICULTY ATO OBTAIN SPARES

AFTER CONSULTATION WITH MANY LOCAL RESIDENTS WE FEEL MORE
REALISTIC ITINERARY AS FOLLOWS:

NOTE TRAVEL TIME ONLY:::

SANAA TO RYAD   10 DAYS
RYAD TO UAE   3 DAYS

25. One of the many telexes sent to Miz and Jim at Islamic Information Services costing anything up to £30 a time, (a week's wages for John and I) pleading with them to send extra funds and explaining that the road conditions (as of 1978) were so poor or non existent in places that we would require a realistic change of pace in our schedule.

26. Yemeni family with whom we shared our mint tea.

27. Soft sand! Soft sand! We had just negotiated a 40 ft sand dune with the help of a passing 4X4 Toyota pick up truck and have stopped for a break before driving on towards the Saudi Border, still far away across the sand.

28. At the shanty town of Al Bogeh we stopped for a tea break whilst this desert policeman, curious to see us, seemed happy to pose before going on with his rounds looking for criminals or bandits!

29. St Mark's Square where John and I made our tourist diversion during the drive back through Europe.

30. Sipping Trappist Beer with Hanna (centre) and John (left), outside a café in the market square at the town centre of Breda, Holland, where we celebrated our epic journey that was almost over. Being well travelled dudes, our neglected hair had by then grown considerably longer.

Yemen

supplies to discover our rations were all but exhausted, but nevertheless found three peaches apiece out of the dusty and very untidy depths of the interior.

We had become used to the visitations by insects, be they ants, beetles or mosquitoes. As usual, on opening the side and rear door, we spread the mosquito net over the van to allow a cooling breeze to waft through the sleeping space but which closed it off to offending insects. Before going to bed I decided to wash my lengthy hair in warmed water. This had now become the one luxury I looked forward to each day as it symbolised the finishing of one day's work and preparation for another. The precious water renewed my belief in the future, was so uplifting and refreshing from the heat and dust of the day, that during our more troubled times it instilled a wonderful sense of well being and delight that lifted the soul and helped sooth tired nerves.

Such simple rewards are the traveller's companion and when living a fairly basic life on the road, provided much needed boosts to a fairly dented confidence. The relief of coming through the hazardous desert and mountains left me almost bursting with pleasure at being alive and so close to mother earth that living on the road had now become a comfort and joy in itself. Meditating over these pleasurable thoughts I eventually drifted off into a deep sleep from the exhausting but exhilarating crossing.

In the morning, we noticed our van was attracting quite a lot of curiosity from the younger elements of a nearby community (see photo of Yemeni family). However there was no harmful intention and they were able to talk to us in broken English about their country and we in return talked of our project. In all we spent three hours photographing the surrounding terrain, talking and sharing cigarettes, whilst also explaining to the assembled audience, the various attributes of our camera equipment.

One particularly bright individual had overcome his shyness and decided to have a closer look through the viewfinder of my twin lens Rolliflex. He was very amused by the inverted image it made on the focussing screen and when the rest of the shepherd family joined us I offered, in Bedouin style, for them to share some tea with us. I filled their thermos with hot water whilst John put some mint tea leaves in it. By their expression of delight, this represented a welcome change from their own ginger spiced tea. When we told the eldest of the group where we had driven from he seemed to get very agitated saying "much danger" and waved his axe in the air. He told us of robbers and "bad, bad people." During this performance we took heed, nodding solemnly. On our return to the van however, the young boys gave us a big grin and in the universal sign language shook their heads indicating for us not to worry too much indicating that the old man had been exaggerating just a wee bit.

Disturbingly, however this account of danger was later reinforced during our stay in *Sanaa* when we were told of a Swiss group, traversing the same route we had taken and who had been attacked with two of the group being killed outright.

Finally we reached the asphalt road at Sanaa and parked opposite the main city gate. John was again offered Quat which he chewed "like a local" but which eventually made him rather woozy. We decided it would be best for him to walk his hangover off and so we made our way to the local market. On the way some little girls came to play around us. One of them fearlessly grabbed one of my arms and using it as a swing shouted for joy as I held her in my grasp, whilst John took a series of photographs. Her mother in full purdah was not so amused and admonished her little daughter (or was it me?), so we left the group to their devices and made our way to the souk.

The market stalls sold anything from sweets to machine guns with ammunition belts thrown in for free. A Colt .45 was going for 180 S Rials (£26), and even came with spare magazines and bullets! Further on was a weathered and aged man in a small stall selling all sorts of munitions from sticks of dynamite to blasting detonators which sat on a shelf just a few inches from his head. There were even some hand grenades. I quickly took a photograph but retired to a safe distance as all the material looked old and was possibly unstable. We realised that most stalls toted a gun or two and it dawned on us that we were probably in the midst of a smugglers haunt.

Leaving the city we drove south along the mountain ridge that bisected the region, to pass through several minor villages on our way to *Sadah*. Along the way was evidence of military action. Burnt out hulks of (Russian built) tanks, armoured personnel carriers and the like, were interspersed with their modern counterparts and demonstrated the struggles that had beset the province over the years.

That night my thoughts turned to home. I decided I needed to get a place of my own when I returned and then develop my career in photography. One thing I would not do was to rush into any headlong commitments for the time being but my thoughts turned more and more to Hanna. She had postponed her own travels to Asia and Australia for my impending return, a couple of months hence. Perhaps we could spend some time in the Lake District? I thought. For now I was getting to know her through the many letters that arrived at the cities we passed through.

I was brought out of my day dreaming as we were about to enter the capital city of *Sadah* and had to make our way to the old souk for provisions. It was full of life and vitality, if a little grubby. To our relief there was no evidence of the arms dealing that we had seen in the northern town *Sanaa*.

Being high up in the mountains we were forced to get into our sleeping bags at night but still slept with the doors open, covered only in the mosquito netting. With hair washed, the dirt and dust of the day gone, the warm embrace of the night air became a soothing cocoon for me. I realized now that I was really acclimatising to life on the road despite the difficulties. But now, at about 1000 meters in *Sanaa*, the night air was so chill that I longed for the luxury of a warm bath.

Sleeping rather restlessly, due mainly to the cold, we both woke up early. Our first task of the day was to assure ourselves of the return journey to Saudi. We first went to the immigration office to get our passports registered, then continued on to the Saudi Embassy to obtain a further visa to re-cross the desert once more.

Inshallah

We were ushered into a very tidy office, and the well dressed official, who had been the ambassador in Paris, took our case on board. He first asked how we came to be in Yemen and we innocently explained. Supported with the letter from Miz we went to great lengths explaining the establishment of the Islamic photo library that we were helping to set up in London and which we were now in the process of taking photographs for.

After our animated explanation covering our long drive he became a little confused if not agitated saying "But how did you get here to Yemen?" We replied " We came over the mountains from Saudi," to which he further questioned: " but what flight did you take?"

"We drove overland through Saudi, across the desert and then through the Mountains to Sanaa."

"But this is impossible!" he replied, and went on: " No foreigner is allowed across this route without permission from Riyadh as it is so dangerous. I cannot take responsibility for your passage so you must return by boat!"

At this surprising turn of events we offered some suggestions to him which included our writing a release note, absolving him or the Kingdom of Saudi Arabia from any liability for our safe passage. This almost persuaded him but at the last moment, fearing that an international incident was in the making, he advised us to visit our embassy and ask them to contact the main Saudi immigration office in Riyadh.

We returned depressed and somewhat apprehensively to the British embassy as a boat passage would, as we had already established, cost the earth, delay our passage, and mean missing out on photographing some spectacular scenery. Afraid that they would become entrapped in a diplomatic wrangle, the British embassy at first refused to help, considering this a private matter. However, as we were working here and not simply tourists, the officer said he would pass on our requirements for further consideration. Meanwhile he could recommend a doctor that the embassy staff used as our hepatitis jabs also needed a booster. The doctor whose name was *Sam*, was well respected by all communities in the city and the embassey thought he may be able to help with our negotiations. We persuaded the official to telephone the Saudi visa section to plead on our behalf but he was still told the same story that had been given to us.

What were we to do? We had to have a re-entry visa or better still a multi entry visa to Saudi to take us to the Arab Emirates and then return from the eastern side across the desert to Jordan in the west.

Although we wanted to go back overland, we thought it prudent to find out the cost of shipping the van from *Al Hodeida* up the Red Sea to Jeddah. Perhaps this was best as the mountain crossing would be arduous and potentially dangerous because it passed through bandit country. Nevertheless by now we were becoming seasoned to the ways of the Middle East, almost looking forward to the challenge of the rough roads that now seemed like highways compared to the soft sand of the desert.

We found a shipping merchant willing to book us but he could only give us a price of 300-400 Saudi Rials (£60) for the passage. A small fortune compared to the price of fuel required for the overland journey and again we would have to wait until a suitable boat arrived which could take several weeks, if not months!

We met up with Sam again to discuss our predicament and to have the jabs we thought prudent to take. With no surgery to hand he took us to his friend, *Paddy Hennessey's* to give us the top up hepatitis jab which was quickly administered. Paddy welcomed us in and after the shots of gamma globulin we (gently) sat down with him and his wife, Rosemary, to a welcome drink of gin and orange and recounted our experiences and worries for the future. Paddy offered to see what he could do for us but meanwhile he made his house available to us.

We returned to the Saudi Embassy again on the 18th of May and some progress with our visa had been made. The diplomatic wheels had been turning slowly and the Saudi embassy had "spoken" to several high ranking officials in both Saudi Arabia and in the British diplomatic sections. The Saudi official agreed that if we got a letter signed by the British embassy, waiving any responsibility for the Kingdom of Saudi Arabia to provide safe passage for us, then they would issue a visa to us without the usual proof of travel, such as sea passage or airline tickets. At that we were ecstatic and thanked him profusely.

That Sunday, we were finally able to pick up our visas from the Saudi Embassy, and with our return passage assured we could now relax and plan our exploration of Yemen.

At this time Yemen was not unified as it is today but divided into two with the northern half being pro western and "tame" whilst the south was strongly influence by Russia with communism being the predominant political influence. There had recently been some border disputes between north Yemen and the southerly Yemen Arab Republic, (forbidden to us), which had now spilled into villages and cities near the border which we were to visit shortly.

Everyone agreed that we should delay our journey to *Taiz* near the southern border in order to see if the terrorist situation worsened there, so we spent the following day helping Paddy with some home chores. and in the evening he took us to a friend who had valuable local knowledge and was a commercial attaché to the British Embassy. We jumped at the opportunity since we had not been able to find the local contact supplied by Miz and so any information about the interior of Yemen would be very helpful to us.

We spent a glorious evening sipping whisky and beer, whilst exploring ideas for photography with some very interesting and influential people. It was here that we met *Rick* who worked for the Wimpy road construction company and in conversation thought that he may be able to swing things to get us into Oman. Like Saudi at the time, they required people to have work there to be able to enter the country and under no circumstances issued tourist visas. Rick was going to arrange for us to photograph some Wimpy construction sites and in so doing obtain work visas to get us through. I also explored the possibility of working back in Yemen after my present contract with Islamic Information had

126

finished, as I was fascinated by the country which had the feel of the "old" Arabia. Yemen to me was not so spoilt as the other countries in the Middle East we visited, that had become dominated by the pressure of commercial western influences.

On our return to Paddy's house we met *Fritz* and *Marianne,* a softly spoken and well travelled Swiss couple who had previously arranged to stay for a few days whilst in transit. That night we talked at some length about a disastrous journey they had whilst in Iran. They had been incarcerated in a prison on some trumped up charge. Though married they were apparently separated into different cells and *Marianne* had been mercilessly raped within earshot of her husband. A traumatic experience for both but one which they were only able to bring to the attention of the authorities once safely away from the police cells. They were eventually released and through the Swiss embassy had made complaints to the highest levels but to no avail. To their horror, they eventually discovered that the incident was being hushed up since their embassy obstinately refused to take the matter any further. So here we sat with them, re-living their experience for us, which highlighted the hazards we faced on the open road and was a stark reminder for us to be careful on the crossing back into Saudi. We were lucky once to get ourselves and the van over without too many problems but would our luck hold for a second time?

Two more days were spent waiting for the Saudi Embassy to return our passports, complete with their letter of passage and visas. I spent the time checking the VW, changing oil, setting spark plugs and ignition timing and finally sorting out the sticking throttle. I could see nothing wrong at the back end by the engine bay, so referring to the manual I decided to remove the metal "skid" pan situated underneath the vehicle at the front, which covered the linkages to the throttle as well as those to the steering column. This is a cover about two foot square and three inches deep and whilst protecting the linkages from the ground below was totally open at the top. As I unscrewed the last few bolts and put a hand up to support the cover, I became aware that it was getting exceedingly heavy and with the last screw undone I could no longer take the weight. Once again my head got a bashing as the metal cover fell on top of me.

Standing up once more at the front of the van, I dragged the pan out to find it full of sand. This had obviously collected during our desert crossing where the "bottoming" of the vehicle in the dunes had scooped sand over the leading edge of the pan beneath the vehicle. At last I could see why the steering had felt so heavy and the throttle was sticking with that amount of sand around the linkages. I emptied the pan and there was now no doubt about it, the throttle no longer stuck and the steering had re-gained its freedom of movement once more!

The delays over the passports had made the days fly by and it was soon the 25th May, a full ten days since we had first visited the Saudi Embassy! One request we had from the ex-patriot crowd we now came to know so well, was to replenish their liquor supply when visiting a place in the south called *Al Mocha*. Here, contraband imports from the African port of Mombassa and Djibouti across the Red Sea, can be obtained at vastly cheaper prices than in the north. This we were happy to do since after all it would be intended for consumption by non-Muslims. Never theless we would still be at risk in the unlikely event of being caught as alcohol of any kind in the Islamic state of Yemen was strictly illegal. Our hosts however had been so kind and helpful to us that we felt it was the least we could do. We asked where to go and who to contact when we got to *Al Mocha* to which Paddy replied, "Don't worry, they will find you! Young boys will come out to your vehicle when you approach the town and take your order!".

We were soon on our way and in the greener valleys of the mountains, maize was replaced by the growing of cereal crops whilst trees were frequent and bordered the many fields and villages we passed. The views from the well kept roads were wonderful, giving John and I many opportunities to photograph the magnificent scenery and local communities. I drove most of the way but often stopped to take roll after roll of film in a very

Yemen

picturesque and photogenic landscape with people hard at work on the land. Unfortunately on my return to Britain my own 35mm slides of this part of the journey were stolen. Sadly, since the folding of the company (1988) we now worked for, I have also not been able to trace any of the hundreds of pictures I took for them either, and so many beautiful sights we passed are now just a memory for me.

Eventually we pulled off the road to camp in the mountains at the village of *Ibb*, a little way from *Taizz*. The VW had performed well but the time spent on the photography meant that we had covered only 212 kms. Nevertheless it had been a tiring day and thankful to have stopped, we sat enjoying the views down into the valleys below when a local passed by and offered us some eggs. We talked with him for a while and he explained that he was a carpenter by trade, and was very amused when I said that in England he would be called a *chippy*.

Writing our letters home we worked out our daily expenditure and with all the delays, repairs to vehicles etc, we decided that we simply had to contact Miz and Jim for a further advance for fuel and expenses. Knowing already, the hot reception this would get, we were nevertheless both quite determined to push on and make our reasonable demands known, come what may.

May was rapidly passing and the 26th had arrived already. We woke up fairly early as the heat was starting to build by 7.30 am. After packing up and with a further drive of only 30 minutes to go we arrived at Taizz and went directly to the post office to find any mail that may be waiting for us from home or, optimistically, from our "contact" here in Taiz, called *Shoki Luckman*. We phoned his office and whilst waiting for him to drive over to meet us we stocked up on bread and other essentials including a treat of Yemeni cake. When our contact finally arrived, he seemed totally uninterested in us, the story of our journey, or helping to set up photography elsewhere in the area. We felt (not for the first time) quite let down after our hardships and were totally at a loss to explain this turn of events or indeed what sort of arrangement Miz had made with him. It dawned on us that so many arrangements had been taken on face value. Our contacts were one of the main bones of contention and we wondered they were just a figment of imagination or wishful thinking.

We had to spend much of time carrying out local research to find places of interest to photograph or even the best routes to take, since the contacts arranged by Miz were all but useless. In hindsight it was a great pity that we had so little time before the start of the journey to carry out extensive research of our own. We were totally dependent on local guides and contacts that we had to find anew which put a burden on the limited funds that were rapidly becoming depleted. Shoki could not even spare the time to have tea with us and in a rather dismissive manner showed us the souk gates, followed by a rapid drive past the Telecoms office to finally reach the outskirts of the town, on the *Hodeida* road. He showed us where we could camp that night, but soon departed to leave us to our own devices. So much for Arab hospitality here!

After this non event, John and I really began to get more annoyed. One thing was for sure, we were going to have to cover the rest of the photography in this part of Yemen with little or no help. Having decided on our campsite for the night we returned to the souk, always a good starting point in the Middle East to photograph any city. We spent 2-3 hrs in the market and then wandered past the main mosque to a slope at the rear, leading to a superb view over the city of Taizz. In the photograph that I took looking out over the city, the mosque stood out to become the centrepiece to a jumble of roof tops and telephone cables.

With one of the classic shots of Taizz captured, I walked back to the market and had a refreshing glass of cold mango juice. Having slaked my thirst, I made my way back to the main gates of the old market to meet John by the van. He already had a kettle going for a much needed cup of tea and whilst sat there, we became surrounded by a large crowd of young men. Keeping a good eye on our belongings they asked many questions as to who we were and where we were from. Suddenly, as if to impress or scare us, one of the lads opened his hands to show us a bat, still living but obviously frightened out of its wits. Before us they spread its wings showing the delicate structures through which the morning light was filtering and proceeded to play with it as if it were a model aircraft.

The crowd then started to press in on us jostling for attention and fearing the worse, we quickly locked up the van and once satisfied that it was secure, made our way once more into the market, while the crowd instantly dispersed. We eventually came upon a curious Jewellery shop, in a side street. Curious in that the little wizened owner, a woman of perhaps sixty, was dressed all in yellow. Even her skin had been painted in *yellow*. Some advertising campaign!

She had an old tin bath full of the most exquisite silver ornaments, many of which must have been sold by the Bedouin or poorer sections of the community, as this old woman distinctly represented the Yemeni equivalent of a pawn broker. The articles of head attire all worked in silver were so beautiful that I wanted to grab a handful of them to take home but alas I had very little money to spare. I had to be satisfied with one piece only, a prayer holder. It had slots either end through which pieces of paper containing prayers could be placed. It was about an inch and a half long with a heavy neck chain also of silver and it is still worn on special occasions by *Hanna*, to this day.

We were only half way through our journey but already our money was now almost exhausted. We urgently needed further funding to pay for our passage back to Europe. We therefore made our way to the Cable and Wireless office to telex Miz and Jim. We had by now got used to the fact that there was no point trying to buck the system and invariably knew a reply from London would take at least a day in sending. There were certainly no mobile phones available then or ATM style cash dispensers so that money had to be telexed through. A lengthy and in our circumstances very frustrating process which simply delayed the journey no end and cost the company even more for food and wages. But these very delays provided the welcome breaks and meeting of friends that otherwise we would have missed.

Inshallah

We left the cable office and made our way out of the city to find a suitable camp site off the main Hodeida road. This turned out to be a slip road used for the construction of a stretch of upgraded tarmac surface and pulling in by an earth mound we spent a very humid and rather uncomfortable night. We woke early, eager to get going and after a mandatory cup of tea made our way back into *Taizz*. We checked once more at the *Post Restant*, cashed one of our last travellers cheques for £100 and filled our containers up with urgently needed fresh water.

Not surprisingly, no reply had not been received to our telex but to crown it all, the post office hadn't any mail for us either. They hadn't had any for months they told us, but a more likely explanation was that they had either thrown it away or opened it for any money it might contain. We were starting to feel a little out on a limb and again and tried to reach yet another contact given to us by Miz but without success. By now we had had enough of this hot and humid city and made our way to the town of *Al Mocha* on the coast to seek ventures new and to obtain our alcoholic booty. The town of *Mocha* was once a busy port trading the world over in the famous Mocha coffee. It was now only a shadow of its former glory and all that remained for us to explore was a very dusty and weather beaten town, hard to imagine the international shipping that arrived here in the 1800's.

At the junction from the main road to Mocha, there was of all things, a full sized military rocket, mounted on a concrete pedestal. We turned off along a levelled but unsurfaced road where the sand turned into a hardened wash board surface with small corrugations about six inches apart. The effect this had on the van was dramatic if taken cautiously. At about 30 mph we felt like we were inside an "out of balance" washing machine with jaw bones being constantly jarred and all skeletal joints rattled until we feared the whole vehicle, and ourselves would fall apart.

Stopping once more to pick up our hub caps that came off incessantly, we decided another tactic would have to be employed to cross this road. Reaching speeds of about 70mph, the suspension now took up all the vibration and the ride proved to be much more bearable.

We drove like this for about 35 km whilst the deafaning sound of the van felt like being inside an empty steel drum with some maniac bashing it on the outside with a hammer. To our great relief, we eventually came to the outskirts of *Al Mocha* whereupon as Paddy had told us, we were met by children touting to sell us anything and everything. Obviously a well trodden path that we had now embarked upon.

We stopped and one sprightly lad jumped up with one foot on the driver's door step and one hand hanging onto the front mirror shouting,

"Whisky! Gin!, Mister" to which we nodded. He indicated that we drive back along the road and then off a little way into the desert and we obliged with the young boy still glued to the van door like a fly in a spider's web. Once there we stopped behind a tall sand dune and were asked what we wanted. I indicated with my fingers that we required twenty four bottles of gin and six bottles of whisky which we would pay for with the money Paddy had given us earlier. The lad nodded and drove off with his companion on the back of a Honda motor bike.

We pondered over the possibility that we had been set up for thieves as yet unknown. The minutes ticked slowly away in this rather surreal situation that we now found ourselves in. About 20 minutes later we eventually heard the sound of a four wheel drive vehicle groaning its way over some nearby dunes.

As it arrived next to us, the older, rather mean looking man driving the vehicle demanded our money first, before exchanging goods, very much along the lines of a gangster movie.

Against our better judgement we passed the monies over to him and immediately he started remonstrating with us,

"This no good." "Not enough."

We repeated the price the boys told us and he agreed yes that is the price."So what is the problem?" we asked. "This not enough for all this gin and whisky!" "Can we have a look." we replied, as we were sure the money was sufficient for the goods requested.

Inshallah

He nodded and on rounding the back of his 4 wheel drive we could see the problem and the reason for the delay in getting back to us.

The Suzuki was full with crates of booze, and it was clear that the young boy had misunderstood my request interpreting one crate for every bottle that I had actually wanted.

The man was not amused and at this point John and I started to get worried. We said how much we really wanted of this haul which led to a further heated argument. During this the man started to brandish a rather worn AK47 and so the little boy intervened. "Ok mister, you buy some more gin, its ok."

My diary recalls that we eventually got away with buying just a couple or so more crates and left the disgruntled seller to return with the rest of his load. We made our way to more open country by the beach and were gobsmacked to be told by a passing Arab not to photograph the port of Mockha itself for security reasons. Security? There was so little to see anyway. We couldn't believe it but pretended to humour him!

Just at this moment an Irishman came to our aid who was working for a Dutch construction company. He invited us back to his air-conditioned portacabin, just outside town, for drinks and a chat and helped us arrange a pass at the police station for the port area close by. Our "guide" took us down to the old port to take some photographs. Once there we immediately became embroiled in an argument with some rather mean looking dock workers about taking pictures, probably because they wanted a bribe and were only subdued when our Irish guide intervened. We decided it prudent to take the vehicle into a secure compound but spent the night awake in the open air, troubled by flying insects, or rolling over on the mattresses which rapidly became soaked in sweat due to the high humidity.

The next morning couldn't come fast enough and rising early we eventually set off back through *Al Mocha,* along another corrugated road to the main route up the coast to *Hodeida.* At the time this road was still under construction and along the way were piles of sand as evidence of workings. We drove at a constant 70mph to overcome the corrugations once more when after 30km or so we inadvertently took the wrong side of a road diversion. Committed to our unintended route and ignorant of any warning signs in Arabic, we flew past a construction gang, shouting at us but it was too late. We drove straight along a length of road just laid with hot tarmac and which was in the process of being covered in loose sand from a bulldozer prior to being rolled flat.

So that was what the piles of sand were along the route we had just taken! I put my foot to the floor to burst though another sand pile already flooding across the road from a mechanical digger and not wanting to get stuck in the hot tarmac I accelerated away. We quickly left behind a very unamused road gang looking at two long wheel ruts down the middle of a perfectly flat and otherwise well constructed piece of road!

We arrived early at Hodeida and in the relative cool of the mid morning found a shady patch of beach. We set up our camp and dressed in swimming gear, cocktail supplies to hand and with the warm air off the Red Sea to soothe tired nerves we sipped our gin and orange, gently drifting off to sleep for a good part of the day. Waking later for a refreshing swim, the water temperature felt the same as a tepid bath. It was washing in cool fresh water from a well supplied by an underground source from the mountains which provided the rejuvenating liquid, not a stone's throw away from the rather saline waters of the Red Sea close by.

Seeing a crowd gathered along the beach, John and I picked up our cameras and decided to explore. It turned out that the whole village had gathered to beach a *Dhow,* (see photo), whilst close by a carpenter and his mate were re-building the hull of one of these ancient vessels. Some are many years old and although the planks may disintegrate in time, the main timber forming the backbone of the keel is much sought after and preserved from generation to generation. Hewn from one piece of priceless timber, they are the most valuable part of the vessel and it was this that we saw the carpenter seamlessly repairing with wooden dowels. The only metal items available are cheap iron fixings which rust quickly in the sea and will rot surrounding wood in no time.

The highlight of the day turned out to be photographing a scene of young Arab boys diving off a dhow moored someway from the beach. They were silhouetted against a gorgeous pink sun-set, that revealed a thin line on the horizon, part of the African coast or an island perhaps? With the sea looking so inviting, I too swam out to the dhow which I climbed onto and dived off. The sea was still warm but the refreshing well water soon had all the sticky salt off my body and swimming trunks after which I returned to the van for our usual dinner of baked beans, egg and chips.

The next morning I woke up early and at 5.30am the sea was now much more inviting being warm against the now cooler air above. I luxuriated for over an hour in this "natural" bath whilst leaving John to enjoy his sonorous sleep. Returning to make a quick breakfast we left at 8 am and took the road to *Hais* which we stopped at for a break of sweets, cold drinks and biscuits before pressing on to *Hodeida*. From there we tried to reach *Salif,* a village further up the coast but the road proved impassable to our two wheel drive vehicle. We diverted onto an alternative road which would take us to the cooler mountains beyond. Winding our way up the mountain passes, beneath the summit of *Djebel Masar* we eventually regained the cooler heights and the sight once more of flowing rivers. These burbled down the mountainsides through meadows in which grazing cattle were eating luxuriant grass, so reminiscent of home and which contrasted starkly with the arid coastal area we had just left.

The villages we met after passing through narrow gorges were relatively unspoilt. They don't have the plethora of TV aerials of the cities but only the odd telephone pole supporting loose wires from which dangle strangely shaped, perfectly spherical nests constructed by a small yellow bird about three inches long, from the long grasses that grew nearby. This was the *Golden-winged Grosbeak, (Rynchostruthus socotranus)*, a startling bird with a powerful black bill and bright yellow flashes in its wings and tail.

Yemen

It is especially noticeable in flight and inhabits the southern tip of Yemen as well as some areas over the Red Sea in Africa.

For four and a half hours we drove, ascending one side of a ridge, to drop down the other across one verdant valley bottom then on up the other side to cross another. From each vantage point we could see the ridges we had just come over (see photo), forming contoured lines, from side to side across the horizon receding far into the distance. After a drive through the most spectacular mountain scenery of the whole journey, we reached *Sanaa* once more.

We met up with Rosemary and dropped off the gin at the house, before setting off once more to the bank to see whether our funds had arrived. With still no reply we returned to Paddy and Rosemary where I quickly checked the vehicle over before settling indoors for the night as we were back at high altitude with correspondingly cooler evenings. We sat around to talk of our journey over the replenished supply of gin and tango (orange sherbet soft drink powder). Paddy told us of his exploits as a pilot during the Rhodesia crisis in the sixties. Apparently when a theoretical goods embargo was placed on Ian Smith's regime, any pilot with an aircraft was running the gauntlet across the borders to drop material into the country and Paddy was no exception. Britain aided and abetted this practice by turning a blind eye.

Sitting down to breakfast the next day I made a list of all the chores that needed to be done. First we had to establish whether Miz and Jim wanted to close the expedition down or send us further funds to allow us to continue to photograph Yemen and allow passage through to the Arab Emirates. Oman by now was looking less and less likely to come off for financial reasons as John and I estimated that we would need at least another £1000 for the return journey and the Emirates were some of the most expensive parts on the whole trip. Oman would increase the amount needed substantially.

We returned to the bank and sent a further telex off to Miz and decided that until we got some semblance of support in a reply, we would take things a bit easier since we had to conserve our remaining money to get home.

The following day we finally got a reply from "the firm", in the form of a rather curt telex, demanding the breakdown of our expenses to date. We had already worked the figures out and were able to send a cable but also explained that we needed to know if the whole venture was now going to be called off as there seemed to be some reluctance for further costs to be covered by them. Also we didn't want to be left stranded as we were now committed to driving back overland and had already arranged visas for this.

Meanwhile, I put in much needed time servicing the vehicle. After a day spent completing the odd job we were entertained by Paddy who cooked us a delightful meal of roast lamb in beer sauce and we also had the company of *Rick* and two visiting engineers. We talked to them over the meal about visiting *Oman* but it seemed that civil unrest had resulted in the deaths of some British oil workers there. With this bad news it now looked even more unlikely that we would be granted visas or that it would be wise to even attempt to go there.

After checking in with the bank on May 1st we discovered there was as usual no reply from Miz or Jim. We were, however, able to pick up some photographs that had been developed in town for *Sam* and took them back to his house where we sat and talked over a seemingly endless supply of coffee and biscuits. On our return to Paddy's I still felt something wasn't quite right with the vehicle as it had developed an unusual vibration especially when pulling away or stopping. I put some mats down crawled underneath and noticed that the rubber engine support on the rear cross bar had broken loose on the passenger side offering little or no engine support at all!

I decided I needed to give the vehicle a thorough inspection and to recheck all the other components. I discovered that a shock absorber had blown apart with oil now steadily weeping from the cylinder. All this was a direct result of the mountain crossing and

Yemen

again the thought that we should have pressed Miz to equip us with a Land Rover kept going over in my mind.

However, I started to work on the vehicle, chocking up the engine and jacking up the side of the vehicle to remove the shock absorber and engine mount. Unfortunately I discovered that as usual, in the cost cutting exercise, the cheapest socket set had been bought by the previous organisers which promptly split apart with the least effort. A new set of tools as well as the spare parts were going to be dear and would substantially eat into our budget of £1000 for the return trip of some 12,000 to 15,000 kms, so we decided to explain the situation and to up date our budget estimate to Miz.

We set off once more to the bank in town and on getting a reply from Miz, we were very dismayed at their reply. Apparently they were blaming us for deviating from the original itinerary and budget and also of being irresponsible with the money. I felt particularly aggrieved as we had stripped the engine down ourselves, saving hundreds of pounds for them, yet still we were getting blamed.

Eventually Miz and Jim sent their own itinerary which set out clearly the mileage we should cover and the time it was to take for us to reach these towns. I have out lined below their agenda and the number of hours driving this would require!

Route to be covered	*Estimated Driving Time*
Sana to Riyadh 7 Days	10hrs per day
Riyadh to UAE 3 Days	8 hrs per day
UAE to Qatar 2 Days	6hrs per day
Qatar to Kuwait 2 Days	6hrs per day
Kuwait to London 18 Days	8hrs per day

In addition to these hours of driving we also had to include photography, rest stops and the like. John and I were at first angry at their total lack of understanding. But anger soon gave way to incredulity and finally laughter since the return from

Inshallah

Yemen along the mountain and desert crossing to *Najran* alone would take 4-5 days depending on conditions and all these times assumed the vehicle performed perfectly over this rough terrain. If pushed too hard the vehicle would inevitably fail as it was simply not built to do the punishing job of which it was asked.

We showed the bank manager the reply to obtain his view on the matter and he replied "No, they don't seem to know about the Middle East, do they!" John and I just sighed in resignation whilst thinking of what to do next.

We stormed back to Paddy's house to compose a reply and rechecked our estimates. By now, what with the cost of each telex at £30 a go and the extra cost of spare parts we knew they were going to be in for a shock and prepared ourselves that they would finally abandon the tour. We talked it over with Paddy and our friends who were unanimous that our employers must be stupid if not irresponsible to treat us like this and agreed with the tone of our reply. Some of the reply from the original telex is reproduced here which put into context the problems of crossing the Middle East. We were fully supported with estimates from local people including the British Embassy staff who were incredulous at the turn of events and felt that we were definitely on the raw end of our deal with Islamic Information Services Ltd

Reply (see also photo)
After consulting with local contacts feel more realistic itinerary

Sana to Riyadh	10 days
Riyadh to UAE	3 days
UAE to Qatar	2 days
Qatar to Kuwait	2 days
Kuwait to London	28 days

In effect we extended the drive time for the Sanaa to Riyadh and Kuwait to London legs of the journey, with the others remaining as per their estimate but with no photography, which we explained would require 4 hours out of every day. We summarised stating that we would require a further 12 weeks altogether for the return trip if it were to include Oman and Bahrain should they give the go ahead but this would depend on us arranging appropriate visas.

We returned the next day to send our more informed estimate (see picture), of times and costs and indicated that they either agree to this, or we would wind up the whole affair as it was now obvious that to continue under that kind of pressure from England would be unsafe, unproductive and irresponsible.

On Friday the 2nd we sent off our ultimatum to I.I.S.L. heartened by the support we had received from the embassy staff who by now were becoming only to well aware of the poor support we had been receiving on our otherwise under resourced journey.

To take my mind off the anger brewing inside me from this decidedly dismal turn of events, I continued with the dismantling of the VW and on closer inspection decided to replace both front shock absorbers, the engine support bar, (which had become severely bent as we had crashed our way over the mountain track), and the rubber engine mounts.

We now felt there was now nothing for it but to wait for a reply from London and with the vehicle unserviceable, as it was partially dismantled, we decided to spend the rest of Friday, (the Islamic holy day) relaxing, taking advantage of the embassy swimming pool and also to finish off reading my novel, The sea above us. As the afternoon began to cool, I went out with Rosemary to the market to buy a chicken for our supper. On the way I trod on something soft but pliable, which stopped me placing the full weight of my foot on the ground in an instant. Thinking the worst I bent down to investigate. I picked up a small bundle of bloodied fur which to my surprise turned out to be a little kitten that had obviously been mauled most probably by one of the many stray dogs. Bathed in the light from a torch that Rosemary carried it mewed a few times and looked up with glazed yet pitiful eyes but finally seemed to give up its hold on life and went limp in my arms.

This event seemed to symbolise the fragility of existence and became a sobering reminder that we all have to take care of ourselves in this life. With the events of the past few days it had the effect of making me determined not to be brow beaten by the ignorance of people back in London and that for safety's sake if we were to press on, it must only be under more reasonable terms. This positive thinking seemed to rally my spirits and on our return I helped cook the meal and put aside my worries for the moment. The next day, Saturday May 3rd, was a normal working day and so we borrowed Paddy's Land Rover as our own transport was unserviceable, to search for spare parts. Things started to look up as sufficient money for repairs had arrived from England and so I left John at the telex office to contact the local cable and wireless facility who we had been told could offer us garage facilities if needed. Meanwhile, I went to VW to purchase the list of spares, which by now had grown in length as I found more and more faults on the van. I finally ended up purchasing two engine mounting blocks, a complete engine support beam, two front shock absorbers and new nuts, bolts, circlips and washers for fixing the parts to the vehicle, along with spare engine oil. In all, this shopping list came to 950 Yemeni Riyals, (£137). A small fortune and a great lump, out of our cash reserves of only £1000 to complete the rest of the trip!

John had also had some success but the garage at cable and wireless was outside the city and in the middle of some radar complex. I decided that come what may I would complete the job outside Paddy's house. I would need extra jacks to replace the engine mount but it was convenient for food and cool shower. The repairs to the engine were fairly straightforward but we had to take the VW to a local garage where new bolts were welded back onto the vehicle chassis to take the rear bumper. After that I took the VW high up into the hills for a test drive. After resetting the tappets, points and replacing the spark plugs, all I had to do now was to check the distributor setting to get the maximum power out of the 1600cc engine. Stopping occasionally to tweak the distributor one way or another I finally settled on the best setting which had the engine turning smoothly but pulling with greater power than we had previously experienced. Was this a good omen, I wondered?

The next few days were spent resting, tuning the engine, re-stocking or cleaning the vehicle. By now John and I were restless to be on our way. We went with Paddy and Rosemary to the new film currently showing at the embassy. To their embarrassment the previous one had been set up only to turn into a rather baudy sex romp. The embassy had to switch it off immediately for fear of offending the local guests, much to the amusement and hand clapping of the ex-pats, including ourselves who sat there cheering the poor projectionist!

The clouds were ominously starting to gather and part of the way through the current film starring Tony Curtis, called "Lepke" the heavens started to open. Remembering the engine gaskets I had left outside the VW on the ground, I rushed back just in time to put them inside the house. Seeing the bottle of Gordons gin on the table, I made up an extra high-strength, orange cocktail, in an empty squash bottle to disguise it and returned with an umbrella, under which the four of us sat huddled, watching the remainder of the film. We gradually became soaked in the warm rain but were comforted by large gulps of the alcoholic beverage from our portable supply which got us inebriated and incoherent by the end of the film.

The next four days we spent arranging extensions to visas for our onward journey since the originals issued in London had almost expired. Eventually we received a further advance of £400 out of the promised £1000 and of this a full quarter of it had been used up for spare parts! At least it was a step in the right direction. We still had not photographed any drilling operations, one of the main commercial activities in Yemen, since water was still in short supply. We drove down to the desert to photograph *Jeff*, an engineering acquaintance of Paddy, at his rig who was now drilling for the precious liquid. The area looked very much like the hills of Petra or Medain Salih and we shot several rolls of the activities there. We decided to sleep overnight and spent an evening chatting round a camp fire, before turning into our sleeping bags and awaking the next day to return the short distance to *Sanaa*.

It was now the 11th June and we awoke to a beautiful day. At Sanaa we went to the souk for what was to be our last look, for on our return Paddy had some distressing news to tell us. He first cautioned us that what we were about to hear must not go outside the four walls of his house, otherwise it would possibly cause chaos and loss of life. We nodded and affirmed our silence.

Apparently the intelligence services of the British embassy had got wind of an uprising in the south Yemen. What wasn't revealed to us then, but what became clear, was that the explosions were part of the preliminary moves in a coup d' etat in South Yemen. *Salim Rubaia Ali,* a moderate in the Peoples Republic of South Yemen and who was pro-unification, had attempted to regain power after being toppled in 1971 by the extreme communist *Abdul Fattah Ismail*. Various factions had been split over the issue of reunification with the north. *Salim Rubaia* had been calling for reunification with the north and could see no option, having been opposed in council and now losing his power base, to the use of military force against the leaders of the NLF (national Liberation Front) of whom his opponent *Abdul-Fattah Ismail* was the leader.

The main coup was to take place on the 26th June, 15 days hence, but already there was increasing incidence of disturbance in both the states of South and North Yemen. As it turned out days later, *Salim Rubaia* failed in his attempted take over of the country and he was subsequently executed by firing squad. This volatile situation obviously could have a knock on effect on Saudi, with implications for our safe crossing since all borders were becoming more jumpy as they were in a state of increased alert. In no uncertain terms Paddy suggested we pack our belongings and move out the next day at first light and basically to "bang over the mountains back into Saudi Arabia as soon as we could!" Our alarm was set for 5 am the next day but despite the situation, I found that I just couldn't get fully awake and snoozed on till 8 am.

Yemen

Once awake, we rushed around clearing our things up and packing them into the van, before saying our hurried but heartfelt goodbyes to Paddy and Rosemary. With hugs and kisses for all their good help we set off once more, this time to the north and homeward bound as fast as we could. We stopped later in the day at Sam's house which was on the way to *Sadah* to say our hurried farewells. It was a traditional Yemeni building of mud bricks, and simply white washed externally, whilst on the inside the rooms were ornately decorated and lined with cushions around the walls, above which hung baskets of flowers. We continued on our way, this time not even stopping to take photographs and reaching Sadaa at 4.30 pm. After adjusting the air pressure in the tyres we made our way up the dirt road to our old camp site by the palms, next to the hill we had stayed at before, on the journey into Yemen.

I climbed the hill once more to look out upon a familiar landscape and take in the spectacular views of the mountains glowing in the deep pinks and cinnamon cast by the setting sun. We were apprehensive for the journey to come and the borders to cross as we were still totally out of touch with the rest of the world's events save for the little transistor radio I had purchased in Saudi and to which we listened intensely for news of the deepening crisis in Yemen. There was nothing yet on the BBC world service so we hoped that the coup must have been kept quiet so far.

I awoke the next day, Tuesday at 7.20 am and put the kettle on for some tea but just felt like lazing for a while which surprized me considering the problems now unfolding in Yemen. Perhaps this state of calm was the optimism that comes out of going back over familiar ground? I had had a restless night, due more to the thought of what awaited us at the Yemeni border just ahead rather than the desert crossing, especially in view of the political problems at the moment. Would we be arrested, or at least turned back as we felt the whole country would be in turmoil by now.

It was my turn to drive and I now became very anxious to get going, so after a booster cup of tea, we started to drive towards the border post which was about 10 kms further up the track. At the same wadi that we had negotiated before I impatiently steered a straight line across, again almost hitting John who had walked the crossing and who now had an expression on his face changing from abject disbelief to horror for the second time. As I passed by only a hairs breadth away, he rapidly jumped out of the way whilst I stopped at the top of the rise the other side for him to jump aboard, settting off once more to the border.

Arriving at the oil barrels we already knew the routine and so got straight out and this time went to the checkpost tent. Once inside we were greeted again and with little formality our passports were stamped. However the official on duty tried to persuade us not to go on as he thought we were mad to cross into Saudi this way, saying it was far too dangerous to go on alone. We decided to risk it in view of the impending fighting and bidding him farewell made our way back to the van to continue across the blisteringly hot mountains to *al Bogeh* and the desert beyond.

We left the border post at 10.30am and pressed on up the mountain slopes to the plateau at about 2000 meters. Here the vegetation changed dramatically to little scrub bushes with magnificent flowers. We carried on trying to make up time and so rarely stopped, since we had got through one border alright but we still had no idea if the Saudi side across the desert, would shut down, when news of the coup broke.

We drove like the wind along the familier track to *Kataff*, where we had tried out the AK 47. We were well within our estimated time but we couldn't get rid of the thought that any delay for photography, may result in our getting stranded in bandit infested no-man's land between Saudi and Yemen if both the borders were shut.

On the other side of *Kataff* was the start of the flooded wadi section where we had become stuck before. There was little I could do to stop the spark plugs getting wet as the engine was so near to the ground but in order to counter the ingress of water to the VW's exhaust I had bought a length of pipe to clamp onto the existing one, thus raising the outlet above water height. I quickly had this mounted but decided to walk over and view the situation anyway.

Walking down to the start of the bad stretch we had become stuck in before, I took some photographs of the water and the wadi itself but had to quickly return as traffic started to build up behind us on the narrow track. When we eventually reached the water pools themselves it was obvious that the level had receded and the van had little trouble negotiating them.

The exhaust extension turned out to be unnecessary and in some respect I was disappointed I didn't have the opportunity to try it out, still it was probably for the best. We soon navigated our way through the wadi and a little further on we came to another chi shop and struck up a conversation with a Yemeni driver over a can of ice cold tea about his neighbouring country Saudi which he thought "no fucking good!".When I told him of our problem securing a return visa in Yemen which seemed to spur him on to become even more derogatory about Saudi officialdom!

Eventually we parted company, anxious to be on our way but a half hour later hit a piece of soft sand in the bed of a dried up wadi. We managed to pull out of it and once free we drove fast to cross yet further areas of soft sand before we hit a hard gravel ridge which threw the VW in the air. The result was that as the front of the vehicle was flipped upwards the roof rack, a flimsy tubular contraption, bounced off the roof, to land with the petrol filled jerry cans with an almighty clatter on the ground.

We stopped and replaced it on the roof but discovered that one of the brackets had come off up the track and in the process a retaining bolt was missing. Searching around the track we had just come down we were able to find the bracket and a passing driver offered us a new bolt from his tool box. Unfortunately this new bolt sheered and in desperation I removed a brass one retaining the number plate which seemed to do the job for the time being. The roof rack continued to work loose and on about the sixth stop, three quarters of an hour later, we were hailed by a couple of Yemenis who were having trouble with a bulldozer used to level and repair the track we were now negotiating.

Inshallah

They couldn't get the battery to start the bulldozer, so after re-fixing our roof rack I went over and had a look. I took the terminals off and on inspection they turned out to be so dirty that I was sure this was the fault. Getting some emery cloth from our van I cleaned the terminals and once replaced we gave the bulldozer another go with the starter. Immediately it burst into life which pleased the two Arabs immensely.

They offered us mango juice for our trouble and offered to share their food, but we pressed on with a wave and much cheering from the crew. The journey from then on was becoming more straightforward but still had to be taken with care. The roof rack was a persistent nuisance, however, and we had to stop many more times to replace it, or adjust the screws clamping the brackets together.

By late afternoon we could see that we were not far from *Al Bogeh* but still in the highlands where it was much cooler and so we turned off the main track to drive across a boulder strewn landscape into a basin shaped area, well out of the way of traffic and any passersby. This was ideal for our overnight stop and as sunset came we took photographs of the wonderful views. To get a better shot of our campsite I climbed onto the roof rack and whilst sitting there John took a picture of me in my dishevelled clothes looking like a lord on his throne, (see photo). On my descent however I inadvertently put my full weight on the sink unit behind the passenger's seat which promptly gave up the ghost and disintegrated. With a little brute force, ignorance and a lot of heaving, I soon had it replaced but in a rather cock-eyed fashion.

I calculated our average speed for this leg of the journey to be an astonishing 26 km per hour, much faster than when we had previously driven this route. Today we had covered 133 km in five hours, including breaks and the odd photograph, which was not bad taking into account the terrain. We delayed our journey only briefly in the morning to photograph the exquisite colours of the desert rocks which appeared volcanic in origin. We then set off towards Al Bogeh making good time down the remaining mountain slopes to the sand shelf and desert below. On reaching Al Bogeh itself we stopped at a chi shop, the same one we went into when last there, and had several cups of sweet black tea. We took several photographs of the area and I managed to persuade a Saudi Bedouin guard to let me photograph him, resplendent in his entirely black dishdash, complete with mandatory AK 47, (see photo).

With the tidying up and other chores done, and petrol and water containers replenished, I set about checking the vehicle for the umpteenth time as the sand crossing was bound to be rough. Letting air out of the tyres once again would help a lot with the grip and flotation on the soft sand. The procurement of a guide was also uppermost in our minds but when offers for this service reached 1000 Saudi Rials (£144), far too much for our modest budget, we decided to go it alone. By this time we had (so we thought) gathered enough knowledge of the area to make it successfully and so we followed a set of tracks into the desert that we hoped would take us in the approximate direction of the Saudi border.

Many of the lighter vehicles set their own paths across the desert and mistakenly we had followed one of these instead of the main route the lorries took. The consequence of this was that we hit very soft sand almost immediately and spent a good deal of time digging out. Time to return to *Al Bogeh* and have a rethink. One particularly bad spot we hit was a sand dyke. This was a long barrier that barred our intended path, far too long to go round and so we made several attempts to get over this and onto the harder sand the other side.

The dyke itself was about thirty foot high and on several occasions we got to within 5-7 meters of the summit before bogging in, having to retrace our steps to try again. We also put markers down to follow, taking advantage of any harder more compacted sand. I just managed to crest the top of the dyke with the VW bottoming out on the sand ridge when, with the engine straining and the clutch spinning to maintain revvs, I eventually pulled over the top and to my horror ran full tilt down the unexpectedly steep bank on the other side!

Resisting the temptation to brake my forward speed I just let the VW roll down with the help of gravity. Fortunately the drag effect of the sand slowed the vehicle down sufficiently to make a reasonably controlled descent. At the bottom I hit a gravel bed, hard enough to stop on and for John to walk to before having a break and thinking about our next move. We were now thouroughly exhausted and becoming paranoid about soft sand which seemed to surround us in every direction. Close by we found some deep ruts left by passing lorries which we decided was the main route through and which we intended to follow the next day. Whilst I stayed with the van, John walked out to recce the track so we could plan accordingly and aim for an early start.

Putting a brew on and listening to *Bridge Over Troubled Water,* I tried to console myself as I wondered if we were going to get out of this mess. John seemed to be gone a long time and getting worried that he may have lost his way in the dusk I put on the side lights for him to home in on, hoping that the battery would not run down. In the meantime, whilst I was waiting, I had talked to a local who passed by and who offered to return the next day at 8 am to take us through the desert to *Al Khadra*. My hopes at this became raised somewhat.

After about one and a half hours John eventually returned, much to my relief and said that the route seemed passable but that there were some soft bits on the way. This, as it turned out was an understatement but for the time being we stayed put and thoughts of the next day were temporarily pushed out of our heads.

After half a day spent attempting to cross the desert, we had come little further than a few kilometres over the 50 kilometre route from *Al Boghe* to the border. However at least we were on solid ground and not far from the main route. After our exertions we ate a simple meal of boiled egg and salt, washed down with orange flavoured "tang", after which we both went straight to sleep. I camped out on the ground as the desert was fairly clear of inhospitable beasties though all through the night I had a troubled sleep, thinking about the driving to come, until in the early morning I finally dozed off.

With a poor night's sleep behind me, I woke at 5.30am and decided to walk the route John had taken to see the lay of the land for myself. After walking for about one and a half hours I decided that this was indeed the main route and that we should follow it whether our guide turned up or not. I returned to the van where we waited till well past 8 am for the guide, by which time the sun had already gained in warmth. The sand had lost its compactness which results from the cold night chill forming a light dew and was by now little more than "hour glass" consistency, flowing with the ease of water.

We set off down the track hitting two rather bad sand dykes on the way. With foot to the floor we managed to burst over the tops of them to continue in the wake of the deep ruts left by passing lorries. Stopping only briefly for a short rest on some more solid ground. We continued along the track until we came to a fork at the foot of a large dune. Taking the left one as this seemed to follow the direction towards Saudi, we turned a corner to find an enormous dune in front of us. It was a staggering forty foot with a slope of about 25 degrees to the top.

We managed to get about half way up before we bedded in and so we dug out and backed the vehicle down to the bottom. Here we were able to turn the VW round on a gravel shelf and retrace our steps a few hundred yards before turning round and having another attempt. We took several tries each time churning up the sand even more and becoming stuck, still only about half way up the dune. On one occasion, as we took the sharp left hand bend by the fork, I was probably going no more than 30 kms per hour but with all the weight on board the VW, we still went up onto two wheels until the back end slewed round. Applying opposite lock we lost a lot of momentum and managed to get only a few feet up the dune that particular time.

By now our nerves were becoming frayed and also the sand had now become so churned up on the dune that we were gradually getting further and further from the top on each attempt. We decided to give it one more go and wherever we stuck we would dig our way out to the top. We got half way up the slope before the back wheels started to dig in. I immediately stopped and we jumped out pulling all available matting from inside the vehicle with us, rubber floor mats, carpets, towels anything that would give support and traction to the wheels. Extricating ourselves was a tedious process of digging sand from under the vehicle, placing mats to the front of the wheels and driving slowly. We had to slip the clutch to give a gradual take up of power and were only able to climb a further five to ten feet at a time.

This all took place under the blazing heat of the desert sun, very much like the scene in "Ice Cold in Alex" starring John Mills, Anthony Quale and Joan Simms. It was a laborious process and extreme care had to be taken so as to prevent the rear wheels getting bogged down. If this were to occur we would probably have had to run back to the bottom of the dune and start all over again. Time and again we would carefully jack up the rear wheels, fill in the ruts underneath, lay mats on top and after lowering the wheels back down, coax the VW a little further. Just as we were calculating how much longer we would be on this stretch, a four wheel drive Toyota Land Cruiser came by and offered us a tow, but said that he had no tow rope! He was quite adamant that very soon we needed to clear the route as lorries would pass this way and that he would help us for 100 SR (about £14) sterling......a bargain!

We first used a rather worn webbing strap that we had obtained in Yemen but this snapped cleanly in half. We then looked to the only remaining possibility which turned out to be the 6 meters of chain securing all the Jerry cans to the roof rack. We unlocked it and took the cans off the roof as they were full of petrol and would release a lot of weight . I was able to shackle one end of the chain to the front of the VW and then the other end to the back of the Toyota using some spare bolts from the tool kit. The 4X4 took the strain and with the chain pulling taut, we both slowly began to get a purchase on the sand.

Yemen

All the time I tried to put the thought of the chain snapping out of my mind, as under such a load it would come flying back into the windscreen of the van. With a struggle and with both engines revving hard, the Toyota managed to pull us to the top with the clutch from the VW starting to overheat and smoke. With great relief we eventually pulled over the crest of the dune and were able to stand on relatively firm sand to unhitch the chain. We paid the driver who left us to our devices as we sat down to have a breather, a cup of chi and of course a cigarette to calm already strained nerves. We took the opportunity to recce the forward route and found only a little soft sand barring our path before reaching much firmer ground.

We returned to the VW which had cooled down, packed all the jerry cans and other belongings back into the van, and set off once more. The route we rejoined was very much as we had remembered, with deeply rutted sand tracks but steerable if taken carefully. My thoughts were that it was the right hand turning at the base of the large dune which was most probably the correct one. No matter, we were on our way, thankful to be back on level ground and what appeared to be the correct track.

A little while later we were stopped by a Yemeni lorry driver on his way from Saudi who asked us for water *(Agwa)* and who confirmed that we were on the correct route. A rule of the desert is that you must stop and offer water or food if asked for. We offered him some from our water bottle and in return he offered us fruit drinks from a pack he had lying next to him on the seat. We had just parted company when I remembered that the Yemeni driver still had our water bottle on board and so ran quickly over to his lorry before it had gone too far from sight. A little embarrassed, I was able to retrieve our only portable bottle without too much fuss.

We continued, but in the harsh midday sun there was little shadow to mark out the track. It was soon obvious that we had strayed off the main path and taking a wrong turning we ended up on softer and softer sand with no lorry tracks in sight.

Inshallah

Stopping on a gravel shelf I reccied the area and fortunately found the main desert track nearby. To reach it we had to negotiate a wadi to find hard ground the other side. We felt, prematurely that we were once more on our way back to Saudi when suddenly, whumph!, whumph! The VW came to an abrupt halt with its front wheels bogged down in a huge rut about two foot deep and filled to the top with the finest gypsum like dust I had ever seen. With the rear wheels still on the hard surface and the nose face down we placed the sand ladders under the front wheels and I tried pulling her out. The VW had seemingly lost all power and wouldn't budge an inch. Alarmed I thought the engine or clutch had packed in after the terrible time spent on the sand dune.

It was then that I noticed that in my haste I had engaged third gear and not first. On the second attempt and in the correct gear, to my great relief, she popped out first time and so I gingerly drove the rear wheels over the sand ladders and brought us finally out of the ruts. This was to be the last problem we had in negotiating the desert sand and with the way fairly clear we pressed on to the border. We passed through two dust storms that by now were blowing from the north and coated everything in a film of grit once again! Thankfully the worst was past us now and we had a relatively straight forward run along the familiar lorry tracks.

Only the occasional sheep or camel broke the white glare of the sand which stretched to the red gravelled mountains beyond, now shimmering in the midday heat. We had made it over the mountains and through the desert. With the hardest part of the journey now behind us, we would soon be onto tarmac road and home free......... or so we thought!

Chapter 10

Return to Saudi

As we drove on following the lorry tracks, the sand thankfully started to become firmer until we eventually reached the Saudi forward guard post 20 km further on. After a brief check of our passports we were directed towards the main border post of *Al Khadra*. On reaching the main camp we gratefully sat in the shade of one of the larger cafes. The main tent which contained several tables was attached to a makeshift cabin where food was being prepared. We were severely dehydrated after our exertions in the desert and longed for a cold drink to slake our thirst. From a refrigerator we took can after can and sat at one of the tables to sit, drink and ponder our eventual escape out of Yemen. We seemed to have come through with only the desert section giving us trouble. But for the Toyota we would still be digging our way out of the sand dune but, "Inshallah" we had again met good fortune. We had accomplished what people here said was an impossible or at the very least dangerous crossing for us.

The passport office was closed and so we had to stay the night and sort out the formalities the next day. The rest of the day was therefore spent cleaning the dust out of the VW and talking to lorry drivers about the route to Yemen, now we were becoming expert at it! We talked to a medic called *Masbah* who spoke perfect English and gave a detailed account of the way of the desert and the Bedouin, including the most notable part of the dress of elder males, the *Jambia*.

This is a curved ritual knife worn in the front and is "The" symbol of wealth for these people and can be quite old as they are handed down from generation to generation. They are usually heavily worked in silver and may contain a bejewelled handle. Some can fetch as much as 30,000 Saudi Rials (£5,000) and can represent an Arab's entire life savings. Some magnificent specimens could be seen at our camp site along with the other symbol of power and influence, the Kalashnikov.

Tomorrow we were to be back on tarmac road once more, a relatively easy journey we thought, to the north and over to the Arab Emirates. How wrong we were as nothing could have been further from the truth. For now though, we slept peacefully, ignorant that the poor advice, servicing and desert conversion in England, coupled with this recent and more difficult desert crossing was to be the cause a major engine malfunction.

The night spent in the desert was too warm and sleep didn't come easily. After the events of the last two days I was also anxious whether the VW would stand up to the remainder of the journey as we still had several thousand kilometres to cover. I woke up at 7am, made tea and met up with our medic friend *Masbah* who we had talked to the night before. He is Palestinian and we talked about the ongoing conflict with Israel. He said his family were living in the Schneller camp for Palestinian refugees in Amman, Jordan, but that he was working here around Najran as the pay was so good.

He had no grudge to bear but like many of his fellow Palestinians felt it was unfair how Israel treated them. They had been pushed into camps on the West Bank and many lived in ghettos in Jordan. What they wanted, as with everyone else in the world, was simply some land to call their own, with the right of self determination.

It is such a shame that now twenty 24 years on, as I am writing these very words, Israel has once again driven tanks into the West Bank and seems to be intent on claiming the land for itself. Yasser Arafat is a prisoner in his own land with Israel destroying all the hard work that has gone into making peace in the area. Just a few incidents, in a tit for tat game across the border, is now setting the whole Middle East on edge. What, one wonders will happen if the oil producing states become embroiled in yet more war?

It appears that nothing has changed in these passing years and as Masbah's story unfolded it left me guilty and desolate that more has not been done to help these dispossessed peoples. He was so helpful, and asked for nothing but friendship in return. Afterwards, he directed us to the passport control office as well as his own medical centre, to get visas and health certificates inspected and stamped. We were still apprehensive as to whether we would be let in as we had no idea whether the political situation in Yemen was worsening.

All the time Masbah interceded on our behalf and was able to speed up the slowly turning wheels of bureaucracy so we were passed through and processed in no time. After only two hours worth of traipsing around the various officials our next urgent task was to repair a tyre that I had inadvertently deflated too much and it had acquired a puncture. Masbah introduced us to a mechanic who very quickly set about repairing the inner tube.

He used a firework repair patch called a Camel. It even sported the same camel cigarette logo and was no doubt a locally made item. It was applied and clamped to the inner tube. The patch was then lit and after about 20 seconds, during which a sulphurous smoke mixed with rubber fumes is given off, the patch is allowed to cool for a few minutes before being removed. What was left underneath became a perfectly vulcanised oval of rubber that is left covering the hole. This was a far stronger and more permanent repair than glue which in the seventies was not as advanced as today and so invariably came unstuck in the desert heat. We then walked over to the café tent, scene of our "Ice Cold in Alex" remake the previous day, to have a couple more cold drinks with Masbah, who offered to provide a guide car to take us to the tarmac road, our link out of the desert and back to Najran. Once on the tarmac road, we parted company with the guide vehicle and soon came to a well with a water pump which gushed fresh sweet water from the deep Cartesian reservoirs, locked up for millions of years below our feet. The water was cascading into several stone tubs about six foot square and about three foot deep. Here the local people were washing clothes whilst children were laughing and playing in the water baths themselves.

Inshallah

After several days on the move and only strip washes to show for it I couldn't resist a wash. However with so many women around I couldn't strip or even take my shirt and trousers off and so I leapt into the tub fully clothed and washed off all the grime of the desert which was soon replaced from the well with sparklingly clean water. As I recounted before, having clean hair was perhaps the one essential I looked forward to as it lifted my heart to have a clean and cool head in the already rising heat of the day. I thoroughly soaped all over, performing a magnificent feat of contortion with my arms to reach all areas beneath my clothes and then sink into the water to rinse off the accumulated grime from days in the mountains and desert.

With much laughter all round from the rapidly gathering crowd of women and children, I stepped out of the stone sink and with a delicate bow to my audience, went back to the van, to let the sun quickly evaporate the water in my clothes. I then filled all the water tanks and our portable bottle, with this wonderfully fresh supply. With a wave to the women and children, and my clothes fully dry, we set off to spend most of the day travelling back north from *Najran* to *Khamis Mushayt*. We reached *Abha* where we stocked up on supplies and then drove on another 20 kms before pulling off the road under a bridge.

The sunset that evening was incredible, and whilst eating our meal and writing up diaries we sat and watched the clouds drift by high above us, casting a variety of pinks and reds over the landscape and leaving the van bathed in a deep orange glow. Balancing the camera on some petrol cans I took several pictures of our campsite before settling down to review the list of running repairs needed on the vehicle after the rather traumatic crossing from Yemen. Roof rack, interior units and bed had all been damaged in the bronco bucking ride and were in urgent need of repair. We intended to be in Taif tomorrow and with Jim, Miz's colleague, visiting contacts in Riyadh, we (ever hopeful), decided to telephone him to delay his departure in order for us to meet up and exchange information, exposed film and letters. This meeting however was not to be, as events were about to unfold that dramatically changed the whole course of our journey.

By now it was the 17th June and the new day started full of optimism. We had just re-crossed the desert and had been allowed back into Saudi and so we were looking forward to exploring the Gulf side of the Arabian peninsula. About 250 kms from our overnight stop we were approaching a steep hill when I noticed the oil pressure warning light flickered on. Stopping to check the oil level I noticed that it had fallen considerably, not a good sign at all! I refilled the engine with fresh oil in the hope that we had simply burnt oil during the crossing and with that we carried on again. Driving no more than 25 kms, the oil light came on once again, and so I stopped to have a look at the engine once more. Opening the engine cowling I could see nothing immediately wrong but from under the vehicle came a small river of oil.

At first I thought we had smashed the sump casing on one of the rocks in the mountain and my mind turned over thinking of ways to externally repair it even if just temporarily. On closer inspection the engine casting itself turned out to be fully intact but oil was gushing from the clutch bell housing, a sure indication that the rear oil seal between the engine and flywheel had failed. I knew this item had been renewed when we rebuilt the engine on Aquaba beach in Jordan and so we assumed something else must have caused it to go fairly recently.

As we were contemplating our next move, some German oil field workers came by in their Chevy pick up truck. They too were on their way to Taif and offered us a tow as we hoped we would be able to get help there. The rope, however, was no more than eight to ten foot and the distance between the vehicles seemed to be far too short for safety. With no other choice we elected to give things a go.

The German driver showed us two hand signals that he would use. One was the opening and closing of a clenched fist, to signify that we should brake, but the second we couldn't believe. He told us he would wave his hand forward to indicate that he was going to overtake! We were incredulous that he would overtake with such a short rope but we were assured that the Saudis drive so slowly that we needed to be prepared otherwise the journey would take forever.

So we started out on our route to *Taif* with me driving and John keeping a look out for hand signals, as well as road and traffic conditions. We soon realised the power of the Chevy's 5 litre engine as it was able to quickly accelerate, even with us as dead weight behind. John's other task soon became one of official cigarette lighter as by now we were both chain smoking our way up north, quite expecting this to be the last journey we would ever make! All attention went on following the rear of the Chevy, taking care not to let the steering wander too much out of line with the tow vehicle in front.

When towed today by the breakdown services a solid bar is used so that the vehicle in front brakes for both vehicles. This contrasts with our situation when a milli seconds hesitation would bring the VW within a midges wing of smashing into the back of the Chevy. We were rapidly becoming more distraught as time went on. On one particularly steep hill there was a long straight run to the bottom and up the other side. However with a line of slowly grinding trucks ahead, out pops a hand from the Chevy and waves frantically indicating that we were about to overtake. We tried to get the German's attention to slow down but they had other thoughts and being inextricably attached, we had no choice but to follow.

I could feel the surge of power as the driver of the Chevy floored the accelerator, jerking our VW to obediently follow and leaving me with the task of holding the steering steady for our lives were literally in my hands. One false manoeuvre and the van, with us inside, would roll over and smash itself to pieces, either with the vehicle in front or into the line of oncoming traffic. We gritted our teeth and puffed even harder at our comfort sticks, whilst the speedometer passed through sixty then 70 to 90 and eventually reaching an incredible 120 kms hour!

Return to Saudi

There was simply nothing we could do except hope and pray, whilst we overtook traffic on our nearside and passed between them and the lorries coming towards us on our outside. This seemed like sheer suicide. With the adrenalin rush still in our veins we then settled back to await our fate to drive at a more leisurely 80 km/hr whilst rapidly diminishing our supply of Marlboroughs that we had on the front dash. We eventually reached *Taif* at about 5.30pm without a stop and the two German lads towed us up to the Hotel Intercontinental where we thankfully stopped to unhitch the VW. We had made it so far and discovered that we had actually covered the journey more quickly being towed than if we had been under our own power!

With very little help from the staff of the hotel about mending the VW, we returned to the van where we met a Frenchman who directed us to the local VW agent. As it turned out this was closed but afterwards he introduced us to British Airways maintenance staff who had a workshop in the city. They were very interested in our journey and immediately offered their garage facilities the following day so that we could remove the engine once more and repair the oil seal. Having filled the sump with oil once more and checked the rest of the vehicle we turned early into bed, exhausted by the white knuckle ride of the day and prepared ourselves for the next day's repairs to the engine. What a day it had been but we were now in good company and quickly fell asleep assured of all facilities needed to carry out repairs.

The following day we returned to the British Airways facility but had to keep filling the sump up, as the oil pressure warning light soon came on and would keep blinking at us impatiently, whilst the VW left an oil slick behind as we drove. By now we were becoming expert at engine removal, taking only about 45 minutes this time to get it out of the vehicle. VW had however designed the engine with a single nut, instead of the usual 6-8 nuts in other vehicles holding the flywheel to the crank shaft. This was secured so tightly it required special tools to undo this! If, like us, you are having to mend the engine with more basic equipment, the nut required the equivalent to placing 125 bags of sugar on the end of a 1 foot spanner, or to put it another way two people standing on the end of that spanner for its removal! In other words it was a brute of a thing to get on or off!

When we finally managed to retrieve the old oil seal, it seemed the heat had probably caused its total disintegration! We would therefore need more spare parts, which meant a further delay until we could obtain them and get them fitted. We later joined the British Airways crew, first at their swimming pool and eventually in their own private cinema to watch "Sugarland Express" starring Goldie Horn. Afterwards we chatted to some of the lads till the early hours about our exploits so far, after which we were put up for the night in very comfortable beds, ready for another day underneath the VW in the garage. What a welcome change!

The work on the engine continued the next day fitting new oil seals and a new release bearing and friction plate on the clutch, both of which had worn out from the mountain and desert crossing. To expedite the rebuild we made the mistake of not stripping the engine completely, for had we done so we would have discovered it to have been full of grit from the desert and damaged considerably from this carborundum-like powder that permeated all mechanical parts. Whether we could have averted its eventual complete failure is impossible to say. Now in our haste to reassemble the engine, we were ignorant of its poor state and pushed on regardless.

I managed to strip a tappet bolt on one of the cylinder heads whilst adjusting the clearances which meant yet another trip to VW. Fortunately they were very helpful as the mechanic there gave me a complete secondhand one in good condition and we quickly bolted it to our engine. With the engine once more installed and with all electrical leads, cables and fuel pipes re-connected we started her up. However it was obvious that all was not well as the rebuilt engine was noisy. This was a warning we should have taken heed of as the oil pressure warning light also kept coming on at low revs, a sure indication that the big ends had gone, also ground away by the desert sand.

162

Return to Saudi

We decided that the engine would need further inspection but as this was going to cost more we would have to get an advance out of Miz as our funds were once again starting to run low. We eventually got through to him and surprisingly he offered to send further funds to us immediately! Unfortunately the nearest city with a branch of the Bank of Credit and Commerce was in *Jedda,* 150kms away and so we decided to divert there. There was nothing for it but to coax the van back as best we could since the run would be mostly down hill! With the prospect of having a fully equipped VW agent there we decided it was worth the risk to get the job done properly.

We woke early at 6am and after a hearty breakfast in the BA kitchen we set off immediately. The descent from the high plateaux to the hotter plains below was through a series of cliff workings, along which the Saudis were building a more modern stretch of road. This required the blasting of rock and so the old road would be closed for several hours after 8am in the morning.

We reached the point where they were blasting and passing over the crest of the ridge, freewheeled down the other side on the old road, some 10 kms in all. This saved petrol but more importantly reduced stress to the engine which by now was starting to labour alarmingly! In fact we were both very tense as at any moment we fully expected the VW to seize up. We seemed to will the VW to carry us the rest of the way to Jeddah and after stopping frequently to refill the sump and let the engine cool, we made Jedda city at 11am.

Once there we limped around in the van, first picking up any mail from post restante and then driving over to Joe's, who we had met a few months before at Dolphin Construction, to see if he could provide any help. Lastly we drove to the large VW facility to get an estimate of the work to be carried out on our engine. The service engineer at VW told us the sorry story. As I had expected, sand had entered the engine through a damaged air breather valve and had then got into the sump oil and gradually ground all the bearings, and other moving parts away until it was ready to seize up. We were very lucky to have made it from *Taif* and…. well….

Inshallah

basically we needed almost a completely new engine! The cost of all the repairs would come to about 3000 Saudi Rials or about £500! This represented our entire remaining budget to return to London. Also we were told there would be a delay due to the current pressure of work unless we could strip the engine down ourselves. Miz and Jim are not going to be best pleased, we thought, but at least we had made it to Jeddah with the van, our film and ourselves intact!

Whilst telephoning from the main post office and making our pleas to Miz, we met George, a German lad, living in Jedda who worked on contract. He offered his driveway for us to take the VW apart again which we accepted. We arrived at his house after lunch and started to extract the engine, with the help of one of his Korean friends. We broke the record and in true pit stop fashion had the engine out and were starting to disassemble it in 20 minutes flat.

As it was now getting late we soon stopped to return to Joe and Brenda's for an evening meal. She had done us proud with roast turkey, roast potatoes and veg which we washed down with some of Joe's excellent homebrewed beer. I was exhausted from the days efforts and said my good nights leaving John to watch football on the TV.

The next day I continued on with the engine, gradually stripping it down to its component parts but all the time feeling slightly dizzy from the sun. The work was slow and by 8am the heat was already building up to a blistering 40 degrees, whilst any engine parts left in the sun became too hot to handle. Coupled with this I was starting to feel the effects of sun burn and decided when most of the parts had been stripped and cleaned that I had had enough. My temper was beginning to fray, I felt sick and knew I simply had to be crazy to work outside in this heat.

The next day we towed our mobile home with its engine parts inside, over to VW to let them get on with the seemingly endless list of repairs. Over the next few days the list seemed to grow and grow as more faults were found in the engine. New camshaft, crank case, shells, con rods, rings, cam followers, oil pump, in fact more or less a complete engine for which the final bill was to come to a whopping 5500 SR or about £800, more than the secondhand cost of the van itself. This was on top of the monies spent in Yemen on other repairs. The cost of these spares which all had to be imported was astronomical and in stark contrast to the little extra cost needed to run a sturdy four wheel drive vehicle as fuel here was cheaper than water to purchase.

Before contacting Miz about this, we discussed whether to pull the plug on the journey or whether the repairs would see us round. As VW were servicing the vehicle I was sure that with a good engine and surfaced roads for the remainder of our journey, the vehicle would pull through. We expected the worst after our showdown with him in Yemen, but Miz surprisingly agreed to send further funds to cover the cost of repairs. We decided to press on with the project but the repairs would cause quite a delay in the schedule yet again. For now, the responsibility of vehicle repairs had been passed to VW and the stress of working on greasy metal with parts too hot to handle in the mid summer heat could be forgotten.

Several days were spent collecting new visas and writing letters to friends, particularly to Han in Holland. By now I had struck up a close rapport through her frequent letters which provided one of the few comforts in my otherwise dusty and rather troubled journey. Back at Brenda's I was also able to catch up on diary writing and plan the rest of the journey. We had arranged for new funds to be sent through to the Bank of Credit and Commerce after the customary request in triplicate for estimates from Miz. This all had to be relayed through the services of the antiquated telegraph office where we were now all but camped out. Meanwhile, we also attended to all the hundreds of other things that needed doing.

The odd few days for the repairs turned into a week and then eventually almost two weeks of waiting, running to the banks, sending endless telexes to Miz and with a little diving in the Red Sea thrown into the bargain. We settled back into the luxury of a slower, less hectic pace of life. We were sheltered from the mid summer heat with all facilities to hand, in the thick walled and cool apartment which we were looking after for Joe and Brenda who had flown back to England to renew their work permits and visas. It was nevertheless frustrating to think that the majority of our delays so far rested squarely on the inadequacy of our vehicle. Now we were again delayed, waiting for the VW to be fixed. John and I spent the time when not taking official photographs indulging in some leisure activities. To have us around meant security for Joe and Brenda and for us it meant shade, fresh water on tap, showers, good cooking, refrigerated beer and ice cold drinks. These were luxuries that made the working day in the heat so much more bearable. John made full use of their stereo, recording music and at one point making a superb rendition of Prime Minister's question time in the House of Commons. We soon became refreshed, gradually recovering from our ordeal in the desert and with it a little restless, as we had spare energy for creativity and even times for pranks.

One that I played on John was to take some chocolate mousse pudding, which looked not unlike cat poo. I placed a dollop on John's camera box which unless closely inspected looked just like the cat had been there. I sat back to await events and could hardly contain myself when he came into the kitchen after a recording session on the hi-fi to retrieve it. His treasured Hasselblad had been well and truly dumped on, or so it seemed, and he hurriedly set about cleaning the case, delivering profanities at the poor moggy, cowering in the corner till I owned up and put John's mind to rest. Such larking though, was quite rare on our journey.

However, that is not to say that whilst waiting for repairs to be carried out, the time spent waiting wasn't uneventful. I had promised to take Joe's large Pontiac car in for a service but I noticed that the rear tyre had been getting progressively flatter and after putting off the job for two days noticed that it was now flat. I decided to put on the spare. American cars are generally built like the proverbial Victorian loo and instead of crawling around on the ground placing a puny jack under the sill as in British cars, this one had a crank jack that is placed under the rear bumper (fender) and it is from here that the car is lifted. Then, having detached the nacell covering the tyre, I was quickly able to replace it with the good spare.

Feeling happy in my work I locked the vehicle and went inside for a cool drink. But I couldn't find the car keys anywhere and at that point I realised I had left them in the boot which appeared to have no manual release and which I had just shut. I couldn't activate the boot without the keys to operate the ignition. *Jim*, an American pilot and friend of Joe and Brenda's, showed me the boot release switch which in most American cars is located in the glove compartment. We traced the wires from the button and hoped to pop the boot catch by "hot wiring" it to the battery. Once ready, I lightly touched the bare end of the hot wire to the battery live terminal and hey presto, the boot lid opened. "Well thank God for that," I said as we were both very much relieved! One benefit to come out of this escapade, was the offer of a meal from Jim which we eagerly accepted !

We visited VW which was rather depressing as they were short staffed and our VW looked sorry for itself with the engine half out. Time was drifting by and nothing seemed to have been done to our van. I went into town to sort more visas and check if money had been transferred yet from London but left empty handed. Over the meal that evening, I talked at length with Jim's wife about our exploits through the Middle East, whilst later talking shop, (photography) with Jim himself.

The next day I finally took Joes's Pontiac into the General Motors agent for a check and hitched a return lift in the back of a Toyota Land Cruiser. This turned out to be a non registered Taxi but the driver still wanted 4 Rials (50 pence) for the short journey whilst the normal fare would have been 2 Rials. This is precisely what I gave him leaving him to try his inflationary tactics on some other poor unsuspecting person!

Up to this point we had divided the time between chores and relaxing but one of the delights of the area was the diving. Like Jordan, the Red Sea nearby offered much for the diver and John was keen to use his equipment at every opportunity. Jim, the pilot rang us the next day and offered to take us up to Seven Palms beach beyond North Creek, as he had just filled up some air tanks.

With a little trouble negotiating the soft sand, we arrived at the water's edge and with the heat building up, John waded into the cool, crystal clear water. I went in to snorkel and plunged over the reef edge into the depths below, whilst John and Jim set up their diving gear. After what seemed about 45 minutes I was about to return to the beach when up popped two familiar heads, describing all sorts of marine wild life in the depths. When John offered me a go on his diving equipment I found it irresistible and readily accepted. This was to be my first time ever and John had often talked of taking me down with him on one of his dives in the Red Sea and decided this was a good time for me to practice breathing through the demand valve attached to the air tank. After his recent dive, there was a little air left for me to explore a deep fissure on top of the reef since John still had the "reserve" left which contained air for just a few minutes.

The fissure was really a bowl within the reef itself, about 30 ft deep and about the same in circumference with soft sand at the bottom, an ideal "training pool" to try out the feel of the air bottle, diving weights and demand valve. So with weight belt adjusted and breathing regularly from the air tank, I dived in whilst Jim accompanied me. Satisfied that I was alright and with nowhere to go Jim signalled that he was returning to the surface as his air was about to run out. I continued to the bottom and sat there holding onto a rock and simply looking about in wonder at the beautiful structure of the coral through the turquoise water, which was teeming with life.

I had completely forgotten I was on reserve and was blissfully unaware of the panic on the surface. At that moment John, looking at his divers watch, realised that my air must be running short and that with no reserve left when it ran out, it would do so suddenly and without warning! Getting worried that I was running into danger he was trying to snorkel down to me as Jim was still offloading his equipment. I was quite oblivious to all this panic on the surface and was in a state of euphoric calm. I don't know what it was that made me look up, but I saw about 7 meters above me John waving his arms and yelling underwater like mad for me to return to the surface. I signalled the OK sign with my right thumb and index finger in the shape of a circle and checked my air gauge to find that it registered zero pressure. Calmly I let go of the rock and I drifted to the surface, stopping half way up for a 10 second break. With about six feet to go the air abruptly gave out but suddenly I was bathed by the glistening waves and sunlight at the surface and able to breath through my snorkel.

Jim asked if I was OK. "Great dive," I said. "It was really something else." I was simply ecstatic.

John explained in no uncertain terms what the panic had been about and reminded me that I should have stayed down for no longer than five minutes when in fact I had stayed down well over this! I know he meant well for me, and it was stupid that I had let the dive go on. It would have been very serious if the air had run out at the bottom even though it was only thirty or so feet down. We washed and stowed John's gear then set about collecting some shells, together with some live conches, which John decided to take back and clean on our return to Joe's house.

The smell that eventually emanated from boiling them in the pan that night was awful. Thank goodness Joe and Brenda were in England. As an alternative less smelly method, I tried to coax one of the molluscs out of its shell by placing it in a bowl of soda water. This seemed to have the effect of making it hick and burp somewhat before eventually coming out to flop all over the place with its poor little eyes waving about and going barmy on their pneumatic stalks. John and I looked on with fascination at the writhing of this little creature and totally forgot to grab it, before it gave one last burp and withdrew for good back in its shell! At this I gave up and into the pot it went.

The next day, 6th July, we still had much to do. We were hoping the VW would be ready to be picked up, which meant a trip to Dolphin Construction to collect Joe's Pontiac. This would allow

Inshallah

John and I to pop into town to pick up money that may have been sent, then drive over to VW to collect the van. Unused to the long length of the Pontiac, I managed to reverse, but only very lightly, into another car whilst parking.

Untypical of our experiences so far, the Saudi driver along with the passengers got out and started shouting abuse and many obscenities at us in English and Arabic since foreigners in the city were lightly tolerated. We pretended not to understand and with raised shoulders and arms just turned and walked away....rather rapidly!

We collected the money and then the van which I nearly crashed in VW's car park, as I had become so used to the power systems of the Pontiac that I nearly collided with another vehicle. This left me very flustered. Two accidents in one day was too much and so John drove the VW whilst I returned to Joe's house in the faster Pontiac to arrive there first. I had just started to unload some shopping when I heard the screech of tyres and the sound of our familiar VW engine. Peering round the front gate with an arm full of shopping I just caught John driving up to the pavement just under the brow of an overhanging tree. A large branch was only about an inch above the roof of the VW which smashed the roof rack off its retaining brackets and with the sound of tortured metal the rack and five full jerry cans came crashing off the back of the van, to land intact but very bent onto the road.

My jaw was left hanging whilst John looked dumbfounded inside the van, wondering what on earth had happened. Well that solved the roof rack problem then, I thought! We were definitely going to have to get another more sturdy one as the tangled heap wrapped around the jerry cans was now no more than scrap! All the money spent in *Taif* welding and repairing the roof rack was now wasted. But as they say, whilst one door closes, another opens, and the problem of the roof rack was soon to be solved in a rather unusual way.

Driving once more to Seven Palms beach the next day we found a jetty to dive from. Having satisfied ourselves that we had covered all the safety checks, we moved off into deeper water through a

Return to Saudi

fissure in the coral. Further and further down we went passing the bright red stag antler shapes of the protruding coral face. Finally the bottom loomed out at us. With my hands out stretched I happily passed my fingers through the tentacles of the anemones that seemed to be waving hypnotically at me and beckoning me to venture further into their world.

I was starting to feel the effects of a sort of nitrogen narcosis. I was literally turning somersaults, happy that we had made the 100ft mark. The result of my exertions meant that I was quickly running out of air and signalled to the group that I would return to the surface.

We returned to a slap-up meal and the next day we set about checking all the vehicle equipment. I adjusted the brakes, which still felt spongy, while John cleaned and stowed goodies in the interior. On checking the engine I discovered that VW had left off an engine mounting bolt and also one of the four connecting the engine to the gearbox! The cause of all our woes, the sand, had entered through the oil breather pipe that now hung down beside the engine. It should have had a new rubber teat on the end allowing any pressure in the crank case to escape but preventing ingress of dust.

The correct conversion for desert driving, we learnt later was to have the pipe extended directly back to the air filter which provides a much better "closed system", and will prevent all ingress of dust. The agents in England had not carried this out with the consequential damage to the engine and the delays we had suffered. Now the rubber teat had been left off the breather pipe once more! This again left our newly built engine critically exposed to sand! In addition we found the tie bars to the steering were also bent so this would mean yet another return trip to VW and more delay.

The next day, we took the VW back to the garage to get the final repairs completed. On the way we passed a Landrover that had been left in a ditch by the side of the road. Although the vehicle looked operational, on closer inspection the whole thing had been abandoned to gather dust and was generally very tatty. What interested us was that it had a full length, welded box section steel roof rack on top. Easily large enough for John and I both to sleep on. A cunning plan was formed.

It should be remembered that in Saudi, stealing is punishable in extreme cases with the chopping off of the left hand. For Westerners this crime usually meant a heavy fine and imprisonment. But the otherwise complete Landrover was not just any vehicle; it was, we convinced ourselves, abandoned and therefore fair game. A daylight raid was out of the question, so we decided to return that evening under the cover of darkness.

Dropping the VW off we got a taxi into town where we bought some film and returned, to pick the VW up and had another look at the Land Rover to check the spanner size needed to release the roof rack. After supper, John and I donned our darkest clothes and in "Pink Panther", fashion drove that night over to the Land Rover once more.

We parked nearby and looked for any signs of police and rehearsed our alibi should we need it. We decided on the "plead ignorance approach" if caught but once reassured we were not being observed, clambered out, pockets bulging with spanners were soon going about the business of "borrowing" the roof rack.

Clambering on top of the roof we had the six or so bolts easily released and quickly had the rack stood alongside the vehicle. Checking that the coast was clear we tiptoed, with pulses racing, to our VW, discarding the rack on the ground to give us another pause to check if the coast was clear.

Everything looked okay and as the rack was too large to fit inside the van we quickly lifted up the rather heavy frame onto the roof of the VW. It was a perfect fit and with a few belly laughs at our rather ridiculous performance, we had the rack bolted up securely and were on our way. Taking a few diversions on our route back to Joe and Brenda's house to "throw" any one following, we arrived and hastily parked the van in the drive and away from prying eyes.

We settled down to a good whisky at bagging the superb roof rack, even if we did feel rather guilty. All the luggage fitted with

Return to Saudi

ease and with so much more security, we were now ready for the next leg. All the tasks had now been sorted. At 5.30am we loaded the van, cleared up the house and leaving a note for Joe, closed all the doors and slipped the keys back through the letter box. It was so quiet at that time of the day that we were out of the city in no time, meeting only occasional traffic. We took it easy as we were still running in the new engine, never exceeding 80kms per hour and stopping regularly for tea or a cold drink. Finally, 230kms from Riyadh we stopped for the night in the desert. Even in the late evening it was still warm and John and I decided to try out the sleeping arrangements on the roof rack.

Finishing my diary and a letter to Han, who by now was featuring more and more predominantly in my thoughts, I climbed up onto my side of the roof rack, so that John and I were lying top to tail on our respective sleeping bags, with thin mattresses beneath. Many stars were visible as there was no light pollution from surrounding habitation. We whiled away the wee hours talking of our trip so far and the lovely people we had met which soon had us falling into a deep sleep in the chilling desert air. This was one of life's greater moments for me and one very happy memory of our time spent in the Middle East. The night passed by in fits and starts as the temperature plummeted. I had to first get into the sleeping bag then pull more clothes and bedding over me to stay warm.

We set off the following day through the desert. The road stretched on for mile after mile and taking turns at driving meant I could continue to read the rest of my book, "Watership Down." It was becoming very hot by now with the temperature reaching well into three figures, the hottest of the whole trip so far, as I recorded 134 degrees Fahrenheit in the van at one point. I leant against the right hand door with my head catching the air stream blowing through the open window. It was far from cooling as it was more like the hot air issuing from a hair drier. But I was able to get some relief by making it cooler with the water soaked *ghutra* that I wore.

Inshallah

Eventually I reached the climax of the book where poor old Hazel rabbit fell asleep in the rabbit hole and woke up next to another rabbit with silver ears and together they take one great leap, Hazel leaving his body behind, to fly up and beyond the warren into the blue yonder. As I turned the last emotive page of text, I looked out over the passing sand dunes becoming rather choked as I realised that we were still far from home. With all the emotions pent up from the trials of our incredible journey that threatened to spill over, I realised how lucky we were to still be alive and free to roam!

As these thoughts passed through my mind, we entered the outskirts of Riyadh. Once in the centre, we searched for the poste restante for news from home. Because there was no official tourism, I had to sign a book describing the company I worked for and put down Dolphin Construction, whereupon I was presented with a beautifully illustrated and expensively finished book. The city had quite a sombre outlook to it. As it is the capital of this major oil producing country, it was strange it was deserted but we took it that most people had probably migrated to the high lands for the summer as the mid summer temperatures here were stupefyingly hot. We next set about photographing the parks in the city centre, where French style water towers dominate the skyline. I took several more photographs of these from the outside and several shots across the city from the inside. Eventually an inquisitive gardener came over and asked what I was doing. Everyone was suspicious of photographers in Saudi and this person explained that there were sensitive communications equipment hereabouts and that it was not uncommon to have film confiscated. As it happened he turned out to be from Pakistan, and after I showed him the letter from Miz he seemed a lot happier.

We talked of his homeland and Nepal which I had visited the year before. He came originally from Lahor and with this common ground we talked at length about ourselves and our families. Since I had studied botany and he was a landscape gardener we became more engrossed in conversation. Eventually

Return to Saudi

all fears evaporated as we freely talked at some length about world affairs and parted good friends, with my film still intact. Poor old John had not faired so well. Returning to the van he seemed to be suffering a kind of shell shock. His film had been taken from him by a police officer and he had only just got away without having his beloved Hasselblad taken as well. Once recovered and not to be left without a record of our visit, John surreptitiously took a photograph of the water tower through some railings and once satisfied that we had covered as much as we dare, we went over to the *Amman Hotel* for a cool drink. We thought it prudent not to try and camp in Riyadh as to do so would invite too much attention and so in the early evening we set off once more towards the United Arab Emirates.

About 30 km from *Khurays* we tried to pull off the road onto some sand but it was so soft, we only just stopped in time before bogging all four wheels down. We still needed the sand ladders to extricate ourselves before we could continue on our way through Khurays and onto *Al Mubarrez*. On the way to the next town, *Al Hufuf,* we found a side track down which we parked. Exhausted from the hard day's drive of 500 kilometres, plus the few hours spent taking photographs in the mid summer heat, we thankfully turned in at 10.30pm eating no more than bread and peanut butter, followed by coffee and orange juice. The night was still cool and we awoke early to take the mandatory shot of the campsite before starting the journey to the Emirates, famous for their gold souks, dhows and beautiful manmade lush green gardens.

Chapter 11

Qatar and The Emirates

The advancing seasons meant that we were now in the hottest part of the year and by 7am it already felt like the midday sun on an English summers day.

We kept up a steady 80 kms per hour and eventually reached the old town of *Al Hufuf*. The roads were quite rutted and full of very deep pot holes but the old town did sport a magnificent old fort, built entirely of mud brick. We stopped briefly to take photographs and once past this town the desert landscape started to change considerably. From what had been low, fairly flat and uninteresting gravel pans, there rose the most exquisite dunes that we had encountered on the whole journey. Some we calculated attained a height of 30 metres.

In places the tarmac had become covered in the shifting sands from the dunes, which is a constant problem here and so we drove carefully so as to avoid driving off the road altogether and becoming bogged down in the deep sand at the edges. Eventually the road led down the coast, to the port of *Salwah*. The furnace heat from the sun high above us, combined with an appalling humidity, made conditions very uncomfortable inside the VW. Compared to the open desert, where we only had to contend with very dry heat from the glaring sands, this humidity never diminished throughout the day or night.

We reached the border with Saudi and passed into *Qatar*, traversing this small kingdom to reach the Emirates on the southern side. The journey was again along tarmac roads that glistened in their sticky, sun roasted way, but by now we had left the large dunes behind.

At the Doha / Juh junction we had the choice of going left and deeper into Qatar but with time pressing we decided to turn sharp right towards the UAE, in the hope of contacting another of Miz's business friends who we were supposed to leave our exposed film with for return to England. Where the roads split some enterprising fellow had built a green painted wood framed tea house, a sort of glassed panelled conservatory with a veranda that all the passing truckers seemed to use. Here we filled up with fuel, from a seemingly deserted garage surrounded by oil encrusted sand. Throughout the furnace heat of the day the lone attendant had to ply his trade and hand pump the fuel from large steel barrels by hand.

We carried on towards the border with the UAE and passed still more exotically shaped dunes. We then passed briefly back into Saudi territory, the only link between Qatar and the Emirates. There are no customs here as to one side is an impassable desert leading to the Empty Quarter that only camels or the best equipped four wheel drive vehicles can travel in. On the other side was the sea and so the single, lonely road takes you only to the UAE. We did notice skull and crossbone signs on the way, presumably to indicate that travellers should not leave the main highway. To go into the Empty Quarter with its rolling sea of sand dunes without sufficient preparation would mean almost certain death through lack of water.

A further two hours through the dunes brought us to the Emirates customs and with the usual bureaucratic fumblings our passports were stamped and carnets inspected. We decided to have a break from the heat of our VW cabin and went to sit in a café. As it was so humid we stayed the night in air conditioned luxury at the café which for 30 Rials (£4) seemed a bargain! The room itself was small but provided a much welcome relief to our heat burdened bodies.

The café was a truckers stopover and provided western meals for all the TIR intercontinental lorries bringing goods from the European markets to the cash rich cities in the Emirates. We were able to dine on steak and chips before retiring to our chalet which even had pipes for running water (we were told) but which were not turned on.

Inshallah

We both slept soundly in the cool of the chalet and on the 13th July set off to reach *Abu Dhabi*, some 350 km away. The taller dunes we had passed in Qatar diminished and gave way once more to the flatter, barren landscape we had come through in Saudi. This was the hottest season and the humidity had reached saturation making this the most uncomfortable part of the journey thus far. Even water soaked cloth around our heads couldn't provide relief from the heat. The high humidity prevented rapid evaporation from the cloth, essential to gain the all-important cooling effect that desert water bags seen strapped to the front of vehicle bumpers also rely on. We were gradually being stewed in our own sweat inside the furnace heat of the van which now approached 132 degrees Fahrenheit. There were constant problems such as the glue on the leatherette finish of the cameras becoming unstuck.

On reaching *Abu Dhabi* we drove through the centre of the city to the BCCI bank, our contact point for further money from Miz. Here we became friendly with the manager who allowed us to use the phone in his air conditioned office. On reaching Miz in London we were not surprised by now at his rather cool and uncooperative reception. It must certainly have been one of his bad days again, as broaching the subject of further funding sent him into paroxisms of rage, blaming John and I again for being irresponsible and negligent with his money.

Very tired from our drive to the city, I was explaining the situation to him in some detail but he simply would not listen to my analysis. He had no concept of the appalling conditions in the mid summer heat under which John and I were now operating and so, after his remonstration, he promptly hung up on me. At this point we just resigned ourselves to the inevitable delays and set off into the city to take some photographs.

Abu Dhabi at the time had developed more advanced Western tastes, than the other, more conservative Arab nations. For better or worse the city boasted some prestigious and photogenic modern architecture. In the central parks for example I was able to encourage an Arab family to pose in the forground with the city spread behind in a panoramic backdrop of fountains, green grass and lush palm trees, all there because of a very costly but effective irrigation scheme.The port also provided wonderful images of maritime life with the working Arabs aboard the ubiquitous Dhows which were used for fishing and transport.

In the early evening, businesses were once again open after closing for the afternoon rest and we returned to the cool of the air conditioned BCCI bank at 7 pm, to see if there was any word from Miz. As usual nothing had arrived and the bank manager consoled us with a cup of tea. By now John and I were finding it harder to become motivated by the project, not only from the almost unbearable climate but also through the seemingly total lack of support from England for what was clearly an over ambitious, under-funded and poorly researched expedition.

However with little choice left but to carry on regardless, we used the phone at the bank to liaise with the contact that we had been given by Miz. Once again, and to no great surprise, we got little response except the offer of the use of his telex machine to call England. The office of the contact was near the harbour and after stopping at Poste Restante we eventually arrived at the local contact's building in great despair. There we sent a message off to the office but instead of Miz, someone else replied from London. The reply was very vague (probably the secretary had sent it) so we were going to have to await events. Meanwhile the so-called "good" contact had nothing else for us and even demanded a fee for the telex to London, a further unnecessary drain on our resources!

Parking outside the office near the waterfront, I now began to read the letters from home to console myself in the fact that at least somebody cared. Hanna, it seemed was thinking of travelling to Australia, soon so I hoped we would get back in time to see her before she left. At this rate and with no more funding, John and I discussed the prospect that we might as well call it a day anyway if Miz was going to remain intransigent. We had just enough funds to get back if nothing more was forthcoming.

Inshallah

The heat, even in the late evening, was unbearable, especially as debilitating effects were increased by the incredible humidity. Lying on the roof rack in the open air with just a sheet covering my otherwise soaking wet body, the mattress below became more and more sodden with sweat that ran freely from my skin into the bedding. I just lay there musing over the day's events, counting off the miserable minutes in my sleepless state whilst listening to the nearby air conditioning fans, blowing their hot exhaust air into the night adding yet more heat to the tepid atmosphere that was simply becoming too much to bear.

All we wanted to do was to take it easy in the daily regime of baking heat which had the local population seeking the coolest shade. Unfortunately our schedule would not allow the luxury of stop overs, taxis, air conditioned rooms or hotel cuisine and our little world now started to grate on our nerves. Already tense from a total lack of understanding from our employers, we had all this to contend with but still decided to stick to our tight shooting schedule. Most days we worked frantically during the relative cool of the early morning, since after that all energy would be sapped from wilting and over taxed and tired bodies.

I decided that the next day we would seek a friendly ex-pat to stay with in the UAE, as I was simply not going to spend another miserable night in the hot house hell on the top of the roof rack! We had no money to speak of and without the use of an air conditioned hotel had to throw ourselves on the kindness of our fellow countrymen. Unlike the reserved atmosphere back in old blighty, the British ex-pat on the whole is a delightful and outward going animal and extremely helpful and generous. With our experience of help from ex-pats during our travels, we unashamedly looked forward to further aid. The next day was spent trying to negotiate some further funding as ours had by now all but run out. The money was so short that we now had no option but to transfer the telephone charge to London to make calls. However, Miz and Jim still had the hump and even refused to accept our reverse charge calls. We were stuck!

Qatar and the Emirates

After several attempts they finally picked the phone up and as always we were first given the re-run of the "funds are critical" sketch. Despite the fact that they were paying only £60 wages for the two of us per week there was apparently, only £400 left to cover all costs for the Arab Emirates, Bahrain, Kuwait and our return trip back to London. We were instructed to accomplish this in 15 days, meaning that we would have to cover an average of 450 kilometres a day, including the time spent for taking photographs!

John and I discussed our options but in the end felt there was nothing for it but to accept their decision and if necessary omit the photography! Optimistically, they wanted even more pictures now, presumably to squeeze the last productive days out of us and we were therefore told to pick up 300 more rolls of film to cover Kuwait on the return leg of our epic journey!

John and I resumed our work and went to look at one of the better built mosques in the city. Standing outside the building afterwards I got into conversation with a couple of British ex-pats, Rick and Penny. I explained our predicament to them and taking one look at my dishevelled appearance, they immediately offered us a room and a shower whilst we were waiting for funds to arrive.

The next few days were spent waiting for Miz and Jim to decide on further funding, whilst our two wonderful hosts kindly showed us the highlights of the city. We renewed our interest in the project and spent time visiting the harbour and the markets, photographing everything from the general architecture to the gold souk and took a prodigious amount of film of the magnificent Dhows, some of which were obviously very old.

Miz and Jim eventually saw reason and now that we had accepted the inevitable demands from England, we got our funds sent to us, care of the BCCI bank, which meant that we could continue with our work in peace. On the 17th of July we woke early to meet another contact at *Sharjah*, just a little way the other side of Dubai. On the way we passed more very spectacular dunes which we spent some time enthusiastically photographing, now that our morale had been boosted by the thought that we would, after all, be able to drive back to England.

We passed through the city of *Dubai* at about midday and of course went immediately to poste restante. We both got mail this time and I once again could sit and read a detailed letter from Hanna. We then drove to the more salubrious surroundings of the Imperial Hotel for a cold drink and also phone our contact in *Sharjah*. In his absence we left a message with his secretary but all further attempts failed to raise any response. We were left totally on our own to sort out a schedule for photography and had to research the area from scratch, which caused yet further delays. What a set up!

Fortunately John had some friends, *Simon* and *Dave*, who were working in Dubai and who offered to put us up for the night in air conditioned luxury. They cooked a square meal for us and even had a supply of girly magazines to hand, reminding us that we had both been on the road for nearly six months now, never talking to women save those from the West. The next day we met up with some Swedish friends of theirs from *Sharjah* who were able to give us a lift up the coast and across the mountains to *Al Fujayrah* on the Indian Ocean and tantalisingly close to the border with Oman. It was here we were told that we could find the magnificent Tiger Cowry shells on the sandy bed of the sea. These are produced by the *Cowry mollusc* and are much sought after since they are "glazed" with a beautiful mottled pattern by the animal on the outside as well as the inside. They range in size from two to six inches long. The animal exudes a sort of mother of pearl over the whole of the outside leaving a shell that is perfectly shiny and smooth, yet reflecting a wonderfully iridescent colour. I soon found fifteen empty cowry shells all clumped together on the sand just waiting for me to pick them up, Inshallah!

After a swim we were also able to get some lovely sunset shots of the Dhows in the harbour and also photograph the wonderfully pink sunset with the dunes and the Gulf of Oman beyond. All too soon though, we had to make our way back over the mountains to

Qatar and the Emirates

Simon and Dave's where we had a very enjoyable meal. The following morning we went to the Saudi embassy in Dubai to pick up our transit visa which unfortunately was valid for one crossing only and no stops which in effect allowed about three days transit. Their refusal to issue a multiple entry visa which we needed to visit Bahrain and Kuwait was because of the onset of Ramadan and the embassy wanted us across Saudi and out of the kingdom as soon as possible during this holy festival!

With Kuwait and Bahrain now off the itinerary, we would have to go from the UAE direct to the Jordanian border on the other side of Saudi Arabia. Having pleaded once more with the Saudi officials for a multiple entry visa but to no avail, we phoned Miz's contact one last time in the hope we could leave our exposed film with him and pick up the fresh stock that he should have waiting for us.

On the way we passed through some of the older parts of the city. No glass and steel structures these. They were traditional mud built houses, with thick walls surrounding deep shaded courtyards. The corners of the building formed small chimneys about two metres square and ten high. The towers cause the warm air to rise up one vent drawing cooler air from another vent in the same chimney. This ancient and natural air conditioning system has no moving parts, does not consume any electricity and produces a cooling air flow even during the warmest part of the year. Magnificent!

It is a sad reflection that in modern buildings more use isn't made of this type of natural air circulation. Instead we use precious electricity and at the same time run the risk of circulating foul, recycled, bacteria laden air that at best leaves one with dry skin and headaches and at worst spreads the deadly Legionnaires disease. However these thoughts were far from us now and we reached the Ambassador hotel to make one last attempt to contact Miz's friend. Still the phone rang with no reply, so we decided to give up and left the fresh film stock with him since we would not be going to Kuwait and our own reserves would last the rest of the journey.

Inshallah

In the hotel we struck up a conversation with a Norwegian tanker captain and over dinner, which he warmly invited us to at his expense, we became enthralled by his deep knowledge of archaeology and the shipwrecks around the world. In his home waters off Norway there are interesting and ancient sites to dive but for him the best were to be found off the coast of Bermuda. While he talked at length, John sat spellbound, whilst I dutifully jotted down copious notes in case I should ever venture to these locations, as my appetite for diving had already been whetted (some would say spoilt), in the Red Sea.

We had a filling meal consisting of mouth watering crab cocktail, steak fillet on a bed of buttered asparagus, accompanied by a very nice Beaujolais. Sweet was an exceptionally rich chocolate cake and after finishing the meal with liquors, we sat in easy armchairs sipping gin and tonics and talked at length about our journey. Our host mentioned that if we would like to delay our journey a few weeks he could put the VW on the top deck of his ship and we could cruise back with him in relative luxury as he was stopping off in Rotterdam!

The offer was very tempting indeed but after so long on the road we both felt that the journey of adventure would only really be complete if we made the return under our own steam. In any case we wanted to push on and didn't want to outstay our welcome with our hosts but thanked him for a wonderful meal and his very kind offer.

We retired to the captain's room to talk at length about our journey, before saying our farewells. Just before our departure he asked both John and myself what our favourite spirits were and gave us a parting gift of Remy Martine and Chivas Regal, together with a pack of 250 cigarettes each.

We left feeling that the gift of human kindness had not completely deserted us and that now the journey was all but over, bar the return to our loved ones, we had found a true spirit of friendship from a like minded soul. It is hard to describe our feelings at being treated thus. Other people, both Arab and European that we had met, had shown an equal kindness. We had combated severe climatic conditions, and the rigours of the journey and came through unscathed. This human kindness left John and I choked since we had received little enough help from our employers who were even now enjoying the fruits of our labours as the film library now contained several thousand quality colour transparencies.

My diary records: "I must make a point of writing up this adventure," hoping that I will be able to share with others, my own story god willing...(Inshallah)!

We left the hotel in the afternoon to return to the gold souk. This is a particularly exotic, very active and famous place as the shop windows literally glow yellow with the huge amount of gold on display. It is well guarded, and robberies are few since retribution is swift for any who try to steal. I was overwhelmed at the variety of goods on display and consequently took a great deal of time before I was able to pick out presents for the people back home.

We drove to the harbour once more, the other main centre of activity in Dubai. Here I was fascinated by the old and wizened looking men who were busy working on their boats, or transporting cargo from one part of the harbour to another. Some of the boats were huge and everywhere bustled with activity before the mid day heat left everything in a state of silent limbo.

On the 21st July we were invited by Simon to the expensive Sheraton Hotel for a final meal before we departed. The main restaurant we were seated in, was full of very expensive looking furniture and exotic, sun tanned people. Although John and I had dressed up for the occasion, we both looked weatherbeaten, with hair, tussled from weeks on the road, and were surely very conspicuous.

The meal was sumptuous, consisting of a mouth watering salad with steak mignion, followed by a very rich ice cream. All around us were very sexy and exquisitely dressed Philippino girls, employed by the hotel, who served our every wish, well almost!

One special attraction at the hotel was the celebrity guest wine waiter who was serving tables close by. I kept looking at him trying to think where I had seen his huge frame and distinctively square jaw before, as he looked so familiar. I quizzed John who agreed, there was something uniquly characteristic about him. The back of my neck started to prickle as he came over to our table to take an order. We decided on a couple of medium priced bottles but all the time I was glancing at him trying not to stare but hoping to remember who he was. As he stood there, writing our order on a notepad it suddenly came to me! He was none other than Richard Kiel, who played Jaws in the James Bond movies. He towered over us as we sat at the table but was not "in character", as his steel teeth were noticeably absent. I tried to be as nonchalant as possible but inside I was bubbling over with questions I wanted to ask but in these sophisticated surroundings thought inappropriate. With a deep, yet unusually soft voice for a man of his stature, he took our order and smiled, knowing that I knew who he was and in return I smiled back, registering that I knew, he knew, I knew. He padded gently over the plush carpet to retrieve the bottles, now cooling in ice, whilst I revealed to the others who he was. On his return we chatted briefly with him, to discover that his appearance at the hotel was a lucrative way for him to earn money between filming contracts. What a contrast of worlds, I thought as we sat there conversing with a film star, in very plush surroundings and comparing it to our own world of roof rack and VW cabin for the last few months. Afterwards the three of us went ten pin bowling, a curious but welcome departure from reading books or writing diaries in the evening and then returned to Simon's for a coffee.

We had to make our way back across Saudi before the main borders were shut and so the next morning, 22nd July, I woke early to check the engine. The tappets were badly in need of adjustment as the cylinder head valves had now bedded in. This meant another dusty grovel under the back end of the van, adjusting the gaps slightly to compensate for the high temperature the engine reached in the summer sun.

We said our goodbye's to Simon and departed at 3 pm for Abu Dhabi. The journey was uneventful and once there we called round to Penny and Rick who were out. In holiday mood, as we were now on the return leg of our epic adventure, we went again to the souk to look for souvenirs and groceries. I bought a citizen diving watch for just £24 compared to £100-£150 it would have cost back in England. The watch was self winding and is proofed, so the manufacturer says, down to 450 metres. The self winding mechanism is magnificent, never needs a new battery and works on movement. Its only drawback is that when the watch is left still for more than a day or two it will stop, but a quick shake has it running again. I still have this watch today and it has become battered and scratched, but still functions well and is as accurate as the day I bought it.

We drove once again to Rick and Penny's house to find they had returned. We were welcolmed in to have a shower and freshen up, whilst they made us a wonderful meal of home made steak and kidney pie with boiled potatoes and vegetables, one of my favourites! What a treat, I thought, to round off our adventure as this was now the last day of the project before the dash to get back across Saudi and avoid the holy festival about to start. The following day we had to renew our cholera injections at the local hospital as we would not be allowed back into Saudi without them. On the way back to Rick and Penny's, we bought more groceries, especially stocking up on baked beans and tinned fruit which in the UAE were no more expensive than at the supermarkets in England.

With a brief stop to give our warm thanks for their hospitality we were soon off on our travels once again, and headed back to Saudi.

Chapter 12

Saudi revisited

After a pleasant and uneventful day driving past magnificent sand dunes, which we had stopped at to photograph on the way into the UAE, we reached the Saudi customs post around 5.30 pm.

We were checked in by the official on duty who seeing that we were to travel across Saudi offered to put us up for the night in the official barracks to awake fresh for the following morning. John and I were at first rather circumspect at this invitation since the military uniforms made us a little uneasy, thinking the invitation to be a set up. It became evident that they meant well and genuinely wanted to help us and so we accepted graciously.

We were welcomed by his friends into a lounge where we talked into the small hours about life, politics and many other topics. We ate fresh dates and drank wonderful coffee, whilst discussing the incumbent problems of the Middle East and Palestine which featured prominently in our collective debate. We also recounted stories of our exploits which amazed them. They simply could not believe we had travelled all the way from London in the VW and were surprised that we had got as far as we had!

Eventually we turned in, but with true Middle East hospitality they offered us freshly laundered nightgowns as well as a gift of a Yemeni *sarong* each, together with juicy dates to take with us. John and I were both feeling guilty that we should have had any bad thoughts about them.

We slept soundly but were nevertheless anxious to resume our drive west to Jordan because of the limitation on the Saudi transit visa and the rapid approach of *Ramadan*.

Having slept well we breakfasted on yoghurt, bread and dates then got the van ready for the days ahead. We were offered a mid day meal before we went but had to decline as time was now pressing and it was still early. However we needed petrol and so

Saudi revisited

drove across the road to the filling station. The fuel was the cheapest we had found anywhere in the Middle East. We filled everything up and also took on board a couple of gallons of oil. We went to pay the bill but to our surprise and delight our friendly hosts of the evening before had already chipped in for us. With many thanks for their kindness, and with an offer to stay longer as their guests, we sadly explained that we had to depart to make the Saudi-Jordanian border in time and must put a good mileage under the wheels that day. Contrary to popular belief in the West, we found the Saudi people a very helpful and understanding race and none more so than these border guards who were most generous and to whom we were most thankful.

The heat was now getting to John who started to feel a little sick and so slept in the back whilst I drove on to *Hufuf* which we made by midday. Here I was directed to the *Damman* road by an Austrian, working in the Emirates who was decidedly fed up with his lot. He was anxiously waiting for his contract to finish just three months later so that he could get out of the heat and return home. I couldn't blame him. The road we took led to the Gulf coast at *Al Qatif* and ran through some spectacular sand dunes on the stretch between *Al Hufuf* and *Damman*. Turning off this highway and working our way back towards the desert interior of Saudi, the long hot tarmac road stretched before me. Mile after mile ran parallel to the Trans Arab oil pipeline (T.A.P.), only 100 yards away on the left. This brings the black gold from the oil fields of the Gulf, across Saudi Arabia, through Jordan and across the highlands to the Port of *Haifa* on the coast of Israel. This must be of great strategic significance but sitting out in the desert it looked conspicuous and vunerable.

The journey was monotonous to say the least, for only occasionally does one meet passing traffic in the afternoon heat, which for most sane people is the time to stop in deep shade. We were anxious to get through Saudi and so I just drove on unhindered, until at one point the road became blocked with a slow moving lorry. I pulled out and overtook at no more than ten to twenty mph but still managed to incite the wrath of the Saudi police who stopped me for reasons unknown. After a rather heated remonstration about which I understood not a word but sat through in placid submission, they eventually gave up in frustration at my ignorance of their language. They let me off the hook with an obvious warning not to do what I didn't know what I was doing, again!

Making sure I was well past any Saudi police check post, I decided to pull off the road. I drove onto a hard, gravel bed to set up camp. Thankful that we were now about 100 km from the sea and in the pleasurable warmth of the dry evening air that slowly cooled, we had finally lost the terrible coastal humidity that had plagued us recently. We were back into our routine and happy to be on the move again. We had covered 537 kilometres including stops and photography, not bad for a day's drive.

The next day I woke early to check the engine. The oil in the air cleaner needed replacing and also the rubber valve on the crank breather pipe had once again come off and disappeared. What a stupid, stupid design. This ineffective and disastrous design had been the cause of a destroyed engine and considerable expense, all for a 50 pence bit of rubber!

I put the old one back on which I kept as a spare, and taped it up to the vent pipe in the hope that it would stay on, as I simply couldn't bear for this engine to get wrecked again! I checked the rest of the engine to discover that one of the tappets needed adjustment. After two and a half hours of extremely tedious driving, a Chevy pulled out in front of us at the next road junction. The driver saw our British number plates and waved us down to see if we were alright. He was from Lancashire and like most ex-pats, worked for the oil companies. He was re-supplying the various maintenance centres and therefore knew the roads well. We were given fresh directions by him, as the sand scoured metal signs were all but obliterated. After a couple of cold drinks which he kindly supplied and with a warning that some stretches were terribly pot-holed, we set off down the road to *Turayf*, following the T.A.P pipeline all the way. It was John's turn to drive, so I caught up on my science fiction novel, "A for

Saudi revisited

Andromeda" and was so absorbed in it that I almost completely lost track of time or our surroundings.

We passed a great many Bedouin, camped in their traditional black goats-hair tents since their herds of camels could still eek out a living from the meagre ration of scrub dotted about this rather uninviting place. They had migrated from the even hotter parts in the south to make use of this comparatively fertile area, but goodness knows how they were able to survive as the gravel desert appeared as barren as any we had seen.

We stopped to have tea breaks and let the engine cool a couple of times. Once by the burnt out wrecks of two huge fuel tankers and then to photograph some donkeys being driven by their owner, the only other sign of life in this part of the desert. The road was still being refurbished in places and at one point the tarmac not only had pot-holes but disappeared altogether. We hit a major diversion and once off the metalled road the vehicle sank into fine soft powdery dust, similar to that which we had blundered into during the crossing from Yemen and which now came up to the van's axles.

Alarmed at this, we drove on with nerves strained and muscles tensed as at any moment we knew it could hide all manner of ruts and holes, just waiting to swallow our VW or smash the suspension. We were dwarfed in size when compared to the huge, long distance TIR lorries and tankers we were meeting and realized our van would provide no protection at all should we run into one of them in the near blinding clouds thrown up in their wake. Even the smaller commercial lorries were finding it hard going through the powder, as they added to the choking clouds that billowed high into the sky.

We could see very little of the sky as we had now entered a dust cloud that again covered everything in a fine grey veil, even though all the widows were tightly shut despite the scorching midday temperatures. Should any lorry have come the other way, we would surely have collided head on and been lucky to survive. After about 20 minutes of worried and rather panicky driving, never letting up on the throttle in case we became stuck, we emerged on the other side of the diversion, to be re-born once again from the twilight zone of the dust cloud into the clear sunshine and fresh air above the metalled road.

I stopped to check the all important rubber dust seal I had taped onto the oil breather pipe and also to open the engine flap again to provide additional cooling for the dust-caked engine. We carried on towards Jordan with the slipstream sucking out the last vestiges of dust from the engine bay and the interior of the VW, leaving a commet trail in our wake.

It was now getting late and we had run our reserves of fuel to an absolute safe minimum. At last we were able to pull in to the only depot for miles to replenish fuel and sink a few cold drinks to wash away the grime at the back of our parched mouths. The locals were greatly amused by our appearance, as we looked like some ghostly grey apparitions. Our hair and clothes were completely caked in the powdered dust we had driven through. We drove another 15 kms until we pulled off the road to camp for the night and inside the van I spread out the roadmap and worked out our distance covered for the day. This turned out to be 646 kms or 435 miles, not bad considering the frequent stops and diversions. Tomorrow we would have to cover the same distance, or more, if we were going to reach the Jordanian border within the three days specified in the transit visa.

The following morning I checked the van again and as we were running in the new engine I changed the air filter and the engine oil, since both were looking quite dirty. For the rest of the day the crossing was fairly routine, driving once again along the tedious stretches of open road that crossed the desert. We stopped only occasionally to refuel or to take one of the detours necessary to circumnavigate the frequent roadworks along the way. We stopped for tea at midday to let the engine cool and later when we neared the Saudi customs at *Zatab ash Shama* we passed a beautiful oasis by some low hills which had a classical Arab fort. This provided an outstandingly romantic sight that could easily have been a set from Lawrence of Arabia.

Saudi revisited

As dusk was approaching we arrived at the Saudi customs where officials proved their usual efficient selves and quickly had our papers processed, despite the fact that our exit card on the carnet was not complete. They amended this for us and soon we were through and travelling the other eight kilometers to the Jordanian customs. Our troubles were now about to begin once more.

Chapter 13

Jordan, the return to friends

We were tired from the day's exertions and the last thing we wanted to meet was a traffic jam. We were now negotiating one of epic proportions, because many vehicles wanted to pass through before the borders closed during Ramadan. Having been helped by the Saudi customs, those of Jordan turned out to be extremely un-cooperative. We queued for ages to have our carnet stamped but when it came to our turn we were simply told to come back the next day. I expect the official was hoping to receive a bribe from us so we felt somewhat betrayed at this example of corruption and discrimination, which we had not met since the Turkish border. Incensed at our treatment, I found a likely figure in command, ordering other soldiers about. I stormed up to the "commander" and demanded an explanation as to why we were not allowed through when clearly everybody else was. He apologised, and to give him his due, arranged to let us through.

Whilst we still had to wait for other documents a heated argument developed between a Saudi and one other traveller at the check post itself. This lead to an all out punch up and like a scene from a cowboy film, the crowd dividing into opposing sides and going to work on each other with fists, legs and elbows. Whatever the argument was about, it clearly caused distinct divisions and became a matter of honour between the two groups. Eventually with the punch up now developing into a minor skirmish we were beckoned to the office where we got our passports and carnet stamped but only after paying seven Dinars backshish.

When we got the vehicle into the queue our turn to be inspected was obviously going to take a long time and so John set about making a cup of tea whilst we waited and watched the outcome of the conflict behind us. After what seemed like an age, our turn eventually came. We were beckoned out of the vehicle as the guards wanted to look inside for contraband. By now the contents were not only dust covered but also rather smelly from the weeks of travelling, even though we had cleaned it thoroughly a few times on the way.

I could see the guards wrinkling their noses in disgust at our van whilst we prepared for a complete search for drugs as in Lebanon. They persevered and accompanied by a great deal of tut tutting they began with cursory prodding with batons into the melee of clothes and other possessions strewn about inside. They then asked me to open the side door, the hinges of which had taken a considerable battering and which were loose. It was at this point in the proceedings that sods law came into play. By now we were extremely tired and annoyed at yet more delays. So much so that I unlatched and flung the door aside with one deft but forceful sweep of my arm. Unfortunately the loose hinges securing the door to the body, which we had intended to replace, gave way. The door kept on going dragging me with it and crashed to the ground just millimetres from the feet of one of the guards. The scene could well have been something from Dads Army and at this point the crowd behind us who had made up and stopped fighting now gathered about and to the annoyance of the customs officers and my embarrasment, started to laugh out loud.

Er.....sorry, I said, making my apologies but the guard was not amused. I made several attempts to replace the door on its hinges but it obstinately would not go back on the rails. Anxious to help us on our way and not to rile the customs any further, various individuals from the group that had gathered about us tried but in vain to replace the door. Finally after a 15 minute struggle the guard gave up on us and shouted at us to get moving...NOW!

Just then I managed to get the lower hinge of the door onto the bottom runner of the van and so I yelled out for some help with locating the rest of the door onto the top runner. Meanwhile John was now under the direction of the guards in front who were angrily telling him to get a move on. He had no choice but to edge slowly across the border whilst I was left attached to the

Inshallah

outside of the side door desperately preventing it from slipping off again. Accompanying me were two other irate border guards holding the end of the door and it was in this very undignified fashion that the attached entourage "crabbed" through the check post and into Jordan proper. As John applied the brakes the door slid forward and Inshallah... seemingly by itself slipped back home and locked itself firmly into the side of the vehicle.

That would do nicely I thought, thanking the officers helping me. I couldn't help but think of the retribution they would exert on the other travellers yet to be searched! With the officials still yelling at us to get out of the way we handed our blue customs card into the main gate. Now, with our entry to Jordan complete we paid the inevitable backshish and hastily drove off.

It was late in the evening and pitch black, save for the twinkling of the stars through the clear skies above. Once on the road to *Amman* and well clear of the customs we stopped on some high ground where there was a soft wind gently blowing through the luxuriant growth of tall grass by the roadside. Today we had covered 868 kilometres (500 miles), a record travelled in one day of the whole trip. We felt it had been worth it though, to reach the cooler climate of Jordan and bring welcome relief from the summer heat endured recently. The temperature was now a lot cooler. The light breeze later turned into quite a forceful wind, waking us at about 10pm to secure our bedding which continued to flap about us on the roof rack until by the early hours, it had once again resumed its pleasantly subdued caress.

After a simple brew of tea for breakfast we set out to reach the capital *Amman*. We passed several barracks, full of military equipment and with much activity evident. We felt sure something was up (possibly the conflict in Yemen or Lebanon) as this state of alert seemed much higher than before. I stole a few photographs of them from the side window just for the record but at the same time we both hoped that trouble wasn't brewing around the corner.

In Amman we first visited the British Embassy where I had arranged with Miz to have our continuation certificate sent for the vehicle insurance. John meanwhile popped to the shops to buy a pump type thermos, common at the time in the Middle East, but virtually unheard of back home. Whilst he was doing this I read through the new insurance policy to check the small print and discovered to my horror that instead of running concurrently with ours and up to 16th September it ran from the 16th September to 16th November, an uninsured gap of a month. I made an expensive phone call back to London to get the problem fixed and to have the correct documents sent on to Istanbul.

Between calls I waited in a nearby café and here met Dave once again. We talked at length about our adventures, over a pizza and a few beers and on his mobile managed to contact Ray who came over and sat with us to join in the heated chat that a happy reunion always brings.

We all went back to Dave's for drinks and he offered to take us to the historical Jordan River Valley to take photographs of Bedouin and some ancient monuments, which we would eagerly have done but for the fact that we were now out of money and couldn't afford the fuel. We returned to Ray's once more, taking him up on his offer of beds for the night, and set about cleaning the van yet again. Meanwhile he prepared a "home coming" meal, of meat balls and potatoes with sweet cornbread and butter accompanied by a very fine wine.

We chatted about our exploits since we had last seen him and later Ray suggested we search for one of the many parties in the city to gate crash. We drew a complete blank but ended up at a very expensive hotel where a round of drinks soon put paid to any spare cash that we had. Crestfallen, we returned to Ray's to watch a movie whilst sipping some delicious Napoleon brandy which he broke open for our reunion.

The following day was spent arranging for the car insurance to be amended and the new documents sent on ahead to Istanbul. As we could no longer trust Miz and Jim to organise the task in time, I left it in the capable hands of my father, who knew the insurance agents personally. Assured that these arrangements were in good hands, we set off back to Amman to visit the

Inshallah

Palestinian refugee camp where our medical friend *Masbah,* who we had met at *Al Khadra* on the Saudi border, had relatives. We hoped that by covering this as a feature for Islamic Information, we could get permission to take photographs.

We were taken to the Palestinian organisation's head office and once they verified our credentials, we were immediately invited to a wedding and told that we could take all the photographs we wanted. We first went to the feast itself where there was much dancing with everyone enjoying themselves immensely. As honoured guests, we were offered the first taste of the food which included a whole sheep's head, complete with boiled eyes popping out of the skull. Untill then we had mainly survived on a rather monotonous diet. Nothing, however, could persuade me to eat sheep's eyes and politely I rubbed my hand over my stomach to indicate that I was full. This worked without causing offence, so I was able to make my excuses and left to photograph some of the exuberant yet exclusively male, dancing.

After the feast was over, all the guests formed a convoy of vehicles. The groom leads and makes his way to the bride's house after the marriage ceremony and has to "kidnap" her and take her back to his own house where the marriage was consummated. The parade was a photographer's delight, accompanied by the spirited whoops of women in pretty dresses and a carnival atmosphere throughout the whole area.

Afterwards we spent another couple of days with Ray and also ventured to the Palestinian headquarters. We hoped to meet with one of the many contacts we had been given and despite a firm invitation to drop into their headquarters, the office seemed abandoned and we also had a distinct feeling they were being wary of us.

Disappointed after a promising start, we returned to Ray's to have a last drink with him and made our preparations for the journey to Syria. Without the help of Ray and Elizabeth we would surely not have completed our tour. We owed them a great deal and would welcome the chance to return their hospitality.

Chapter 14

Syria, the hunt for souvenirs.

We set off the next day taking about one and a half hours to reach the northern border with Syria. Once over, we drove to Damascus where we spent some time souvenir hunting in the souk. I bought another traditional Saudi robe (*thobe*) and a wooden chess box inlaid with mother of pearl. Afterwards we scouted around for a place to park overnight and ended up outside a school in the city centre. We went to the same café which we had visited before, to have barbequed chicken, chips and salad. In this more tolerant and westernised country the meal was for once accompanied by a beer and so for a while we could relax, write up diaries and contemplate the world we had journeyed through.

The following day was thethe beginning of August. On our return north we had thankfully left the summer heat of the southerly lands behind whilst passing through the undulating highlands, with a lush covering of plants, trees and crops of all sorts. We felt we were well into our return journey even though we still hadn't left Syria. The refreshingly green landscape contrasted so much to the desert that we had been immersed in for so long but which was rapidly becoming just a memory.

At Aleppo we again visited the souk to take some additional photographs and seek out souvenirs. I decided to buy a Saudi style head cloth which was a kind of white muslin with tassels knotted along each edge. John and I then entered into a very protracted discussion with some merchants over pricing of carpets. We were told they cost anything from 200 to 1,700 Jordanian Dinars (£150-1300), which was far too expensive for our meagre pay and so we had to suffice with a little "window shopping" only.

I decided to experiment with some photography in the catacombs of the market, using the minimum aperture and a long shutter time of about five seconds. These came out as intended, with a perfectly exposed carpet stall (see photograph) and the blurred outlines of ghostlike clients looking for bargains. Time was soon passing and we reluctantly left the market, symbol of the start of our journey in the Middle East, six months before.

We drove out of Aleppo picking up a Syrian soldier who was hitching to his barracks near the border with Turkey. We chatted about the seemingly large increase in military movements since we were last there to which he became rather evasive and so we closed the subject at that. We dropped him off before arriving at the Syrian border where we decided to stop over. Whilst dining on our usual beans, egg, chips and tea, some British lorry drivers seeing our English number plate strolled over and in the ensuing conversation told us of the preferred and prettier route back through Turkey.

This, they said would avoid the hassles of suicidal lorry drivers whilst still sticking to the more reasonable and quieter roads across the central parts of Turkey. To our relief we could avoid many of the pot holed arterial routes that had nearly caused us so much grief on the way out.

Chapter 15

Turkey, a change for the better

The next morning after a gloriously cool night through which I slept soundly, we were up for 6.30 am. We made our way to the customs where they processed our papers. To save time, John arranged the carnet to be cleared whilst I persevered with the passports. For some reason the officials were trying to delay our transit, presumably in the hope of a little extra *backshish* but I was having none of it and eventually some heated verbal persuasion eventually got the bureaucratic wheels turning. Once more, after a brief vehicle search, we were waved on. With perfect timing John had just finished processing the carnet so he was able to jump aboard as I moved off and that was it, we were through!

We passed the ancient Roman ruins again on the track through no-mans-land between the borders of Syria and Turkey but we dared not risk stopping to photograph them (which was forbidden) in case we were being observed. Expecting to be searched once more by the Gestapo like woman from before, we approached the Turkish customs with some trepidation. To our relief she was absent and the carnet and passports were stamped in double time. To save further bother we didn't mention the hundreds of extra rolls of film we carried and had picked up from one of the contacts on the way. From the official, John also received an impressively large stamp in his passport which he was very pleased about, since mine was by now full of current visas as well as those from my journey to Nepal the previous year. Many commented that I seemed exceptionally well travelled!

We were ushered through and on the other side a hitchhiker waved to us frantically and I stopped to offer him a lift. Immediately I was set upon by an irate Turkish taxi driver accusing me of stealing his fare! He even grabbed my arm as I drove off and with great difficulty I controlled the steering with one hand whilst fending off this madman and jamming the accelerator peddle hard to the floor. We pulled off down the road shocked and a little shaken by this event, leaving the taxi driver as a diminutive speck on the horizon.

We dropped the hitchhiker at the junction between *Antioch* and *Iskendrun*, then turned off towards what we thought was the road to Antioch. We realised we had taken a more minor route instead and immediately circled round, to pass the crossroads where we had left our hitcher only moments before but he seemed to have vanished into thin air! We now had to make our way up the mountains to *Iskendrun* and then *Tarsus*, through some breathtaking countryside but realised we were desperately in need of petrol. A national strike had left many of the petrol stations dry as we passed through one after another only to be waved on. We eventually had to break into our reserves on the roof rack. Otherwise we stopped only to buy melons and biscuits and for a coffee break at a rustic, yet tidy cafe by the roadside.

At *Tarsus* we stopped for John to change one of our last travellers cheques for £30 and whilst we waited, were quizzed by the very attractive female desk clerks about our journey. It was only with the greatest difficulty that we tore ourselves away to resume our journey! The countryside we passed through was a carpet of green with tall mountain pines. We continued on the highway up and over the mountains. This required nerve and an occasional heavy boot on the accelerator as we had to be prepared to overtake at any time due to the slow grinding procession of HGVs blocking our way.

We kept up a good pace though, and arriving at one garage were allowed our ration of three-quarters of a tank of fuel. Later at the *Konya* turn-off we found another garage who let us have two further jerry cans. So little by little we re-stocked with fuel in case the shortage was much more widespread in Europe. Driving on we came to some open countryside where we pulled onto a side road for our overnight stop, about 60-70 km from *Konya*.

Turkey - a change for the better

Whilst we mused on the day's events, a shepherd boy came by driving his many sheep and introducing himself as *Nebi Gakel*. At first he was too shy to talk to us but later opened up and in the course of conversation he told us that he had come from the village of *Cumra* nearby.

He spent some time, animatedly talking to us throughout the evening. The day's log showed we had covered 520 kms, far enough for us but not as much as Miz would have liked. Still he would now have to wait our return as we were not going to risk wrecking ourselves or the vehicle at this stage.

The next morning dawned bright and sunny and with a few low clouds scudding above us. This was a considerable change from the last few months where the only clouds had been the wispy traces of alto-stratus, high in the cobalt blue sky that would neither screen the searing sunlight, or bring rain to the parched lands. The puffs of white candy-floss above us, now left the impression of almost being close enough to touch and were a reminder that we had now travelled far to the north and into cooler climes. After our ablutions and a cuppa, John piled everything into the van whilst I took some black and white photographs of the surrounding area. The fields were flat but full of stubble and close to some ancient agricultural machinery, rusting amongst the wind blown hay which made for a photogenic picture.

We left about 9.45am and drove to *Konya* where we intended to stop. The town itself was very clean and full of tourist shops, again quite a contrast for us. We found that in no time we had already passed through the town and so decided to press on, unfortunately missing a stop at the old mosque there which dates back to 1200 AD. Further on we came upon some traditional wells using a beam lift and counterweight to draw water. The skies were deep blue and we even saw herons flying close by. The fields had been recently harvested and the brown stubble was now dappled from the shadows cast by the clouds above. This made a truly romantic country scene with the wells in the foreground, a simple reminder of the poorer parts we were passing through.

We travelled accross more rolling countryside, full of the most beautiful shades of irridescent green from the grasses bending in the gentle breeze. This brought us to the small town of *Polyadin* where we stopped to buy provisions. In the market square someone had strangely deposited a huge block of coal, about a metre cube, with a "for sale" sign on it. We photographed this unusual object and went about our chore of purchasing provisions, most importantly potatoes, as we were now suffering from chip withdrawal symptoms.

The town's folk were extremely friendly towards us and inquisitive as to who we were, since we looked nothing like the usual tourists who passed through. In one shop where we bought cooking oil and eggs the shopkeeper offered us a coffee whilst we told her our story. More and more people gathered to listen to us as we became the "old timers" recounting our adventures. We drank up and said our good byes making our way back to the van and waving enthusiastically as we left. Passing a pony and trap on the outskirts of the town I got John to stop whilst I jumped up onto the roof of the VW. From my vantage point and through the viewfinder I now saw an older, rather plump woman, seated in the trap who took her scarf off and waving it at me, gave a wonderful toothless grin....what a welcome to Turkey!

We made our way to *Aksehir*, eventually coming to a large roundabout, in the centre of which were two, full size Mig 15 aircraft on display. Not wanting to miss this unusual monument, we stopped and I took a couple of shots, only to see a military barracks right behind them. Fortunately no one saw me with my camera for we should surely have been arrested or otherwise berated as had happened before and so we quickly continued on our way through town. We eventually found ourselves in a very English looking countryside, overcast with a thick, grey blanket of low hanging cloud.

This was a mighty unnerving change from the last few months, leaving us with a sense of claustrophobia since the clouds almost seemed to close in on top of us. Even though, it was the hottest month of the year, we felt that by comparison to Yemen and Saudi, it was quite cold to our thinned blood, making us don extra layers of clothing.

The sunset that night was magnificent and John and I took turns with my tripod to take shots with our respective cameras between throws of the frisbee. This was another indication of the change in temperature since to burn off energy in this way was unthinkable in the heat and humidity we'd endured further south. The towns looked more European and some houses even sported well tended gardens, which made our thoughts turn more and more to home and the future which lay ahead

The day had provided the first familiar surroundings of Europe after our six month journey and tomorrow we would enter Istanbul, the true gateway from Asia, back to our homelands. John and I sat and talked of our intended plans when we got back and what life held in store for us. It was a rather melancholy moment.

Next morning we had a long drive to Istanbul taking in some spectacularly mountainous countryside, full of green grass and sheep, with trees and shrubs in the higher fells. As we neared the town of *Ismit*, the hills gave way to flatter farm land, interspersed with the increasing presence of industry. At *Ismit* we reached a junction with the main highway and as we were turning off to go to *Istanbul* John gave out a sudden whoop at the sight of two gorgeous girls hitching a lift. Unfortunately I had already reached the new by-pass before John could get me to slow down and we were unable to stop in time, leaving us (probably for the best) to journey on *sans- femmes.*

We reached the city centre at 1 pm and on our way to the Blue Mosque, went straight to the post office to collect awaiting mail. I was delighted to receive five letters, four from Han and one from my parents. John sadly got nothing from either friends or family and looked pretty dejected so I read him a few of mine from Han. We went up to the Blue Mosque where we parked the

VW for the night and were soon deep in conversation with fellow travellers there.

John meanwhile had bought some black and orange enamel paint to add a few touches to the decorative appeal of the vehicle. Exhilarated at the thought of reaching the gates of Europe, we decided that the epic journey needed some token of celebration and so we set about painting the journey on each side of the van complete with road map and place names of the major towns, cities or other places of interest that we had passed through. While I concentrated on the front of the vehicle John completed the rear, the whole tapestry being meticulously followed from a master plan drawn on a piece of note paper. This of course attracted interest from passers by and fellow travellers, who gathered around us to ask about the places we had visited and how easy it was to get there.

This included an Australian called Bob and his New Zealander companion Ann. There was also an elderly couple who had come by camper van from the picturesque village of *Fordingbridge* in Hampshire, close to where I had worked as a river biologist two years before. They knew the *Downton* salmon hatchery and we talked about my work there and some of Bob's less secret work for the MOD at Porton Down.

We spent the next day resting and preparing for the drive to Greece. In the morning I used the washing facilities of the YHA with its hot and cold running water before prevailing on John to go to the souk for one last walk about.

Whilst John stayed in the city to have the Turkish bath he had promised himself on the outward journey, I returned to sit in the park by the Blue Mosque and chatted to fellow travellers. I talked once more to the elderly couple we had met before who, it turned out, had also driven to Finland and were accomplished travellers in their own right. As the day grew warmer and with little else to do, John and I finally completed not only the painting of the map on the van but were ready to celebrate and paint the town red on our return to Europe.

Turkey - a change for the better

On the morning of our departure, 7th August, I went over to the American Assurance building in the Tam Vai district, to pick up our insurance documents which my father had informed me would be ready for collection. To my great relief they were in order but only with a couple of days to go before the old ones expired. The American in the office there was very helpful and explained that he was in the process of moving to Croydon in England to become head of the Middle East operations. I returned through heavy traffic to our old parking space where I had left John and found that he had meanwhile been chatting up four girls hitch hiking through Turkey. When I rejoined him we all decided to walk to the New Style pie shop for coffee, cake and a chat. Later, John and I returned to the van where we had arranged to meet up with *Max*, a German making his way back to the Turkish border and who had cadged a lift from us earlier in the day.

We said our goodbyes to the other travellers, envious that some were only just starting out on their own adventures and then set off through the suburbs of Istanbul to officially leave the Middle East behind us and enter the last phase of our journey back through Europe. We arrived at the Turkish border with Greece, the one where six months earlier I had nearly run over a border guard and where the customs officer had kept us waiting whilst he finished watching a football match on his portable television. We were apprehensive on approaching this particular border for we felt certain that we would be given a rough time going through.

However the whole area had been transformed and cleaned up completely. The ominous green clad and slovenly military personnel had disappeared, leaving only smartly dressed police to deal with the traffic. All the broken down or impounded lorries had been removed and the tarmac forecourt even had white lines painted for vehicles to park. Whilst we parted company with Max, instead of having to go to a seedy hut, the border guards (leather Gestapo coats gone), kindly came to our van in immaculate police uniforms and very quickly dealt with our passports.

Inshallah

They didn't even ask for baksheesh so we were through and on our way inside 30 minutes. I was still stunned by the changes and when we turned round to look back we could see that road signs had been erected with the legend *"Welcome to Turkey"* painted clearly for all to see. What a change had taken place in just a few months! Whether this was for show or that real political changes were afoot we couldn't be sure, but it was with relief that we had passed through that particular customs without delay and were heading towards Greece.

Chapter 16

An incident in Greece, a near miss in Yugoslavia

At the Greek border, further up the road we again had little trouble getting through apart from having to negotiate a traffic queue. Whilst we waited, some American hikers, *Kit, Crissy* and *Dave* asked for a lift. They were going to *Athens* via *Alexandroupoli*, a fishing port on their way through to the rest of Europe.

We made rapid progress once away from the border, driving across flat and fertile countryside between rolling hills that led down to *Alexandroupoli* on the coast. I realised too late that we had passed through the busy town before anybody was aware. They were not unduly concerned and were happy to come a little further with us. We passed through the university city of *Xanthi* where we bought provisions for our meal later. One shop proved irresistible as it was selling exquisite pastries the likes of which we had not seen for months. But alas, all our money had now been spent on fuel and we had to make do with the wonderful aroma emanating from the extractor fan at the front of the shop.

We drove on, arriving at a beach I remembered from our previous visit in March and pulled onto the sand to camp. It looked idyllic but soon thousands of midges, mosquitos and sand flies came to greet us and even though the evening was still warm I quickly added more layers. I donned long trousers, then socks and shoes, and eventually huddled on a chair with a jacket pulled over my head to protect my ears, still getting bitten in a million and one places. It was a miserable place but we enjoyed our fried chicken and talked for several hours over a bottle or two of wine. I managed, somehow, to sleep like a log that night despite the attentions of the flies.

Inshallah

The next morning we woke to find that fishermen were already about their business on the mud flats by our van and were busily catching eels and shellfish. We were soon on our way to *Kavala*, another delightful Mediterranean fishing port about 40 kms further on. We stopped to look around the town and after shopping for provisions we sat on one of the terraces to have a coffee. The shops eventually closed for lunch and so we passed the time in the shade of a white awning having a delicious meal in the front of a sea food restaurant, of freshly cooked fish and newly baked bread. We sat drinking cool beer and enjoying the exquisite meal whilst the sea breezes blew a warm and tender caress to us from the quayside close by. It was sheer heaven. *Chris,* who was a vegetarian, had to plead with the waiter to bring her baked beans and potatoes instead of meat. I thought this to be quite ironic since John and I had travelled most of the way around Arabia on this staple food. Here we now were, having a real break from this diet, as the fish we ate was fresh and such a welcome change. It had been almost unobtainable throughout our journey, except in a few coastal areas and even then only at expensive restaurants which our budget precluded.

We set off to *Thessalonica* once more. Some way down the road, I saw *Chris's* rucksack drop off the top of the van and thought this strange as it had been tied securely to the roof rack. We returned a few hundred yards to pick it up off the road and discovered that Dave's was also missing. Luggage had been moved about with items gone from the roof rack itself and inside the van. We returned to report the theft to the police and after a lengthy episode, bought more vegetables and some wine at the market for later. We set off again towards *Thessalonica.* As it was getting late and we were feeling extremly tired from our upsetting afternoon, we decided not to waste time looking for a suitable lay-by but at the edge of *Kavalla,* pulled off the road to an official campsite. Here I managed to fill up our water containers with fresh cool water but realised our hopes of getting into it quickly were dashed as a long traffic queue we had joined wasn't moving at all. After a brief discussion, we decided to drive on.

Stopping overnight on another section of beach it was my turn to cook, so I started sorting the luggage out inside the van to make some more space when to my horror, I now discovered my own bag full of camera equipment had also gone missing. I fought down a cold rage at this intrusion into our world. Stupidly we had left rucksacks and other luggage on the roof rack, safe enough in the Middle East but now an open invitation for thieves to liberate them. Perhaps this was poetic justice for taking the Landrover roof rack in Saudi. Allah perhaps also works in mysterious ways. This would now mean a return trip, waisting more valuable time, to add these items to the police report the following day. That would have to wait, for now as I cooked us all a splendid curry which we washed down with large helpings of wine. We were all rather sleepy after the days events but one positive aspect was that the beach we were now camped on, was insect free and with the sound of the Mediterranian lapping at the shoreline close by, we were all quickly soothed to sleep on the soft and still warm sand.

With the first rays of light from the breaking dawn, I drifted out of my deep sleep and awoke to an absolutely still day. The shore beckoned to me for a bit of beach combing and putting on my *Yemeni* sarong, given to me in Saudi, I wondered along the line of flotsam washed up by the tide. I came upon a solitary flower, struggling amidst a pile of debris on the sand to cling onto life, which I decided simply had to be photographed. With my remaining camera, I took a close up of its colourful petals by lying on the sand, whilst in the background the disc of the early morning sun was rising up behind it.

By now the first warming rays were beginning to touch my skin, helping to sooth away the worries of the previous day. As the others were still sleeping I quietly returned to the van to retrieve my mask and fins before traipsing down to the water for a swim. I was fully submerged, when I noticed the sea was full of jellyfish. My first instinct was one of panic and to dash out of the

211

water but as I had not been stung I willed myself to stay and investigate these creatures further. I was fascinated by their slow undulating movement through the water which seemed such an efficiently evolved mechanism.

Playing with them I tried one experiment where I pushed water at them which had the effect of making them instantly change direction, against the local current that I was producing. The next experiment I tried was to look at the behaviour of individual cells that waft the plankton laden water towards its digestive system. These are called *coenocytes* and by pouring a handful of sand over the topmost part of the "umbrella" of the jellyfish, I could clearly see the individual grains of sand being moved along by the tiny cilia, (waving hairs) of these cells. They were working hard to pass the sand along and over the side of the jellyfish which sank in a curtain of silica to the sea bed below. After a further half hour amusement I left the creatures to their own devices and swam back to the shore.

I was starting to relax completely, now that the journey's end was in sight and without the pressure of work, or the intense heat sapping every ounce of strength. After months spent in Muslim countries, many of which will not allow strangers to mix with women, I began to think of Hanna, feeling the need for female company and was also distracted by the proximity of the two attractive women, now sleeping by the van. My eyes were drawn to the sight of *Chris*, now innocently curled up into a foetus position and whose only covering was a swimming costume of the thinnest fabric, revealing every curve of her body. Guiltily, I pushed my yernings aside, contenting myself with making tea and writing up the events of the past 24 hours. Soon the rest of the motley crew began to wake and I passed cups of tea around before having a hurried breakfast and taking a photograph of the group. We then doggedly set off back to *Kavalla* to report the other missing items.

The stolen camera bag was quickly added to the previous report and by 11.30am we were once more on our way to Thessalonica. I started to become very tired and depressed as I was worrying

An incident in Greece, a near miss in Yugoslavia

too much about the loss of my trusty Rolliflex and asked John to take over. I moved to the back of the van to have a sleep. Crissy was also there and together in the small space we slept side by side. I lay there dreaming the minutes then the hours away until all too soon we reached Thessalonica, the current destination of our companions.

We drove to the railway station and sat down for a coffee, chatting nervously amongst ourselves until Max got himself a lift to Austria. Finally we kissed and said our goodbyes to the others, before setting off ourselves, towards the Greek border. We arrived well in time and quickly passed through into Yugoslavia where, to my surprise, I was able to cash one of my Lloyds cheques to boost our exhausted funds, something unexpected in those days before credit cards took over.

It was now the 10th August, two months since we had left Yemen and just under a month since leaving the UAE. It was John's turn to drive and I continued reading my novel whilst keeping a watchful eye on the changing scenery and the road map. We decided to take the much prettier coastal road this time and passed through some spectacular mountain scenery once again, driving along tortuously winding roads hewn out of the deep gorges.

We stopped to fill up with fuel when a VW combie like ours and a Ford Capri with British number plates turned into the garage forecourt. The two families turned out to be related Syrians who had settled in England but were on their way back to visit their homeland. One group living in Birmingham had a son who, dressed as a Syrian spoke with a broad Brummie accent, while a girl from the other group lived in Kensington Gardens and had taken on the rather posh lilt of the *Sloane Ranger* set. These two very distinct dialects bore no relationship to their actual wealth and seemed out of place because until recently we had been immersed only in the very different regional accents of Arabic. Whilst chatting we were able to give them a few of the more interesting accounts of our exploits throughout the Middle East which had them aghast at the risks we had taken.

Inshallah

For the first time in months it started to rain and with it the temperature plummeted. Whilst John was driving I casually leant forward to turn the heater on and blow warm air from the engine to the blower inside the van. The heater hadn't been used in months and the crossing through the deserts, and mountains in Saudi and Yemen had left huge deposits of fine dust in the vent pipes. These now blew out and formed a thick and clinging fog inside the van. John only just managed to see through the swirling particles of dust to the windscreen.

Some way further on we started to pass a wooded area and were able to drive the VW into this. It was now a lot cooler and so the mosquitoes only gave us a minor problem. Waking early the next morning we were sitting having our morning cuppa when we noticed that a herd of sheep had taken an interest in us and were now surrounding the VW. They looked excitedly at the interior of the van in the hope of some scraps, but eventually walked away in a disappointed silence.

The scenery we now passed by was spectacular, and skirting the endless mountains and inlets we came to a fork in the road. We had a choice to either catch a ferry that crossed directly over to the other side of the estuary or to motor round. We chose the ferry and as we later discovered the other road would have added an extra 90 kilometers!

Whilst in the slowly moving queue to the ferry, we passed a car by the roadside that had broken down. I quickly looked at the components of their engine and cleaned all the electrical contacts and terminals. This soon had the engine roaring into life and with gleeful thanks from the occupants I returned to the van. The crossing took only minutes and we were soon back on the winding coastal road. At one point we came upon a line of stones along one side at a particularly bad corner. We slowed to find a huge lorry had broken down just round the bend and even at our slow speed it came as a sudden shock to find the way almost completely blocked! We were now both stressed up and tired from this hazardous driving and had a break. We sipped a refreshing cuppa, admiring the blue sea close by, before setting

An incident in Greece, a near miss in Yugoslavia

off towards *Split*, a rather inhospitable looking industrial town along the coast towards the Italian boarder. Some 60 km the other side of Split, we came across an over crowded but well kept campsite, heaving with camper vans and tents. Most were German or Dutch and after a few circuits of the miniscule road within the site we found a piece of open ground near to the sea which was unoccupied. However it was a 30 degree slope, too steep for most vehicles to attempt. We persevered and having backed down we set about with rubble and boulders to build a platform under the tyres and soon had the VW parked level, with the kettle already steaming for a brew.

The site was well provisioned, with excellent facilities, allowing us to have a wonderful and much needed hot shower, a perfect remedy to the privations of camping.

But with this civilised site came other trappings. Opposite us a family was desperately trying to get their barbeque to light but only succeeded in making a smelly cloud of pungent fat laden smoke. Fortunately they gave up, leaving us to sit in peace and to write up diaries.

The next morning we had a swim and while close in to the shore the water tended to be warm. A few feet down however, it became much colder. Even so, we took the plunge and I snorkelled down to the sea bed, about 30 ft below, as there was so much to see. Eventually it became so cold that we both had to return to the van to warm up. This was a stark contrast to the Gulf which had been many degrees warmer.

We attempted to leave at about 11.15am but had to make several runs to get the van up the slope and over the loose gravel. We ended up with many spectators and several people joined in to help push the van up the rubble strewn bank. Whilst John settled the bill, I waited behind the wheel and got into conversation with a couple of Australians who told their tale of woe. Apparently they had only just entered *Yugoslavia,* when they had their vehicle smashed in an accident. They were left unhurt but were now somewhat delayed and were reduced to hiking around the country to see the sights, while their motor was repaired. I knew that feeling well, and told them of our exploits and of the engines we had managed to get through in our epic journey! We now drove on to *Ryeka,* still passing through really beautiful countryside, similar to that of the Lake District. Now we were able to keep other luxuries like chocolate in the van, as it was so cool that it wouldn't melt! This was wonderful, as was the availability of fresh milk and sliced bread, consumed with pieces of sausage on which we gorged ourselves as we drove towards the border.

At the Yugoslavia customs they merely waved us through but on the Austrian side they became very curious about our map on the side of the van. They gave the vehicle a cursory search and were highly amused by our animated tales of adventure, illustrated by the the decoratively painted map.

By now our official money had run out and we were only able to replenish our fuel when I cashed another of my cheques for thirty pounds. We filled up but I was desperate to buy some more 35 mm film for my Pentax as this was the only camera I had left and we still had so many places to pass through on the remainder of our journey. Excitement though, was rising every mile nearer to home. We were overflowing with stories we wanted to tell and yet we still had a wanderlust that drove us to see as many sites as possible on the route back and to eke out our journey to the very last moments.

Venice was so close to our route, that we felt a diversion to this famous city was irresistible, even if we had to dip into our own savings to pay for the extra mileage and the ferry crossing to get there.

Chapter 17

Love and spaghetti in Venice

We passed several car wrecks but eventually got onto the road to Venice, the first real stretch of motorway since leaving Europe six months before.

By now I was also discovering other items missing that were with the stolen camera bag. A crucial letter containing Han's phone number was also stolen and with no other means of contacting her before we arrived in Holland, I quickly wrote a letter giving our estimated time of arrival, and posted it that night in the hope it would arrive before us.

Sunday August 13th, was Dominion Day and I woke early to the call of nature to find the loos being cleaned and therefore closed. The cleaner woman had no suggestion as to what I should do and shrugged. There was a ticket office I had spotted and which had just opened for the ferry passengers close by and so I traipsed over to see if I could have any luck there. I crept past the ticket office just inside and had my fingers wrapped around the door handle to the gents, when a head poked itself round the office window to say it was for official use only! Blast! This was getting silly.

I went back to the van and tried to forget about ablutions and set about making a brew. Eventually John woke up out of a deep slumber and we sat and drank some warming tea. With yet more liquid inside I decided I would have to go to the loo someway or another. I tried the gents again but it was locked. Inspiration came to me just then as I tried the ladies and found it was open so I shot into one of the cubicles to my great relief. I then waited whilst other occupants came and went and at a suitable lull in the proceedings, put my head around the door to check that the coast was clear and made a dash out of the building, before being accosted for indecent behaviour. What a palaver that had turned out to be, and significant in that this sort of thing had never been a problem during the rest of the journey. Now back in so called "civilisation", it seemed that even basic necessities for fellow human beings had a bureaucracy all their own. I realized I was no longer a curiosity but just one of the crowd and at this thought my ego took something of a dive. Next time, I decided that I would just go in the street and damn offended eyes. We closed the curtains and covered all the windows, locked everything up and took our gold and cameras with us, in case of a repeat performance of the break-in we endured in Kavalla. To be sure we would still have a vehicle on our return, I even took the rotor arm off the VW.

We walked down to the quayside to pick up the ferry. We didn't have long to wait until one arrived, upon which a flood of people poured, with most of them staying in the stuffy and overheated passenger cabin. John and I stayed on the open deck as we had now fully acclimatised to the outside life and made our way to a wooden bench as it was too nice to be cooped up. We found the journey to Venice was over almost before it had begun and on arrival we wandered around the landmarks, taking in *Rialto* and *St Marks Square*, all full of tourists but still magnificent places to visit with plenty to photograph. Especially photogenic were the many gorgeous Italian women! They sat with affluent nonchalance, sipping coffee and generally displaying themselves to the world as if they were supermodels. In one of the many cafes we had a very expensive but small plate of spaghetti.for 15,900 lira (£8), the price we had been accustomed to paying for a three course meal. We were so short of money that I even had to go and change my last three pounds sterling that I had kept for such emergencies. We had walked several blocks before I realised that I had forgotten to pick up my Pentax camera from the cafe table. Losing both cameras would be unforgiveable so I quickly ran back in a state of shock, not expecting to find the camera but coming close to the table that we had been sitting at, found it was still there! Inshallah, God was indeed good to me that day! Strolling through the back streets, we came to a large

Love and spaghetti in Venice

building and rested in the entrance lobby of the grand marbled mansion which we took to be some kind of library. Eventually a man dressed in white trousers and jacket came over, looking concerned and asked in English what we wanted. Confused when we replied that we were simply resting and intended to look at the library, he explained that this was no library, and that we were sitting in the accident and emergency department of the hospital. Ah! That would explain the medicinal smell I couldn't place when we entered.

We left and went our separate ways to explore and photograph the streets on our own but once back at our rendevous at the quayside I sat down for a rest, whilst waiting for John to return. My mind which was musing over the days events was suddenly alerted to the fact that a soft feminine voice was asking me something. On looking up there was another of those stunningly beautiful Italian woman, asking me for a light for her cigarette. My heart skipped a few beats and my lungs stopped breathing whilst I took in this gazelle, now standing close beside me.

She was expensively and well dressed and wearing a perfume to suit but I decided, definitely was not trying to proposition me. I managed to regain another breath by force of willpower and at first, tried to light her cigarette with a match but the wind kept blowing it out. I was already in a scene from a *Fellini* film and with heart pounding, I took the cigarette from her full and inviting lips and placed it in my mouth next to mine to light them both myself.

The taste of her lipstick on the filter of this expensive looking slim cigarette became intoxicating and in a flash wild thoughts passed through my mind. In a few seconds I had it alight and gently passed the cigarette back to her inviting lips once more. She smiled and after inhaling, thanked me softly with a parting "ciao" and a wave, before turning her elegant body away from me, to board the ferry and out of my life forever. She left a wafting cloud of her intoxicating scent behind that lingered sufficiently for me to ponder this exquisite meeting in my mind. From what seemed from afar, a familiar voice piped up, "Its friggin cold out here!" John had at last returned to bump me out of my daydreaming and I went on to explain my recent meeting which he listened to, absorbing every detail.

We made our crossing on the next ferry which soon had us back on the mainland, where we offloaded our belongings into the van. We were off, to the next town of *Cortina,* up in the mountains before crossing the border back to Austria. To this day I always associate Venice with romance and very beautiful women but have yet to return to refresh my memories of this time.

Chapter 18

Austria, a missed opportunity

We stopped for fuel and had a conversation about the weather with the attendant in French. This conversation was more out of politeness than anything else and it felt curious to be talking about such a mundane item as the weather after six months of travel. Now we were following main roads all the way. The deeper into Europe we went, the less interest we attracted as travellers. We now began the process of letting the European culture wash over us once more and become yet another anonymous vehicle amongst thousands. By now I was thinking more and more of Hanna, the woman I had met in Nepal. She had taken so much care in writing to me throughout our journey that I felt sure we were destined to be together as life-long partners, despite the romantic opportunities that still presented themselves. We continued to drive through Austria, giving a lift to two gorgeous girls who invited us back to their tent. Even this couldn't dissuade me from the journey ahead and my reunion with Han, (sigh), and after dropping them off at their campsite we drove on.

Stopping overnight in the mountains we thought that we were out of money to pay for the camping but rummaging around in the various crevices of the van, we came up with 250 Austrian schillings (£12) and a £1 note. With this we paid for the camping, a lump of cheese, an egg, a potato and even a quarter litre bottle of wine! We cooked our meagre meal of egg and chips but the wine did its trick and soon had us off to sleep, ready for the next stage through Germany.

The following morning was warm and sunny, causing the van to heat up inside. I was quickly up and taking in the fresh crisp air, strolling up the hill behind the camp site and photographing the surrounding valley on the way.

Inshallah

The clarity with which sounds carried was astounding and standing there it was possible to hear the faint noises of habitation drifting up from the valley below. I could see the wisps of gently rising vapour, driven up by the sharp sun to condense into brilliant white clouds high above us. The huge mountains were a splendid hue of green and pale blue and even in these summer months the high peaks were still capped with patches of snow. I drank in the scene with mixed feelings that our journey was nearly finished but thankful that we had safely accomplished our task. We had our morning cuppa and whilst John went for a shower I proudly painted a further extension to our map on the side of the van, much to the amusement of the other campers. Whilst we drove through the mountains, the farmers were busy at work as we passed little hamlets on our way to the top of the pass from Cortina to *Toblach*.

Turning left onto the *Bruneck-Brixen* road we discovered that we had overshot the turning off the motorway and were headed up the toll free *Brenner pass*. As we were already on the old road we decided to carry on along this winding and far more interesting, route instead. We were thwarted later on when we still managed to take another wrong turning down a slip road, still ending up back on the motorway. This eventually took us to the Austrian customs where the police were quite interested in the maps on the side of our vehicle and asked us if we had just come all the way from Yemen. We explained our journey once again which eventually satisfied their curiosity but only after they had made some amusing comments at our expense. They let us through and we were back in Austria. We stopped off further up the motorway at a very modern looking restaurant to fill up with fuel and have a coffee break. Here we met an Austrian hitch hiker, called *Jhose*, who we offered a lift to and in return he bought us a wonderfully rich cake each, and a glass of milk which seemed to contain about 75% cream. After our usually modest meals accompanied by sweet black tea it was a welcome piece of free gluttony for the journey's end.

Chapter 19

Germany, Autobahn to Holland

At the border with Germany the customs were checking vehicles thoroughly and as we had advertised our route on the side of the van we were given a real welcome by the police. We had our passports photocopied, perhaps as a standard terrorist counter measure, and even Jhose's Austrian Euro pass was thoroughly checked. We stopped later at a small village to buy some provisions as I had been able to cash another thirty pound cheque at the border. We stocked up on eggs, sausage, biscuits and some medicine for John as he had now acquired a jippy tummy once again, probably from all the rich dairy foods we were now eating.

The rest of the day was a monotonous drive along the autobahn past Munich and Stuttgart until we stopped in a lay-by for the night, close to Frankfurt. We had travelled 653 km, which was not bad as averages went but poor considering the quality of the roads we were travelling on. It put into perspective the stressful hours spent driving through the Middle East, achieving much greater distances. We had then also put up with the heat, poor road conditions and most of all, the appalling drivers.

On August 15th, we woke up late (by Middle East standards) at 8.30am and I was flabbergasted at the technology the Germans had put into having a pee. The loo on the lay by was an ultra modern and windowless stainless steel cabin. There was a coin slot outside to start the machine up, whereupon it opened the door to allow you in. On exit it flushed automatically and every once in a while sprayed itself to clean all surfaces. How clinical, I thought to myself and what if you get stuck inside on a self cleaning cycle? The thought made me shudder and I decided this was technology going too far. Give me a sand dune or a forest any time! An Australian couple we had met earlier came over to the van to have a chat. Over breakfast we had a long talk, during which the girl tried unsuccessfully to find a solution to John's *Chinese* puzzle ring.

Later we entered *Cologne* and there parked up to visit the famous Cathedral, the Kolner Dom. Similar to St Pauls during the WWII blitz of London, it was one of the few buildings almost unbelievably left undamaged, in the otherwise gutted city. We staggered the 509 steps to the top of the tower, stopping to look briefly at the bells on the way up. The main one was the heaviest, weighing, so the guide book informed us, a massive 25 tonnes. We were grateful it wasn't rung whilst we were there as the smaller ones were deafening enough on their own!

After the austere attitudes to sex in the Middle East it was a culture shock to visit the red light district, which was on open display and a featured tourist spot in the heart of the city. Famous for its sex shops, there were also peep shows which at that time were a revelation to me as they were so new on the market. The porn magazines, common today, were a real eye opener and seemed to cater for every taste known. I was struck by the feeling that the liberalisation of attitudes in Europe had come at a price as they contrasted deeply with Arabia and the Islamic code practiced there. People here traded in fantasy, not at all connected to the real world and in that sense something was missing in the spirituality of everyday living

It was a welcome change when we returned to the main square by the cathedral, where a crowd had gathered around a pavement artist. With a pallet of chalk he was drawing the most exquisite reproductions from photographs of old masters, whilst close by, a couple of musicians played familiar tunes for their supper.

Chapter 20

Holland and destiny awaits

Leaving the tourists to their wanderings we made our final run to the border with *Holland* and by late afternoon had reached the town of *Breda* where Han had her flat. Finding it through a labyrinth of small cobbled streets we came to the area called Nieuw Haag Dijk. This is a delightful student area in the old part to the south of the main town. Here John parked, whilst I walked over to the house and rang the doorbell. *Mrs Hoppenbrouwer*, Hanna's landlady opened the door and invited me in. My last letter had arrived just in time so that she had been expecting us.

Han was not there as she had gone to her parents house in *Baarle-Nassau*, 25km out towards *Tournhout* on the Belgium border. However I was welcomed and was able to use the phone in the hallway to let Han know that we had arrived. After a break of almost a year since our meeting in *Kathmandu* and a brief chat over coffee in a nearby cafe, I was finally able to talk to Han again. Her soft lilting voice was heaven and after what seemed the briefest of moments to catch up with news, John and I arranged to stay at her flat as she would come over the next morning.

At 7 am I awoke, dressed and then tidied the mess John and I had made in the flat, just in time before the door bell rang. I rushed downstairs to be greeted by a smiling face which after all these months I was able to see once more. Han it turned out, had brought all the ingredients for a hearty English breakfast including tomatoes, bacon and eggs, fresh bread and a very aromatic ground coffee.

With a hug and a brief kiss we went upstairs to talk about my travels in Arabia. After months of enduring the highs and lows of our own little world, John and I were overflowing with stories. Ian patiently listened as we recounted in detail our exploits, only

225

breaking in with the odd question here and there when she lost the drift of our English conversation.

We swapped presents and I gave Han the Cowry shells from the Arab Emirates, as well as the silver chain holding the Yin and Yang which I had purchased from the gold souk there. Han in return gave me a beautifully made shirt which I still have, a tree pendant made from enamelled copper and hung from a thin leather necklace, and a scarf woven from Nepali wool, all made by her own fair hands.

Later in the day we drove in the VW to Baarle Nassau where I met Han's parents. A wonderful couple who I was nervous of at the time but who I have come to love fondly in the years since. Her mother very efficiently went about cleaning all our laundry which had suffered considerably over the months of travel.

Replete, washed, and laundered, we set off back to *Breda* having arranged with some Belgian friends of Han to have a homecoming party on the following Saturday. Once at the flat John was able to contact *Jan* who we had met on Aquaba beach and who some months earlier had arrived back from Iraq to the University in *Vageningen* and who we also invited to the party.

We spent the rest of the day exploring Breda, taking in the delights of the street cafés through the long summer day, strolling casually from pub to pub. We finally sat on the terrace just off the market square and next to the church, sipping glasses of strong, heady Trappist beer, before returning to Han's flat and to talk away the evening over another hearty meal.

For now, I was complete and laying with Han in the early hours, I once more dreamed of the desert and the million and one thoughts from the events that had unfolded and the people we had met. Now that the struggle to simply get round and photograph what we could had drawn to a close, I felt the whole journey had been worth the effort. That we had completed the journey at all is still quite amazing to us. We had managed to bring back many classic and unique photographs despite the heat and breakdowns, and had many times fallen back on the goodness of those we met, which is a tribute to the kindness that exist in folk of all nations.

Holland and destiny awaits

If this journey taught me one thing, it was the reminder of a genuine interest in the traveller, and that the help we were offered locally, more than made up for the hardships we were put through. We were privileged to be able to take part in this journey, coming as it did between bouts of aggressive fighting and feuding in the countries we visited. Most of all I am grateful to those we met on the way, who willingly shared their life, their culture and their homes, with us. As I sit and write these final words it is with great appreciation that the hand of human kindness and understanding offered to us time and again, still lives on throughout the world ....Inshallah!